P O L I T I C A L
P H I L O S O P H Y

2

2

The System of Philosophies of History

LUC FERRY
Translated by Franklin Philip

THE UNIVERSITY OF CHICAGO PRESS • CHICAGO AND LONDON

Luc Ferry is a professor at the Sorbonne and the University of Caen.

The University of Chicago Press, Chicago 60637
The University of Chicago Press, Ltd., London

01 00 99 98 97 96 95 94 93 92   5 4 3 2 1

Originally published in Paris as
Philosophie politique, 2:
Le Système des philosophies de l'histoire.
© Presses Universitaires de France, 1984.

Library of Congress Cataloging-in-Publication Data

Ferry, Luc.
  [Système des philosophies de l'histoire. English]
  The system of philosophies of history / Luc Ferry ; translated by Franklin Philip.
     p.   cm.—(Political philosophy ; 2)
  Translation of: Le système des philosophies de l'histoire.
  Includes index.
  ISBN 0-226-24472-5
  1. History—Philosophy.   I. Title.   II. Series: Ferry, Luc.
Philosophie politique. English. 2.
D16.8.F45313   1992
901—dc20   91-20948
                                                                    CIP

♾ The paper used in this publication meets the minimum requirements
of the American National Standard for Information Sciences—Permanence
of Paper for Printed Library Materials,
ANSI Z39.48-1984.

To

Miguel Abensour

and

Jacques Rivelaygue

CONTENTS

vii

CONTENTS

ABBREVIATIONS

B   Fichte. *Beiträge zur Berichtigung der Urtheile des Publicums über die französische Revolution.* In *Schriften zur Revolution.* Frankfurt: Ullstein, 1973.

BH   Heidegger. "Brief über den 'Humanismus'" ("Letter on Humanism"). In *Wegmarken.* Frankfurt: Klostermann, 1967.

E   *Hegel's Logic; Being Part One of the "Encyclopedia of the Sciences",* Trans. William Wallace (1873). Oxford: Oxford University Press, 1975.

FL   Fichte. "Einige Vorlesungen über die Bestimmung des Gelehrten" (referred to throughout this volume as "Fifth Lecture"). In *Sämmtliche Werke.* Berlin, 1965.

IUH   Kant. "Idea for a Universal History with a Cosmopolitan Purpose." In *Kant's Political Writings.* Trans. H. B. Nisbet. Cambridge: Cambridge University Press, 1970.

LH   Heidegger. "Letter on Humanism." In *Basic Writings: From "Being and Time" to "The Task of Thinking."* Ed. David Farrell Krell. Trans. Frank A. Capuzzi and J. Glenn Gray. New York: Harper and Row, 1977.

LH   Alexis Philonenko. *La Liberté humaine dans la philosophie de Fichte.* Paris: Vrin, 1966.

PS   Hegel. *Phenomenology of Spirit.* Trans. A. V. Miller. Oxford: Oxford University Press, 1977.

RH   Hegel. *Reason in History: A General Introduction to the Philosophy of History.* Trans. Robert S. Hartman. Indianapolis: Bobbs-Merrill, 1953.

SK   Fichte. *Foundation of the Entire Science of Knowledge.* Trans. Peter Heath and John Lachs. New York: Cambridge University Press, 1982.

ABBREVIATIONS

SR   Fichte. *The Science of Rights*. Trans. A. E. Kroeger. New
        York: Harper and Row, 1970.
SW   Fichte. *Sämmtliche Werke*. Berlin, 1965.
VG   Hegel. *Die Vernunft in der Geschichte (Reason in History)*.
        Hamburg: Felix Meiner, 1955
W   Heidegger. *Wegmarken*. Frankfurt: Klostermann, 1967.

INTRODUCTION

Politics and the Philosophy of History

1. Totalitarianism and the Philosophy of History

Having devoted, along with a number of other persons,[1] the past ten years to an exploration of the German idealist philosophies, I have reached the conviction that a knowledge of this intellectual period is crucial for an understanding of our own time; that our own theoretical and political debates are rooted, though as a rule unknowingly, in the philosophical structures whose ultimate bases were never so clearly and profoundly disclosed as in the German philosophers. We know the famous judgment of Heine, a polemicist as gifted as he was heedless of nuances, that the doctrines of Kant, Schelling, Fichte, and Hegel would "beget revolutionary forces just waiting for the right moment to fill the world with admiration and dread." We also know the hoopla with which this era has been invested today by people who, on the pretext of exposing the roots of totalitarianism, have used metaphors as dubious as they are pathetic, and quotations as artfully selected as they are truncated, to conjure up the ideal prototype, so welcome in France, of the German philosopher as super-rationalistic, fanatical, pan-German, and (why not?) anti-Semitic.[2] Each of these writers saw or thought he saw—probably the only grain of truth in the image—that the central political question of our time, democracy versus totalitarianism (for this is a matter of two sides of the same question), is rooted in the German thought of the nineteenth century.

Need we accept a diagnosis as hasty as it was muddled and, without any form of trial, cry like the urchin Gavroche in *Les Misérables:* "It's Fichte who's to blame! It's Hegel who's to blame!"? Wouldn't it be better to dismiss this murky philosophy as pseudoscientific twaddle and to adopt in all security the intellectual "bastion" that Anglo-American positivism could then represent for "serious" minds? I con-

fess straightaway that both these attitudes seem to me to spare themselves what is still in question: a real analysis of the connection
between our modernity, both theoretical and political, and German
thought. Hence my plan to present these ideas in such a way that,
without waiving the requirement of textual honesty (immediately excluded by the polemical prejudices mentioned above), is not reserved for archaeologically minded scholars or even the "technicians" and historians of that era in philosophy. This book discusses,
therefore, the structure and potential political effects of the various
philosophies of history born of German idealism or, as is the case in
the phenomenological tradition of Martin Heidegger and Hannah Arendt, of a critical distancing from the thinkers of this period.[3]

The reader may legitimately wonder why I am attempting the
presentation from the vantage point of the philosophy of history. This
choice is not arbitrary: it reflects the philosophy of history's quite
special and intermediary status between the domains of politics and
"pure" philosophy. (I'll come back in a few pages to what I mean by
pure philosophy.) This status—which has largely eluded historians
of philosophy, few of whom are concerned with political matters—
was probably best revealed in several contemporary analyses of Stalinist totalitarianism: every one of them, we emphasize, proceeds
from a *political* analysis to a critique of "the" German philosophy of
history and then to a critique of philosophy proper. Following the
pioneers that were Hannah Arendt and Raymond Aron, Cornélius
Castoriadis has given us an exemplary description of this approach:

> If there is a true theory of history, if there is a rationality at work in
> things, it is clear that the direction of this development must be en-
> trusted to specialists of this theory, to the technicians of this rationality.
> The absolute power of the Party—and, within the Party, of "the cory-
> phaei of Marxist-Leninist science," to use the admirable expression
> coined by Stalin for his own purposes—has a philosophical status,
> based on reason in the "materialist conception of history." ... If this
> idea is true, power must be absolute and any democracy is merely a
> concession to the human fallibility of the leaders or a pedagogical
> technique of which only the leader can measure out the correct dos-
> ages.[4]

This passage, whose equivalent we find in most of the writers who
have attempted a genuine interpretation of totalitarianism,[5] clearly
shows the intermediate status of the philosophy of history: it indicates, though in a voluntarily schematic fashion, how a political phe-

nomenon like Stalinism is immediately understandable as "based on reason" according to a certain conception of history. (Here we should avoid an unfortunate confusion: Castoriadis is not uncovering a real causality, but merely an intellectual origin.) Briefly described, this relation may be stated as follows: political phenomena like the absolute power of the Party, the preemption of any democracy by a class of technicians, the absence of pluralism, and the like, are understandable and intellectually thinkable when they are related to the idea, *in part* inherited from German idealism, that history is a process both rational and controllable, hence capable of serving as the object of a "science" that, unlike all other sciences, claims to have total knowledge of its object as well to set forth the ends for human action. From politics to the philosophy of history, we are thus referred to a third level, that of philosophy proper: (let us say provisionally) to a certain one-sided definition of what forms the nature or texture of the real in general (hence of the historical real as well); for what quite obviously underlies the philosophy of history Castoriadis is attacking as the intellectual origin of Stalinism is the purely philosophical thesis that the totality of the real is both rational (everything is explainable, at least in itself, if not for us who may be unable to various degrees to get a full view of this rationality, and precisely the degrees between us and the "genial guide") and controllable at will (manipulable in the way reality is when we do a scientific experiment in the laboratory).

Thus, because of philosophy of history's intermediate status, it is at this central level that I have chosen to begin my discussion of German idealism and its phenomenological critics, and this precisely because my purpose is not to do the work of the historian of philosophy, but rather to show how the philosophies of German idealism still have a few secrets to yield about how to regard our own political era.

In view of the example mentioned, however, the issue might seem already settled, "philosophy of history" having already been repeatedly "refuted" from every quarter, so that in our Western democracies, at least, it survives only in some uncommonly stiff-necked ideologues who fortunately are on their doubtless too slow but nearly certain road to extinction. And whatever the nuances or divergences separating them, the non-Marxist analyses of totalitarianism, the leading one being Arendt's, already have essentially completed the critical task whose tripartite approach I have mentioned: an analysis of the political phenomenon, a description of the "Germanic" philosophy of history, and a deconstruction of its philosophical presuppositions.

I will admit straight off that I have been a bit disappointed by this work as done by thinkers who were non-Marxist or who were turning away from Marxism, despite the legitimacy of the enterprise and the occasional depth it displayed. Not that I would have expected Marxist criticism to produce a genuine interpretation of Stalinism: such an attempt has always seemed to me essentially impossible, for the tools of the criticism would share too many of the assumptions of the object it claimed to be criticizing.[6] These interpretations, primarily inspired by phenomenological thought,[7] have generally seemed to me in danger of committing two errors. The first is to conflate a mutually contradictory multiplicity of philosophies of history under the single label "the philosophy of history." The second error is to criticize the so-called philosophy of history from the standpoint of phenomenology, which I shall argue makes *any scientific work in the field of the social and any ethical view of politics and history impossible.*

This point probably calls for some explanation: the phenomenological criticisms of totalitarianism and of "the" German philosophy of history have ended up leveling three charges against this philosophy of history:

(1) Rationalism which, even in the guise of historical materialism, is actually Hegelian in origin has been criticized for applying the "principle of reason"—the principle that no event in the world takes place without a reason and, as such, is not inexplicable—to the whole of the historical real. The unqualified assertion of this principle—or in Hegelian terms, the assertion of the perfect rationality of the real (everything in reality is intelligible, at least in itself)—has been attacked for its conclusions, mainly because it inescapably leads to thinking of history as a *continuous* process, one that in its very essence excludes any mystery or possibility of *radical novelty,* each event, each "stage" being necessarily connected with the preceding ones by a causal nexus. According to a similar view, it has been thought that behind this necessity in the direction of history, behind the rejection of novelty so vigorously denounced by Arendt in her *Origins of Totalitarianism,* there emerged the disavowal of pluralism so imperishably expressed by Simone de Beauvoir: "Truth is one, error is multiple. It is no accident that the Right professes pluralism."[8]

(2) The unlimited extension of the principle of reason could then be attacked as a negation of the autonomy and transcendence of legal and political phenomena. The line of descent from Hegel's criticism of "abstract rights" to the Marxist criticism of human rights is clear: it lies in the same rejection of "formal reason" or "ideology," here considered in "historicist" fashion as simple *products* of history that it would be illusory to try making radically autonomous—it mattering little, as it happens, that the autonomy of the political be won, against Hegel, over "objective reason," or against Marx, over the economic infrastructure.[9] Boundless confidence in the effective incarnation of the principle of reason, whether it is honestly defined or not as an idealism (honestly because it is idealism that it is about, i.e., an identification of rationality and reality), ended up, in other words, confounding the real and the ideal, denying that it was possible in judging history to refer to an authority that was higher than and external to the laws supposed to be governing it (small matter *here* that these laws be those of absolute Spirit or of socialist legality).

(3) The idea that the real was wholly masterable and controllable (an idea that was not, for once, at all Hegelian in origin), that man thus could "enframe" it and have it at his imperious disposal, was analyzed, under the names "voluntarism" or "activism," as one of the prime intellectual sources of Stalinist terrorism.

2. The Limits of Phenomenological Criticism

From this threefold criticism, whose various artisans can easily be guessed, it was obviously necessary to come up with a "new" idea of history based on some "other" philosophy. It was chiefly in reference to Heidegger's deconstruction of metaphysics (largely taken up in France by Merleau-Ponty) that this "new" idea of historicity could be elaborated. Part 1 of this volume discusses at some length the nature and limits of Heidegger's deconstruction of metaphysics as the prototype of the phenomenological critiques of totalitarianism. Let us say for the moment that in Hannah Arendt, a student and disciple of Heidegger (even if this fact is disturbing because of Heidegger's political choices, the fact remains inarguable),[10] this new idea of historicity, crystallized around the concept of action,[11] involved a genuine destruction of the concept of causality, because—at the philosophical level, and insofar as the totality of the real was subjected to it—this concept of causality was precisely the very principle of the phi-

losophy of history of which totalitarianism was intellectually supposed to be the latest manifestation.

> Newness is the real of the historian who, unlike the natural scientist
> concerned with ever-recurring happenings, deals with events which
> always occur only once. This newness can be manipulated if the his-
> torian insists on causality and pretends to be able to explain events by
> a chain of causes which eventually led up to it. . . . Causality, however,
> is an altogether alien and falsifying category in the historical sci-
> ences. . . . Whoever in the historical sciences honestly believes in caus-
> ality actually denies the subject matter of his own science.[12]

Therefore, the task was attributed to the antitotalitarian thinker, not
of claiming "to know the mysteries of the whole historical process"
after the fashion of those "ideologies which are never interested in
the miracle of being,"[13] but of "detecting this unexpected new"[14] that
is the mark of all genuine historical action; and the "substance" of
history was defined as the "interruptions of some natural series of
events, of some automatic process, in whose context they constitute
the wholly unexpected."[15] That this "new" idea of history as discontinuity or, to repeat one of Arendt's formulas, "chain of miracles"[16]
was backed by a philosophy that led to the pure and simple liquidation of any use for the principle of reason or causality, and to a consideration of the real as irrational, was something Arendt did not hesitate to assert: "[I]t is precisely this infinitely improbable which
actually constitutes the very texture of everything we call real. . . . It is
because of this element of the 'miraculous' present in all reality that
events, no matter how well anticipated in fear or hope, strike us with
a shock of surprise once they have come to pass":[17] thus we have a
clear and clean articulation ("it is because of," Arendt tells us!) between a "new" philosophical idea that refuses to see the real subjected to reason and a "new" idea of history denying any form of
causality in it. Drawing conclusions about history from his purely
philosophical criticism of the principle of reason, Heidegger too was
to condemn the illusion of causal continuity in these terms: "Epochs
do not let themselves be derived from one another and set on the
track of a continuous process. There is nevertheless a tradition from
epoch to epoch. But it does not run between epochs like a ribbon
that ties them together; the tradition comes every time from the con-
cealment of the destination" (from what Arendt called, repeating Heidegger's expression, the "Miracle of Being").[18]

As I have suggested, the phenomenological criticism of German
metaphysics seems to me in danger of committing two errors.

Let's begin with the simpler one: How can we not see that, despite the validity of the criticisms mentioned, the abandonment of the principle of causality makes not only science impossible, but also, paradoxically, ethics (which Heidegger has the virtue of making quite clear in his "Letter on Humanism")? From the viewpoint of Heidegger's or Arendt's phenomenology, once the three criticisms of "the" philosophy of history are made, what task can we assign to the social sciences? Certainly, the historian or social scientist who postulates the perfect rationality of the real could founder in a paranoid delirium of which it would be only too easy to give examples. How, on the other hand—and Max Weber, who was hardly a Hegelian, saw this very well—can we expect to produce any intelligibility in the social sciences when the principle of reason or causality is *altogether* illegitimate? And how, on the practical level, can we maintain the possibility of an ethical appreciation of politics (which does not mean that we will confuse the two realms. Who, moreover, could "honestly" claim to be able to do without this possibility?) when any form of voluntarism is condemned for the "terrorism" it potentially (and genuinely) harbors? How can we preserve a minimum of "the moral view of the world" (and without this minimum, what would be the meaning of "the banality of evil" of which Arendt speaks so well?) if human actions are not credited to some intentional causality of the human will, but only considered "miracles of being"? Let us grant for the moment that it is naïve—naïve in the way only metaphysicians can be—to think that man is the author of his acts through the free causation of his will. In this case, don't we have to draw the conclusion—the very conclusion that Heidegger so well accepted—that ethics in its essence falls within the province of the metaphysical illusion that the subject is the cause of its acts? For fear of the theoretical and practical implications of causality, its abandonment by phenomenology represents a fine instance of throwing the baby out with the bath water.

Hence the two questions that will be continually at the heart of this book and define what is truly at stake in it:

(1) Can we preserve some use for the principle of reason or causality, a use that is by definition indispensable to any form of explanation (for what is an explanation but giving a reason?), without granting that this principle inevitably leads to a superrationalistic and historicist philosophy of history? In short, rather than deifying or destroying the principle of reason, is it possible to limit it? Between the rationalism of the various metaphysics of history and the irrational-

ism of the phenomenological criticism of these metaphysics, is there a philosophical position that is not a pious wish or an honest skepticism or a simple appeal to good sense, but one that is genuinely explicable and coherent? In other words that may better bring out the current relevance of these questions: Can political philosophy— which, in creating its own theoretical space, grants the autonomy of politics and in so doing must criticize the principle of reason—be reconciled with the social sciences which, like the other sciences, cannot function without this principle?

(2) Can we keep a "moral view" of the world of history and politics—hence a practical and even voluntarist view—without this "moralization" of politics resulting in that confusion of two domains we know can lead to a logic of terror first illustrated in modern times by Jacobinism?

It has been said that the phenomenological criticisms of totalitarianism run the risk of committing a second error: that of conflating under the name "philosophy of history" or "metaphysics of history" an antinomial plurality of representations of historicity. These expressions, as most often used by professional critics of totalitarianism, are indeed equivocal, and ignorance of this could stand in the way of any truly rigorous understanding of the intellectual origins of totalitarianism.

3. Some Tasks of Philosophy Issuing from German Idealism

To restore the plurality of ideas of history stemming from German idealism—a plurality that again is in danger of being glossed over by the generalizing anathemas of "metaphysics" or "the philosophy of history"—I would like to sketch an approach that is the reverse of the one referred to here as a paradigm of the deconstruction of totalitarianism: instead of going from politics to "the" philosophy of history and then on to pure philosophy, I shall start with pure philosophy and from it "deduce" this possible plurality of ideas of historicity.

The problem here concerns the definition of what I have been vaguely calling "pure philosophy." Philosophy is often viewed as intellectual gymnastics without any specific object, or as the learning of we-don't-quite-know-what kind of "critical thinking" of which we see dimly how these grounds alone could enable us to define an autonomous discipline (as though the mathematician, biologist, social scientist, and so forth, did not think or go through their own "intellectual gymnastics"). There certainly exists a body of literature unanimously considered "philosophical," but one might still be hard put to indicate exactly what this adjective means. These works, if only by the use of concepts they convey, doubtless seem different from any form of narrative—which seems to set them apart from what is usually taught as literature—but they still do not concern a specific object, as do the empirical sciences.

Now, to identify the real source of the plurality of possible philosophies of history, we must have a minimal but exact definition of the tasks of pure philosophy as they may be identified from German idealism and the phenomenological criticisms of it. This is indeed indispensable, for we have seen how any philosophy of history is inseparable from a philosophy on which it rests.

To confine ourselves to the essential thing—to what is strictly necessary for a real understanding of the philosophical foundations of history—I will say that, at least from German idealism on, philosophy includes four main elements and is defined by four fundamental tasks. Here I shall merely indicate these four stages in a formal way, without trying to show or even to justify what may be abrupt or arbitrary in this or that aspect of this "definition." I beg the reader to proceed through the rest of this book before making a judgment about what this introduction just sketches in order to set forth hypotheses and to clarify the stakes without which the very plan of this work could not be expressed.

(1) Unlike the empirical sciences, philosophy does not concern any particular existing object. In the language of Heideggerian phenomenology, we could say that it does not bear on any "beings," but "merely" inquires about the features common to all "beings," to all particular objects, and does so before we have concrete experiences of them ("before" here having a logical and not a chronological sense; happily, we begin seeing objects before we start doing philosophy): this means that before I have seen or touched this or that particular object, I can know, completely a priori, that it must have a certain number of properties without which it could not be held to be an object. I know, for example, before I see a table, a chair, or a tree, that these things will share the property of being located in space and time, occupying a certain portion of this space, being to some extent identical to themselves (i.e., of having a certain permanence through the various modifications they undergo in time), possessing, in a sense yet to be specified as regards the philosophy of history, a reason for existing, or, if you will, a cause, and so on. From this first viewpoint, then, philosophy may be defined as *an ontology*

(giving this term the very precise and somewhat unusual meaning that Kant sometimes did and, following him, Heidegger) *of the a priori definition of the objectivity of the object,* of what constitutes the essence of objectivity in general (which, in his book on Kant, Heidegger calls by the suggestive expression "ontological pre-comprehension," meaning what I know about the object before having it present in front of me. An example from set theory may make this sense of "ontology" more intelligible. In mathematics we define a set by stating a property to which a certain number of elements corresponds (the elements that are classed under this property). Now if I wish to give an a priori definition of an empty set, that is, one to which no reality corresponds, I state a property that explicitly denies one of the criteria indicated by ontology as constitutive of the definition of objectivity. Thus, for instance, if I admit ontologically that an object, to be an object, must be identical to itself, it is enough that I deny the principle of identity, that I posit the property $X \neq X$ as the defining property of my set, and I will have with certainty defined a priori a set in which no element can be included. Someone who understands this example also necessarily understands what "ontology" means here. If we think about the operation for obtaining this definition of the empty set, we see that it assumes, if only implicitly, that I have an idea or criterion for the properties without which an object could not be represented as existing. And I have this criterion completely a priori; I have no need to know that no element corresponds to the property $X \neq X$, no need to consider the empirical objects one by one to see if by any chance there was one that corresponded to this requirement. This general definition of the objectivity of the object (of the "beingness of beings," Heidegger would say) is, we dare say, the first and chief object of any philosophy. Its first task is to describe and enumerate the set of the criteria without which an object could not be thought of as such. Plato was doing this when he distinguished the Form (that which is stable and identical to itself) from the sensory (endlessly variable and changing), as was Aristotle when he set forth his table of "categories." Incontestably, however, it was not until German idealism, and probably Kant, that this enumeration could claim to be truly systematic. Without going into detail about this work in ontology, we may say that the two basic criteria accepted by the German idealists (but not only them) as essential to any definition of the reality of the real are the principle of identity and the principle of reason. (The reader has probably already noticed the problems encountered under these circumstances by the attempt to limit the principle of reason in its application to history. I shall return to this point.)

(2) Once this ontology is described—which, once again, was done in a seemingly definitive way, at least in philosophy, in Kant's *Critique of Pure Reason* (certain Kantian categories have been denied or deduced in a different way, but to my knowledge no new ones have been added)—we may still inquire about its origin, that is, about why we think of objectivity in general just this way and not some other, according to these criteria (identity, reason) and not according to others; we may also ask why these criteria seem to be common to humanity (a community that is attested to—if we asked for a sign of it, for example—by the ability of the sciences that use or have used these principles to be universally communicated and discussed) and thus form the basis of an ethical point of view, that of intersubjective communication. This question about the origin of ontological structure has been given two types of answers.

(*a*) The first answer consists in seeking a reason, a grounding for this structure, thus, as it were, by redoubling it by having one of its constitutive elements (the principle of reason) function on it. This cause has usually been found in God, creator of the "eternal verities" of ontology. Hence the terms that Kant and later Heidegger used to designate this type of answer: "onto-theo-logy," because the explanation of this community of structure manifested by ontotheology rests on a certain theology or idea of God as the basis of philosophical truths. In this sense, the "materialist" attempt to deduce ontological categories from a material basis—for example, for explaining the emergence of the principle of identity from a "social relation" like the barter—still comes under ontotheology, even though it represents a secularized version of it. This sort of "ontotheologizing" was attacked first by Kant and later in a rather similar way by Heidegger. It is obviously impossible here for me to give the details of this criticism (to which I shall return at some length in part 1 of this volume). Its principle, however, may be stated quite simply: it condemns ontotheology as circular by showing how, in forming the basis for ontology, it is already forced to use ontological principles, so that the foundation remains purely subjective and paradoxical.

(*b*) Hence the second "answer" to the question of the origin of ontology, an answer that in Kant and Heidegger (we cannot overemphasize how much Heidegger read and reread Kant!) deconstructs the question itself, making its circularity explicit, and concludes this deconstruction with the thesis that it is impossible to find a true basis for ontology and thus to give a definitive answer to the question of the ultimate source of the philosophical structures of our thought.[19]

(3) Inquiring early on about the origin of ontological structures, philosophy may later question the relation between the modes of thought that define objectivity and the real itself. Isn't there some misconstruction, even absurdity, in defining a priori structures of objectivity while, for its part, the real itself (concrete objects) could very well resist submitting to these structures? Concerning this last point, our studies of German idealism have led us to propose three "models"[20] of philosophy or, if you will, three paradigmatic answers to this central question. According to the first model—the position of those whom Kant and Heidegger call "metaphysicians"—the real is thoroughly and "in itself" subject to this ontological structure, and hence in this sense wholly identical and explicable, in short, according to the Hegelian formula, completely "rational." We call this position the Hegelian model, for, among the modern metaphysicians, it was clearly Hegel who went furthest in systematically working out the philosophical limits and implications of the assertion of the rationality of the real. According to the second model—basically the position of Heidegger's phenomenology—existence is essentially inconsistent with the principles of identity and reason, and, as Arendt stresses, is characterized by "difference" and "mystery." According to the third model—most vigorously articulated in Kant's *Critique of Judgment*—the real, without being *in itself* and thus in advance completely rational or identical to the ontological structure, is still no less rationalizable, the ontological structure then being used as a method for explaining or understanding the real and without this explanation or understanding being guaranteed in advance (as they would by definition be in the Hegelian model). Part 1 of this volume is a detailed analysis of these three modes of answers to the question of the relations between ontology, as an empty structure, and the historically real.

(4) As ontology, philosophy may still inquire about the question of ethics, that is, to consider just modern practical philosophy, about the ends that man can and should set himself in relation to other men. In modernity and especially in Kant's *Critique of Practical Reason,* the question of ethics takes the form of an ontology in the sense indicated, that is, an attempt to define objectivity: one can soon be persuaded of this by a brief analysis of what Kant saw as the moral end of any human action. Kant distinguishes three types of possible ends, which rise progressively to the domain of what is properly eth-

ical, that is, the domain of objective or universal ends. This is the real significance of Kant's famous distinction between suitability (which consists uniquely in the consideration of the means for attaining the ends particular to a given subject), prudence (which is directed to more general ends, such as health, which may be considered common to the human race as a biological species), and morality proper, which consists of setting for oneself ends that are valid universally and unconditionally (for example, never to treat others purely as a means).

With the inception of German idealism, in the *Critique of Practical Reason* and then in the writings of the young Fichte, philosophy thus expresses what we could call "practical ontology " or a theory of practical objectivity ("practical" here broadly meaning "of ethical concern" or, if you will, "concerning the ends of man"), for it tries to indicate in a general way what ends we must necessarily hold to be objectively valid and then try to bring about. Consequently, practical ontology assumes a minimum of two "conditions of possibility": first, it implies that the ideal and the real not be perennially identical, for otherwise the very concepts of an end or the "ought" would by definition lose all meaning: so that for me to propose actualizing some end I consider good, this end (please excuse the truism) must be not yet actualized and may even never be: despite its apparent triviality, this point is of extreme importance for the understanding of the plurality of philosophies of history, for we can see that it implies a calling into question of the Hegelian rationalism in which the real and the ideal have coincided from time immemorial (at least in itself or from the viewpoint of God). The second condition of possibility for practical philosophy is thus freedom, meaning the possibility for the human subject to actualize, as much as material circumstances permit, the ends that practical ontology represents as objectively (meaning universally) valid.

4. The Plurality of Modern Philosophies of History

Once stated, this brief sketch of the four basic elements defining philosophy, or at least German idealism (a description of theoretical ontology, questions about its origin, its relation to the real, and a description of practical ontology), may yield a more precise understanding, starting with their true roots, of the various philosophies of history whose plurality has perhaps been poorly discerned in the phenomenological criticisms of totalitarianism which conflate them under the conglomerate expression "the philosophy of history."

We will take as a hypothesis that, based on ontology, there are only five conceivable philosophies of history.

(1) The first philosophy of history is the embodiment of theoretical ontology, that is, Hegel's assertion of the absolute validity of theoretical ontology for the totality of the real. To form the continuistic and superrationalistic idea of history—certain aspects of which I mentioned at the start of this introduction and which Hegel so masterfully set forth under the name of the "cunning of reason"—requires positing that the real is wholly and in itself consistent with the principles of identity and reason. The expression "cunning of reason" refers to the mechanism by which Hegel saw the rational being actualized by its seeming opposite (for example, law by the selfish passions, peace by war, and so on) so that the totality of the real is rational, for even that which seems to be opposed to rationality in fact works toward its perfect actualization. For Hegel, Reason does not mean a formal rationality or ideal that is the opposite of a rebellious, contradictory, or chaotic reality, but, according to the formula that best expresses the nature of this system, the identity between itself (as a result) and its opposite (the seemingly irrational process that produces it). From this perspective, the "moral view of the world" so dear to Kant and particularly Fichte is but a pure illusion and the very idea of praxis evaporates, the real and the ideal being in themselves forever reconciled. The only definition of freedom that is fully compatible with this idea of history is therefore "the understanding of necessity."

(2) The second philosophy of history is the product of an effort to see what I call "practical" ontology as genuinely embodied in human reality. Unlike the first philosophy, it conceives of history as the result of a free human praxis, meaning the process in which man externally imposes a transformation on the real in the name of a universal moral ideal (if you like, a "program") that remains forever transcendent and whose actualization is never guaranteed.

Before discussing the other three philosophies of history—which in fact merely take stands about the first two—we should clear up the misunderstanding in which these two quite distinct philosophies are mixed together under the same name and their political implications confounded. Contrary to widespread opinion, neither of these two philosophies of history by itself represents an intellectual source of totalitarianism. As I have tried to show elsewhere,[21] the political upshot of Hegelianism *alone* would be merely a form of quietism ultimately rather similar to classical liberalism. (Who, for that matter, does not see the intimate connections between Hegel's theory of the cunning of reason and the liberal thesis of the "invisible hand" or laissez-faire? If the liberal idea of history is one of "physiocracy," Hegel's "spiritocracy" scarcely differs from it on a practical level and, whatever else we may say about them, all conceptions of history up to Toqueville's are reminiscent of Hegel's thesis of a hidden providence.) The "logical" practical outcome of a representation of history in which all of the real is working by itself toward the ultimate actualization of the rational would be a wait-and-see attitude, for the good and simple reason that the real is already in itself (embryonically) identical with the rational (since everything real is consistent with the principle of reason). In short, Hegel's idea of history is in all respects closer to Montesquieu's than to Stalin's (to be persuaded of this, read Hegel's remarks about Montesquieu in the introduction to his *Science of Right*). Certainly conservative, Hegel's idea of history nevertheless essentially excludes any form of activism or voluntarism: for example, despite his approval of the consequences of the French Revolution (the emergence of political freedom and the modern state), Hegel remains one of the most perspicacious critics of the Jacobin terror.[22]

For its part, the moral view of history resulting from the embodiment of practical ontology, and thus aiming to transform the real from the outside for the sake of a universal ideal of practical reason, essentially implies a certain violence with regard to what resists the actualization of the moral ideal (a violence that Hegel's theory renders quite superfluous by positing that the real links up, by itself, with the rational). Even when it takes the extreme form of Jacobin terror, however, this violence cannot be confused purely and simply with the violence of totalitarianism. Arendt herself soundly proposed a distinction between three forms of political terror:[23] (*a*) the terror, which might be called "normal" in revolutionary times, involved in the elimination of opponents of the Revolution—eliminations that are obviously carried out in the name of moral virtues, as testified to by models of the kind represented in the writings of Robespierre and Saint-Just, long before those of Trotsky and Lenin; (*b*) terror associated with an ideological project that views a certain end as not just a moral necessity, but a "scientific imperative" as well, a typical example being the "dekulakization" forced on Russia in the late 1920s. Here we are on the threshold of (*c*) totalitarian terror, which—in a third image, one particularly recalcitrant to rational or "moral" explanations, if not ideological ones—leads to the great Stalinist purges and the appearance of concentration camps. So we see that, following Arendt's classification (repeated by Raymond Aron in his *Democracy and Totalitarianism*), the terror engendered by an exclusively moral view of politics corresponds at most to only the first form and not to the two others. In other words, Jacobinism is not totalitarianism.

Hence it is odd that most critiques of totalitarianism, especially those inspired by phenomenology, have confounded these two quite different philosophies of history under the same name. All the odder because they are sufficiently antagonistic as to constitute a real antinomy: either the real is rational and under these circumstances there is no need to act, or we should actualize a transcendent moral ideal on earth and under these circumstances the real is not yet rational but demands to be transformed. Thus, the passage from Castoriadis cited earlier is extremely problematic: "If there is a rationality at work in things," he is in effect telling us, "it follows that the job of actualizing it should be confided to those who are specialists at it." On the contrary, shouldn't we think that someone who admits the perfect rationality of the real has no need to entrust some practical task to anyone at all? And, conversely, someone who thinks that a practical task should be carried out well would be caught in a glaring contradiction if he or she admitted that the real is somehow already rational. So the logic of totalitarianism is by no means self-evident.

(3) For a political phenomenon like totalitarianism to be possible, one must not take up only one of these conceptions of history, but associate and combine them in the monstrous and absurd composite represented by the third philosophy of history derivable from ontology. According to this philosophy, the historical real is not only wholly rational in itself or from the viewpoint of those who hold the keys to its interpretation, but also (and, contrary to what Castoriadis's text leads one to suppose, this is extremely odd) perfectly controllable by one or several conscious wills. In short, this third philosophy of history is not merely theoretical, like Hegel's, or practical, like Fichte's, but represents the fantasy of a unity of theory and praxis or, in other words, the fantasy of a "revolutionary science." To appreciate the "originality" of this third philosophy of history in comparison with the first two, we should perhaps recall that on the one hand Hegel always clearly distinguishes between the philosopher and the man of action, between the understanding and the will: while his

philosophy represents an attempt to reconcile the two aspects, this reconciliation is effected through an attack on the viewpoint of the will (the moral point of view) as a pure illusion of finitude, and by not ranking it equal to the theoretical point of view (see pp. 41–42), and on the other hand, that Fichte employed the greatest rigor in condemning any rationalistic or deterministic conception of history. I think that it is only in the socialist tradition, beginning no doubt with Saint-Simonism, but especially with Marxism, that there appeared the idea of a science that would have the capacity not only to offer a complete understanding of historical processes (which assumes the rationality of the real), but also to determine the ends of human action (which excludes this rationality, but implies a practical point of view). And it is in the very writings of Marx that there clearly emerges the absolute contradiction which this third philosophy of history focuses on yet still claims to reconcile: in Marx we indisputably find an account of ideas borrowed from the first two philosophies of history. The preface and the penultimate chapter of book 1 of his *Capital,* for example, clearly develop a theory of historicity in which the process leading to the *end* of history is marked by stages linked, in Marx's phrasing, by an "iron necessity," with the "inevitability governing the metamorphoses of nature." Nor, however, can one be unaware that in other passages Marx calls on human praxis in order to actualize the end of history which his earlier writings still seemed to describe as absolutely necessary. Most of the debates in the Second International centered on the question of which of the two models was the more "orthodox," and whether it was obligatory to let the process run its course by itself (a view that for the reasons indicated I call Hegelian) or, on the contrary, to "hasten" it (in relation to what, moreover?) by means of a revolutionary praxis (the Fichtean model). Therefore Marxism cannot be reduced to either Hegelianism or Fichteanism, for it represents an attempt to combine these two conceptions of history, even though they are rigorously antinomial in every way. And it is precisely in this respect that, to take up a frequently debated question, Marxism has some relation to Stalinist totalitarianism, which Marx would have certainly disavowed.

(4) The fourth philosophy of history that can be thought of as based on ontology, rather than combining the first two philosophies, rejects their assumptions. This is basically the position of Heidegger and Arendt, both of whom refused—in the name of a deconstruction of "metaphysics," and even a criticism of the theoretical and practical aspects of ontology—to think of history as rational or controllable,

as involving a theoretical or practical causality (in Arendt's terms, history should not be thought of as either "nature" or "the product of work"). I have already said how this deconstruction, which concludes that the historical event ("the action") is a pure "mystery" or "a miracle of Being," runs into what I think is a considerable difficulty through the a priori prohibition of any theoretical or practical view of historicity (any "explanation" or "ethical" appreciation).

Our four philosophies of history may thus be presented in the form of the following diagram (fig. 1).

(5) Because of some theoretical and practical difficulties in these four philosophies of history, I thought it desirable to propose a fifth conception of historicity, based on a reading of Kant's *Critique of Judgment*, which, without combining (like 3) or abolishing (like 4) the applications of the two ontological structures, attempts to limit them in order to articulate them. Only such a limitation and articulation would allow for answers to the two questions asked: how can we avoid giving up all explanation out of a concern to avoid the Hegelian model, and how can we avoid giving up all ethical assessment in order not to risk terrorism: in short, how can we find a solution other than the certainly radical but totally fruitless one offered by phenomenology? It is obviously impossible in this introduction to indicate the detailed content of this fifth philosophy of history. Let us say provisionally that in principle it consists in limiting ontology by considering it not a dogmatic truth, like a law of reality itself, but merely a method, even a "horizon of meaning" or a viewpoint for thinking, and that it is precisely through this first limitation that the two elements of ontology, the theoretical and the practical, could be articulated without contradiction. Let us also say, for informational purposes, that in the social sciences, this conception of history—which to my knowledge has never been definitively formulated from the viewpoint of ontology—could find an embryonic illustration, notably among the neo-Kantians, thinkers like Wilhelm Dilthey or Max Weber, in the well-known distinction between explanation (a matter of theoretical ontology) and understanding (a matter of practical ontology).

5. Questions Raised by the Conflict of Philosophies of History

Before examining these philosophies of history in detail, I should give a systematic summary of the problems that I propose, if not to

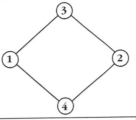

Combination of the first two points of view in a "revolutionary science": history as intelligible and controllable.

Theoretical ontology applied to history (absolute extension to the real of the principle of reason) (Hegel).

Practical ontology applied to history (revolutionary transformation of the real in the name of a universal) (Fichte).

Abolition of the first two points of view in a deconstruction of ontology: history as "miracle" of Being, in essence inexplicable and not controllable (Heidegger, Arendt).

Figure 1.

resolve, at least to explore down to their ultimate presuppositions. Then and then only can the plan of this essay can be set forth intelligibly.

The differences between the first four philosophies of history may be reduced to two central problems: a theoretical problem with some practical implications, and a practical problem with some theoretical extensions.

(1) The first difficulty—on first approach a purely theoretical one—lies in the very antinomy formed by the philosophies of history (1) and (4), that is, in the antinomy whose thesis could be expressed as follows: "Everything real is rational, that is, identifiable and explicable at least in itself, if not for us," and whose antithesis is: "Neither in itself nor in its rational basis is anything real conformable to the principles of identity and reason, but everything real is actually difference and mystery." It is easy to see the epistemological consequences of these two statements as well as the theoretical interest they generate. The thesis seems to guarantee the possibility of science and particularly the human sciences: How can I pursue a project of scientific explanation without assuming in advance that the real I am dealing with is rationalizable? Isn't this assumed in psycho-

analysis, for example (and I have deliberately picked an example that I am fully aware will inevitably startle certain readers—I will return to it), when it postulates that every act, even the seemingly most trivial (a slip of the tongue), has not only a meaning but also a reason for occurring: in a word, is not just a simple "accident"? For its part, the antithesis aims to preserve the discontinuity and mystery of the real, to preserve the autonomy of human phenomena from rationalistic reductionism, an autonomy that, to be asserted, definitely assumes the breaking of the principle of reason that may connect everything with everything and thereby reduce all apparent (relative, as they say) autonomy to a dependence of fact (regarding unconscious impulses, the infrastructure, and so on). To counterbalance the shocking example above (and to square myself with psychoanalysts), I hasten to add that the phenomenological model is also present in Freud's writings (Jacques Lacan, who had read Heidegger, saw this), for the assertion of the dynamic unconscious—some forever undecipherable and unrationalizable obscurity—may also illustrate the antithesis in that it restores an intrinsic dimension of mystery to human action. Far from being surprising, the fact that a single idea, in this case one of Freud's, cuts across two antinomial models poses in all its clarity the theoretical problem I am trying to set up: how do we think of a use for the principle of reason that leads neither to a rationalism that turns into a delirium of interpretation, nor to an irrationalism that, out of a fear of reason, overwhelms us with mysteries? I add that today, at least in France, we can use much the same terms to describe the relations between sociology (which has for the most part determinedly clung to the thesis) and political philosophy which, after brilliantly deconstructing its chief object, totalitarianism, is wearing itself out in a scarcely concealed repetition of the antithesis. (Totalitarianism? A radically new, unheard-of, mysterious reality—a new "face of Being." The origin of the state? A "mishap," an "irrational event" that it would be absurd to claim to explain, and so forth.)

Because it basically concerns a problem in theoretical ontology (the status of the principle of reason), however, this seemingly merely theoretical antinomy actually conceals a practical problem whose importance it would be hard to exaggerate. When we take a close look at the two members of the antinomy, we see that both the thesis and the antithesis link up, whether they want to or not (and of course for opposite reasons), in the same negation of practical ontology, the same negation of any "moral view of the world," of any ethical view of history and politics: the thesis because it considers all intentional action (all will to actualize an ideal external to the real) as an illusion of finitude (see the analysis in chap. 1 of Hegel's critique of the moral view of the world); the antithesis because it sees a metaphysical illusion in the subject's claim to be the conscious cause of its actions (see the analysis in chap. 2 of Heidegger's deconstruction of ethics in his "Letter on Humanism"). Thesis and antithesis are paradoxically in agreement about the same practical or rather "a-practical" attitude, whether that described by Hegel in terms of "contemplation" (see Hegel's use, at the end of his *Encyclopedia*, of the Aristotelian expression *noesis noeseoos* to characterize this attitude) or by phenomenology in terms of "releasement" (*Gelassenheit*). Thus, in answer to the naïve scholar who asks him the "voluntaristic" question: "So what in the name of heaven should I do?" Professor Heidegger imperturbably replies: "We should do nothing, merely wait,"[24] since we are not "ourselves the source or basis of our actions, and "we" merely "should" with "releasement" open ourselves to "the miracle of Being." Arendt discusses this passage in these terms: "In modern times and above all in the modern age, much has been written about the will, but despite Kant, despite even Nietzsche, not very much has been found out about its nature. However that may be, no one before Heidegger saw how much this nature stands opposed to thinking and affects it destructively. To thinking belongs '*Gelassenheit*'—a serenity, composure, release, a state of relaxation, in brief, a disposition that 'lets be.' Seen from the standpoint of the will the thinker must say, only apparently in paradox, I will non-willing."[25] Why? Because authentic thinking is thinking of the "miracle of Being," thus denouncing the illusion of the metaphysically naïve will that claims it is not Being that is the "ground" (let's not forget the quotation marks) of action, but the conscious subject. We thus see that hiding in the theoretical antinomy formed around the principle of reason is—as Theodor Adorno said in his *Negative Dialectics* (and this aroused his antipathy toward this phenomenology which in other respects he definitely admired)—the same liquidation of any ethical viewpoint in favor of thinking (even if, once again, thinking is defined *here* as thinking of the identical, and *there* as thinking of difference).

(2) But the second problem, seemingly connected only with practical ontology, involves the same formidable symmetrically converse theoretical problems. By itself, this problem can be stated quite simply: how can we preserve an ethical view of politics without flirt-

ing, even unwittingly, with Jacobin terror? The theoretical questions raised by this should not, however, be underestimated. There are two main questions, and this precisely because they are raised by the relation between practical ontology (of the moral view of the world) and the two opposing philosophies of history in the theoretical antinomy:

(*a*) The first question, clarified if not resolved in Kant's *Critique of Pure Reason,* seeks a possible agreement between the two antinomial terms formed by the principle of reason (the basis of the Hegelian model) and the idea of freedom underlying the moral view of the world: if I set out to actualize some ideal on earth, or simply some end I take to be good, I am obliged to think of myself as its author, the first beginning of my action—which essentially denies the principle of reason that always condemns this moral view as an illusion and tries to find the real reason for my action in some social or individual unconscious (through a "genealogy") (by way of example, read Engels's letter to Bloch in September 1890).

(*b*) The second question stems from the confrontation between the moral view of the world and the phenomenological idea of history: how, without foundering in metaphysics, can I claim to be the first cause of my actions? It isn't because it would be nice to be able to think of myself as a free being, and one eventually capable of ethical actions, that this representation is not a sheer illusion—precisely that illusion which consists in not thinking the truth of Being with acquiescence [*Gelassenheit*]. We thereby see that the genealogies of the ethical subject may be conceived both from the viewpoint of rationalism and that of phenomenology. How can I preserve an ethical and critical view of the world if I am "determined" by something external to me, be it Reason or Being, mechanical cause or "mystery"?

I must say that my innermost conviction is that all three philosophies of history at stake in the two central problems, theoretical and practical, set forth here are uncircumventable; in other words, it is strictly impossible for us permanently to eschew reason, "mystery," or ethics, and that even if they enter into a multiplicity of contradictory entanglements, taken together, these three elements still constitute our philosophical situation: hence the lack of interest to me of philosophies that interminably claim, or have claimed, without succeeding (that is impossible), to uphold one of these three positions against the other two. Hence also the project of articulating these three views by exploring these contradictory entanglements down to their deepest roots.

Right from the start, however, the whole enterprise could be undermined by a suspicion: if we straightaway take our stand in modernity, don't we risk missing the true philosophical point of view, the one that the thinkers of antiquity elaborated before the intervention of the "decline" initiated by Galileo and Descartes? This new "quarrel between the ancients and the moderns"—which already breaks out in Nietzsche and the German romantics, and was to become a central theme in Heidegger's thinking—was transposed to the field of political philosophy by one of Heidegger's former students (who occasionally deviated from his teacher): Leo Strauss. Strauss reached two conclusions about the circumstances that make political philosophy possible: the survival of political philosophy involves a critique of historicism (agreed), but this can only be done through a return to "classical" (ancient) thought, all modern political philosophies being irrevocably headed toward a radical historicism.[26]

Thus, Hegel's vision of a univocalness of—even a fundamental "complicity" ("in the final analysis") between—the modern philosophies of history (beyond their apparent antagonism) thus suggests a paradox that calls for some reflection. Freely commenting on Leo Strauss, Pierre Manent unhesitatingly asserts that the opposition between "realist" thinkers (for whom the real and the ideal must coincide) and "idealist" thinkers (who value the ought, the split between the real and the ideal) is purely fictive, Hegelianism actualizing the unity of these two traditions at the same time as it reveals the illusory nature of the pseudoantinomy that they create: "Machiavelli, Hobbes, Hegel—this is the line of development of political thinking in the form of realism or the sacralization of fact. Rousseau, Kant, and again Hegel—this is the line of development of modern thinking in the form of utopia or the sacralization of right. Hegel is the common term of these two lines of thought. We know he considered his system the completion of philosophy; at the very least, he completed modern philosophy by realizing and uncovering the unity of his apparently twofold and contradictory plan."[27]

I have already elsewhere attempted a critical analysis of Strauss's claims, and this is not the place to review them;[28] we have seen how, far from being simply apparent, the plurality of modern philosophies of history can be literally "deduced" from the structures of ontology and the questions inherent in them. It of course remains to be shown, however, that the plurality that is merely *possible* at the level of this "deduction" is both real and legitimate (irreducible). So we should consider the question of the historical emergence of this plurality before we undertake not to reduce this plurality to a Hegelian synthesis, but to grasp its articulations. And we should first look at the emergence of the basic duality of theoretical (rationalist) and practical (ethical) philosophies of history, for they form the central core around which the other philosophies of history are gathered.

6. The Emergence of the Plurality of Philosophies of History: German Idealism and the French Revolution

There is absolutely no doubt that we could find numerous forerunners of the "theory of the cunning of reason" as well as of the "moral view of the world."[29] In my opinion, however, Kant and Fichte were the first to come up with a systematic formulation of these two philosophies of history, and this was prompted by the conflict dividing German philosophers on the subject of the French Revolution:[30] as we shall see, our two philosophies of history are initially the only two possible responses, from the viewpoint of the Enlightenment, to the "reactionary" attacks on the Revolution starting in 1790. The study of the political context giving rise to the theory of the cunning of reason and the moral view of the world will enable us to see not only the "practical" stakes of these two philosophies of history, but also to spell out further the plan of this study.

As has been noted in all the analyses of the *Rezeptiongeschichte* of the French Revolution,[31] philosophers in Germany saw the events as a presentation (*Darstellung*) of the theoretically triumphant notion of subjectivity: the Revolution was seen, at least initially, as a product of the Enlightenment, the moment when "man ceased to be governed by external wills and obeyed only his conscience," in "the inner light we each possess";[32] speaking in the name of reason, the Revolution immediately confounded its cause with that of man becoming the foundation of his own destiny, in short, with the cause of freedom understood as subjectivity.

Having said this, we know how in 1790 the public's initial enthusiasm[33] began to give way to a reactionary criticism that was later fueled by the Terror: inspired by Burke's *Reflections on the Revolution in France*,[34] writers "Burkized" with greater or lesser talent, as Alexis Philonenko notes,[35] Rehberg's 1793 *Untersuchungen über die französische Revolution* [Investigations into the French Revolu-

tion]³⁶ proving the best pamphlet against the upheavals in France—
the one to which Fichte replied with his *Beiträge zur Berichtigung
der Urtheile des Publicums über die französische Revolution* [Contri-
butions toward the correction of the public's judgment on the French
Revolution]. Rehberg's criticism was essentially directed at "the idea
of a politics based on reason and not on facts,"³⁷ that is, the very one
the German public had at first most applauded in the Revolution,
including Gentz who, before he too became a "Burkite," wrote to
Garve in 1790 that France presented "the first example of a form of
government based on principles, and a system that is consistent."³⁸
In other words, Rehberg attacked the Revolution for attempting to
deduce practical politics from theory, in particular from Rousseau's
Social Contract: as "a political system deduced uniquely from the
laws of pure reason,"³⁹ the Revolution could only fail to solve the
concrete problems of the "real world" and prove itself impotent;
furthermore, by giving power to the will of all, the revolutionaries
fell victim to a confusion caused by pure theory: Rousseau's subtle
distinction between the general will (reason) and the will of all (a
result of the passions) was bound to be lost in the transition from
theory to practice, and bound to lead to the empowerment of the
arbitrary will of all, dominated—owing to human weakness—not by
reason, but by blind passions: thus, not only was theory powerless,
but it also gave rise—by being able only to betray itself when put
into practice—to the system it claimed to destroy, "in which the civil
constitution depends on arbitrarily determined principles."⁴⁰ Faced
with this aberration that produces the excesses we are now witness-
ing (in 1793), it is clear, concluded Rehberg, that politics must come
back from the ideal to the real, from theory to practice, and—assuming its separation from theory—base itself primarily on the "observation of the age, the places, and the social, historical, and moral
relations of the people,"⁴¹ in short, to give up being a science and to
be merely a more modest but less perilous empiricism.

These criticisms are well known. We may not, however, truly
understand them and the reactions they provoked among the *philosophes,* the defenders of reason, until we see that this attack is in fact
a repetition of an earlier one: politically, it exactly reproduces a first
philosophical attack on the Enlightenment which had taken place
during the *Pantheismusstreit* [pantheism dispute] beginning in 1785.
Disregarding the particular issues in the conflict,⁴² we recall that the
quarrel about pantheism was primarily between Friedrich Heinrich
Jacobi and Moses Mendelssohn, with Jacobi criticizing "rationalistic"

philosophy as ill suited to thinking about reality and life while seeking in faith that which "uncovers and reveals existence," and with Mendelssohn responding by defending reason and speculation against a return to empiricism and religiousness.[43] Now, clearly, starting in 1790, the criticisms of the political "rationalism" of the French Revolution merely repeat the arguments already voiced by the opponents of rationality during the *Pantheismusstreit;* one can give two clear proofs of this:

—The reference to an indispensable empiricism consistently serves to separate theory and practice, and this works against the search for a politics founded on reason: we have seen this reference in Rehberg; we can see it just as much at work in Burke's *Reflections* in the will (which, oddly, uses the same metaphors to repeat Aristotle's criticism of Plato's philosopher-king) to grant political power to "the farmer and the physician, rather than the professor of metaphysics. The science of constructing a commonwealth, or renovating it, or reforming it, is, like every other experimental science, not to be taught *a priori.*"[44] In his reply to the "Burkites," Fichte clearly stresses that this empiricism amounts to a thinly disguised irrationalism, that is, the position defended by Jacobi in the quarrel with pantheism:

> I can certainly share with you wherein lies the authentic point of conflict between you all and us. You don't really wish to completely ruin relations with reason, nor with your generous old friend, the Beaten Track, either. You wish to cleave yourselves between the two, and thereby manage to fall into the uncomfortable situation of being unable to fully satisfy two such cantankerous masters. Go ahead and follow with resolution the feeling of gratitude that attracts you to the latter; then we'll know where we stand with you. . . . A rational reason for this you could not cite, since *here you are leaving reason behind.* (*B* 107, emphasis added)

In other words, it is irrationalism, which Jacobi had already used to oppose the Enlightenment in 1785 and which reappeared in Burke in 1790 and Rehberg in 1793, that is at the core of counterrevolutionary empiricism.

—Fichte's diagnosis is so sound, at least in the German context, that it would even be possible to support it today on a factual test: in 1790, even before Burke's writings appeared, Jacobi wrote a long letter in French to the Academician Jean François de La Harpe, who supported the Revolution and presented it as the work of the philosophes, in which he attacked the revolutionary claim to have found "a fixed way of being governed by reason alone."[45] And Jacobi then uses against the Revolution the arguments he had used five years earlier against the Enlightenment: "Reason was never the only thing with us up until now; considered as an abstract being, one of pure reason, she seems to us neither legislative, nor executive, but purely judiciary, purely applicative of given determinations to given objects. She is a superb lantern-holder; but by herself she could neither enlighten nor move. . . . We hate this insolent reason who has neither heart nor guts, who has nothing but sacrifices to lay before us and who orders us about as if we were made for her, whereas she is made for us."[46]

Clearly, this attack on reason in 1790 represents a resumption of the attack that had taken place in 1785 against the Enlightenment.[47] Under these circumstances it was natural that Kant, who in *What Is Orientation in Thinking?* had responded to the first attack in 1786 with a ringing defense of reason, also undertook to respond to the second in 1793 with the book *On the Old Saw: 'That May Be Right in Theory, but It Won't Work in Practice.'* Kant completed his response in 1795 with his "Perpetual Peace," but in 1793 Fichte too attacked the "Burkites" with his *Beiträge,* his first important piece of writing, and thus entered on the political scene with a text that runs parallel to Kant's. This parallel has been luminously pursued by Alexis Philonenko,[48] and there is no need to cover the same ground here. I wish merely to stress that the two responses, Kant's in "Theory and Practice" and Fichte's in the *Beiträge,* employ two philosophies of history in a political defense of the French Revolution, but the two philosophies of history are quite different and so conclude with quite different defenses of the Revolution:

(1) Kant's defense concedes to Rehberg that human weakness (the selfishness of inclinations) definitely runs the risk of introducing a solution of continuity between theory and practice: human nature is[49] too wicked for the idea of duty (theory) to have direct application to desires and plans (practice). But Kant still rejects Rehberg's two conclusions from this disparity between theory and practice: the assertion of the futility of all rational theory and practice, and the justification of the most conservative and authoritarian politics. (Because human nature is wicked, the rule of law must be imposed by every means.) To respond to Rehberg with a defense of the principles of the Revolution, the only thing Kant could do—given that he began with the idea that human nature is wicked—was to develop an idea of history in which selfish inclinations came to limit themselves

27

precisely because of their confrontation with each other. This was the thesis defended in 1795 in his "Perpetual Peace": the political problem (to create the maximum amount of freedom and a minimum of constraint while achieving the maximum amount of justice and security for all) is "insolvable, even for a people composed of devils (if only they possess understanding)"; for—on condition that a constitution is drawn up such that these people whose "private attitudes conflict" are forced to set a limit to their selfishness—they gradually come to realize that it is in their own interest jointly to curb their inclinations in such a way that "these beings behave publicly just as if they had no evil attitudes." The political stake of Kant's thesis is clear: we should not expect the solution to the political problem to come from the "moral" action of the authoritarian state externally imposing the rule of law on selfish individuals; he rejects the antimony, used for arguing against the Revolution, between freedom (which would bring about anarchy and a state of war) and despotic authority (which could secure merely order and civil peace): without the need for a despot, it is enough for the state—*certainly necessary*—to provide the selfish inclinations with an enclosure that sets a limit to them, and then these same inclinations may be freely deployed within these limits, and, by holding each other in check, produce "the better effect." The state is justified as the minimum framework within which these inclinations are played out, fashioned as they are by "the great artist of nature herself [whose] mechanical course . . . visibly exhibits the purposive plan of producing concord among men, even against their will and indeed by means of their very discord." [50] Historical necessity ("the mechanical course") thus achieves the rule of law without individuals truly willing it, without some transforming action imposing it: human nature has no need of moral improvement, for "nature's design" is actualized by the very fact of this "unsociable sociableness." Contrary to a widespread interpretation, Kant's reply to the reactionary objections was not at all moralistic, for he made no appeal to good will. Kant's writings thus take a political stand that is explicitly based on a conception of history, one of whose descendants is undeniably, mutatis mutandis, Hegel's theory of the "cunning of reason," [51] and about whose speculative prerequisites there are grounds for seeking.

(2) Fichte, too, based his defense of the Revolution on a conception of history: denying the thesis of human weakness that Kant had conceded to Rehberg, Fichte starts with a *neutral* state of nature and can thus assert that the history of humanity is fully *open* and hence is

the history of Freedom acting, and the arbitrary limitations imposed on this freedom should be done away with, thus actively creating the conditions for its full flowering. As we have seen, the political implications of this defense are quite different from those of Kant's:

- Kant's solution justifies the state as an enclosure necessary for a productive interplay of selfish inclinations; Fichte's solution seems to lead to a negation of the state in the affirmation of the rule of freedom;
- Kant defends less the revolutionary process (which is in no way indispensable, since it is "the mechanical course" of history that produces the state of civil peace) than its effects, that is, its contribution (at least up to the excesses we know about) to the creation of a civil constitution in which the inclinations hold each other in check; Fichte defends not only the effects, but also the process of the Revolution—which expresses freedom at work in history; in this sense, only Fichte is properly a revolutionary.

So we have two political positions (Fichte is a revolutionary, Kant is basically a reformer) and two conceptions (mechanist, activist) of history. Fichte unfolds the modern idea of historicity in which the subject is the motor in history: for him, the subject in action in history appears as the human subject (free action); but Kant's theory of "nature's plan" sets forth a different philosophy of subjectivity and a different conception of the subject of history: the very movement of the real is deployed *as if* there was a providence at work that was manifested in the discernible finality in the course of the world. In a word, Kant formulated what was to be the main point of Hegel's point of view,[52] to wit, the idea that there is a rationality at work in history, but one that escapes the awareness of particular subjects.

I of course do not mean to "reduce" Kantianism to an embryonic Hegelianism: we shall see (in chap. 3) that, whatever its ambiguities,[53] Kant's philosophy of history consistently differs from Hegelian rationalism (from "realism" or "historicism" in Strauss's sense of the term) in never positing the idea of a cunning of reason or "nature's design" as other than just a hypothesis or "conducting thread" for the philosopher's reflection (and never as a dogmatic truth). Nevertheless, Kant's philosophy of history differs from Hegel's more in its status than in its doctrinal content. As for this content, we may think that the fundamental duality of the modern ideas of history had its philosophical formulation with the writings of Kant and Fichte just mentioned. I can now make clear the plan of this book.

—*Plan of this book.* In part 1 I take up the first problem (see sec. 5 above)—the problem caused by the antinomy of rationalism and irrationalism: as I have said, this antinomy is first and foremost of a theoretical kind. It poses an epistemological question: whether and to what extent does the principle of reason govern the totality of the historical real? In part 1 I propose to begin with a discussion of the practical consequence of the fact that both thesis and antithesis, rationalism and irrationalism, lead to the elimination of the ethical viewpoint that we have just seen adopted by Fichte. I think this method has two advantages: first, it enables the nonspecialist reader of the history of German philosophy to grasp the stakes of this antinomy, stakes that would probably be attenuated by a purely theoretical discussion of the status of the principle of reason. Primarily, however, to have done with the thesis that modernity is thoroughly homogeneous, it will be necessary to show why, in their very antinomy, neither Hegelianism nor phenomenology definitively succeed in radically (without remainder) eliminating the ethical point of view. Therefore, after examining Hegel's criticism of the moral view of the world (chap. 1), then phenomenological criticism of Hegel (chap. 2), I shall come back (chap. 3) to the question of the status of the principle of reason in history, whose absolute affirmation or absolute negation in Hegel and Heidegger respectively explicitly leads to the elimination of the ethical point of view.

Once it is shown that the moral view of the world cannot be dismissed in either the most coherent rationalistic metaphysics or what is probably the most radical criticism of it, we can in part 2 consider the problems raised by the practical philosophy of history, particularly the antinomy it in turn forms with rationalism (with mechanism).

The reader may be a bit surprised when comparing this plan with the deduction proposed here of five philosophies of history, that it does not take thematic account of the third or the fifth. There are two reasons for this: on the one hand, what will be said about the theoretical and practical philosophies of history as well as the antinomy they form is sufficient, without further need for specific elaboration, for criticizing any pseudoscientific attempt to arrive at a dogmatic combination of rationalism and voluntarism (the third philosophy of history). On the other hand, the final chapters of each of the two sections, as the reader will easily see, bring out in a rigorously parallel way the two fundamental aspects (on the theoretical and practical levels) of the fifth philosophy of history whose conclusion shows that it is nothing other than the articulation of the nondogmatic elements of rationalism, voluntarism, and phenomenology.

The Antinomy of Rationalism and Irrationalism: From Hegel to Heidegger and from Heidegger to Kant

For Hegelian Readers

Some readers will surely be startled by the beginning of chap. 1, for I thought it best not to address directly Hegel's central question about the existence of *contingency* in history. The conclusion of the chapter attempts to make up for this apparent shortcoming. For now, however, let me say that this absence reflects neither some ignorance on my part of Hegel's writings on this question, nor a misappreciation of his criticism, in the introduction to his *Principles of the Philosophy of Right,* of the "sociologism" that, before its time, was represented by the idea of history set forth by the adherents of the "Historical school." As becomes clear by the end of this chapter, I merely attempt to show that Hegel's position inevitably lends itself to two different interpretations: *either* we admit that the contingent exists in history, but in that case Hegel's critique of Kant's and Fichte's criticism (particularly the formal, strictly Kantian conception of the *concept*) seems untenable; it was in this sense that Theodor Häring could say of a passage Hegel wrote about the contingent: "There is no doubt whatever that all this fundamentally contradicts the fact that Hegel made it a point of honor to conceive [*begreifen*] all determinates as integrated in the totality, even/also the spatiotemporal ones, if only as subordinate elements, if only by way of principle";[1] *or* one starts with the critique of criticism, with the plan to go beyond the merely formal conception of reason (the concept), and then the contingent has to be "deduced" and one founders in a "fantastical" idealism (a reading proposed by every critic of Hegel's idealism from Schelling to Marx and Kierkegaard). In my opinion it is the first member of this alternative that is philosophically and philologically the most plausible: as I shall try to show, it makes most problematic the thesis of Hegel's "transcendence" of criticism.[2]

The Hegelian Philosophy of History and the Rationalist Negation of the Idea of Praxis

1. The Basic Features of Hegel's Theory of the "Cunning of Reason"

We have seen how *in principle* a rationalistic philosophy of history inevitably has to make a radical criticism of what it regards as the naïve idea of practical freedom. This judgment can also be confirmed *in fact* when we see how, from Tübingen to Frankfurt, Hegel's philosophy of history, starting with positions initially quite close to those of the young Fichte, gradually changed through a criticism of its starting point, as Bernard Bourgeois has shown very well:

> At Frankfurt Hegel discovered the specific relation between moments of time that makes time an irreversible creative process, a genuine historical evolution. He granted increasingly great importance to historical time as the source of the various human contents that at Berne he located *in* time, but whose origin he saw as essentially human freedom understood in a seemingly formal and voluntaristic Kantian-Fichtean sense. From then on, Hegel was to go beyond this twofold formalism of time as pure form, pure medium, and of freedom as the autonomy of the will.[1]

It is clearly impossible here to spell out the details of the development of Hegel's thought or to show how it grew further and further away from an ethical and practical view of history.[2] So instead of a diachronic study of the development of his philosophy of the cunning of reason, I shall pursue a synchronic study systematically indicating what could be called the most important features of this theory, that is, the ones making it radically anti-Fichtean. (In discussing these features, I am obliged to repeat certain remarks made in the introduction. This irritant seemed to me less serious, however, than the ones inevitably caused by a more allusive treatment.) On the basis of this analysis, we can return to the question of how this conception of history eliminates the Fichtean view and hence presupposes a genuine internal criticism of Hegelianism that aims to determine the exact point at which this rationalistic conception of history precludes Fichte's plan for a moral view of the world and a basis for the idea of praxis.

(1) According to Hegel, in the final analysis the fundamental "presupposition" of the theory of the cunning of reason is the idea that "reason governs the world and so also governs and has governed world history. In relation to this in and for itself universal and substantial reason, everything else is subordinate, its servant and means" (*VG* 87; *RH*).[3] As such, Hegel's philosophy of history suggests that it is a deterministic theory, one in which historical events are connected indissolubly or necessarily. It should be stressed that, at the level of history, Hegel's theory of the cunning of reason is a direct consequence of the unlimited use of the principle of sufficient reason according to which everything has a reason for being.[4] This amounts to postulating not only the universal validity of this principle, but also the absolute intelligibility of the real, the fact that everything real is explicable and hence that one can explain [*rendre raison*] every event in history,[5] even those that clearly do not *seem* to bear the stamp of universality and rationality. It is also noteworthy that this assertion is reciprocal, and we may posit that every unlimited assertion of the principle of sufficient reason (or another version of it, the principle of causality) implies an idea of history as the cunning of reason, for it implies the necessity of thinking of the real as entirely explicable, meaning completely rational "de jure" or "in itself," if not "in fact" or "for us." This simple and possibly trivial-seeming observation, however, helps us appreciate all the problems of a criticism of the cunning of reason, problems that can be summed up as follows: Can we give up making unlimited use of the principle of sufficient reason? Doesn't the desire to explain the real "objectively"—to find some logic, whatever it may be, in the sequence of historical events—imply the use of the principle of reason (or causality) and hence a view of history as the cunning of reason? Under these circumstances, isn't every scientific or "objective" approach to history fated to reintroduce Hegel's theory of the cunning of reason, whether that is desired or not?[6] Hegel's answer to these questions is quite clear: it is impossible to limit the principle of reason, and it must be wholly valid for history if "this reason is immanent in historical reality" and "achieves itself in and by this reality" (*VG* 87; *RH*).

(2) Hegel's deterministic view of history is also idealistic, for it

implies the identity of the rational and the real, the latter being posited as completely "explicable." In this sense, we see that this view of history strongly depends on a certain application of ontology, on a definition of the real as a priori subject to the two logical principles underlying Leibniz's *Theodicy:* the principle of identity (the real, being identical with itself, is identifiable) and the principle of sufficient reason. The theory of the cunning of reason thus depends on the ontological postulate that the real is a priori and basically consistent with these two logical structures of rationality.

(3) Thus, the theory of the cunning of reason is dialectical: it presupposes that reason is realized through its opposite, unreason, that is, the chaotic interplay of particular self-interests and passions, through its "other"; as such, the opposite or "the other" of reason is in reality merely an *apparent* otherness, for it partakes, if only instrumentally, of an overall rationality. And we can easily show how this fundamental dialectical structure—reason being realized by its *apparent* "other"—is specified in a multiplicity of seemingly antinomial pairs that can in fact be reconciled through dialectics: this way, law is actualized through force, the universal through the particular interplay of inclinations, spirit through the natural process of clashes of self-interest, consciousness through the unconscious, and so forth. Thus, the three terms by which we have hitherto defined the cunning of reason ineluctably refer to each other: every idealist thought— every thought of the unity of the real and the rational—is necessarily dialectical and deterministic, and vice versa: reason is dialectically realized by its apparent "other" because the irrational is necessary for the actualization of reason, and hence everything real—which is rational (explicable)—is useful and necessary.

(4) In essence, the theory of the cunning of reason implies the radical negation of the very idea of praxis, the reduction of the ethical point of view (the point of view of free action or the Fichtean "ought") to a pure illusion connected with the subject's finitude: "the consummation of the infinite End thus consists merely in removing the illusion that makes it seem as yet unaccomplished" (*E* 274, addendum to §212), the illusion of praxis in which one supposes that the Good, far from being actualized in the world from the beginnings of time, must be still introduced into it. If the real has been completely rational from the beginning of time, the very idea of praxis— the idea of a transforming action performed on the real by a subject to make it better—is absurd, and this for two reasons:

—First, this idea necessarily presupposes the possibility of making decisions, that is, the possibility for the finite subject to think of itself as the author of its actions and not as the plaything of some external force; but this supposition is contrary to the principle of sufficient reason which excludes any possibility of a first beginning in the world: for if one is free to initiate by oneself a series of events in the world, the real would not be rational (wholly explicable), but arbitrary and dependent on the will of each finite subject. Understood this way, a belief in freedom is thus an illusion of the Hegelian "common consciousness."

—Second, if the idea of praxis is wholly illusory, that is because reason is not in reality formal; reason is not a simple empty form, a simple "plan" or merely ideal "program" with which one projects information onto or transforms the real (matter) from the outside. If, however, we take seriously the proposition that the real is rational (and how can we not when we refuse to reject the principle of identity and the principle of reason, that is, the preconditions for any logical thinking?), then reason is the totality of what is, not an abstract form similar to what Kant and Fichte call "practical reason." So the idea of praxis—the idea of a transformation of the real and a plan of rationalization that is not yet carried out but *ought* to be, and hence is merely formal and ideal—must thus itself be explained using the correct idea of reason as the totality of the real; it is then necessary to "explain," "give reasons" [*rendre raison*] for the appearance in the finite consciousness of the formal theory of reason expressed by the idea of praxis; it needs to be shown how the real by itself gives rise to the "ought," the illusion of praxis or voluntary decision, for "this is the illusion in which we live" (*E* 274). In the end the solution to the question is fairly simple: it consists in showing how what we as finite beings take for a free [voluntary] project, a praxis, is actually wholly determined by the historical process in which we are situated; it is the very movement of history that creates the illusion of praxis, and this illusion should be dispelled: "In the course of its process the Idea creates that illusion, by setting an antithesis to confront it; and its action consists in getting rid of the illusion that it has created" (*E* 274). It is noteworthy that we find this form of the negation of praxis in every theory of the cunning of reason, even the so-called materialist version. Thus, for example, Marx gives economic "content" to Hegel's theory of philosophical rationality only after he reduces revolutionary praxis to a mechanical effect of the process of accumulating capital: "Along with the constant decrease in the number of capitalist magnates who usurp and monopolize all the advantages of this process of transformation, the mass of misery, oppression, slavery, degradation and exploitation grows; but with this there also grows the revolt of the working class, a class constantly increasing in numbers, and trained, united and organized by the very mechanism of the capitalist process of production."[7] The idea of praxis is radically denied when conceived in terms of production (hence causally, in terms of the principle of reason) resulting from a process external to it, which Hegel brilliantly summarizes as follows: "[T]his dialectic is not an activity of subjective thinking applied to some matter externally, but is rather the matter's very soul putting forth its branches and fruit organically. This development of the Idea is the proper activity of its rationality, and thinking, as something subjective, merely looks on at it without for its part adding to it any ingredient of its own. To consider a thing rationally means not to bring reason to bear on the object from the outside and so to tamper with it, but to find that the object is rational on its own account."[8]

The assertion of the total rationality of the real thus necessarily results in the elimination of any *critical* or *ethical* (meaning external) view of the world in favor of an exclusively internal, immanent criticism that is in reality confounded with the understanding of the object studied—because the object has for all time been consistent with what it should be. Or, as Hegel says in a remarkable passage in which he sums up his own philosophical journey compared to the (supposed) positions of Kant and Fichte, it is the point of view of "the understanding" [or "Intelligence"] that eventually replaces that of the "Will":

> While Intelligence merely proposes to take the world as it is, Will takes steps to make the world what it ought to be. . . . It is here that we meet the contradictions that are so bewildering from the standpoint of abstract morality. This position in its "practical" bearings is the one taken by the philosophy of Kant, and even by that of Fichte. The Good, say these writers, has to be realized: we ought to work in order to produce it: and Will is only the Good actualizing itself. If the world then were as it ought to be, the action of Will would be at an end. The Will itself therefore requires that its End should not be realized. In these words, a correct expression is given to the *finitude* of Will. But finitude was not meant to be the ultimate point: and it is the process of Will itself which abolishes finitude and the contradiction it involves. The reconciliation is achieved when Will in its result returns to the presupposi-

tion made by cognition. In other words, it consists in the unity of the theoretical and practical idea. Will knows the end to be its own, and Intelligence apprehends the world as the concept actual.(*E,* addendum to §234, p. 291)

This criticism implies a certain conception of the will and also a rejection of the point of "ethical finitude" that should here be restored (since, aiming to reduce and supersede the ethical dimension—the Fichtean point of view—Hegel claims to stand beyond any such dimension: a claim whose legitimacy needs to be evaluated):

—Hegel's theory of the will may first be regarded as a broadened version of Kantianism. Like Kant, Hegel saw the essence of the will lying in self-positing or autonomy: "On the one hand, the task of science is, roughly speaking, to overcome this contingency; as in the range of practice, on the other, the end of action is to rise above the contingency of the will, or above caprice" (*E,* addendum to §145, p. 205). Thus, "the genuinely free will 'should' include free choice as suspended [*aufgehoben*] "(*F.* 206). The will thus corresponds to its real concept only when it becomes practical reason, that is, the universal moral will and not a particular will: "The Practical Reason is understood by Kant to mean a *thinking* Will, i.e., a Will that determines itself on universal principles" (*E* 86). Thus Hegel seems to echo Kant's concept of autonomy. To Kantianism, however, he adds the idea that the universal will should not be opposed to the free will, to the particular will, but reconciled with it.[9] From the practical point of view, the sign of the finitude of the moral view of the world is the indefinite disparity between the universal will and the particular will (which results in the imperative form taken by the moral law).

Furthermore, according to Hegel, this point of view is not only dangerous,[10] but also contradictory and indefensible: for the moral will claims to wish the Good to be eventually actualized; but if that were the case, the very standpoint of moral action would vanish. This sheds light on the roots of Fichte's formalism: in reality, the moral will wants itself (as a *process*) more than the Good (as a *result*) because—value inhering in the moral intention and not in the result of the action—the actualization of the Good would eliminate all moral intention and hence the Good in a contradiction that Hegel sees as involving an appeal to the "bad infinity" created by the putative solution of an ideal actualizable only ad infinitum: "Consciousness has . . . to bring about this harmonious unity, and continually to be making progress in morality. But the consummation of this progress has to be projected into a future infinitely remote; for if it actually came about, this would do away with moral consciousness.... The consummation ... cannot be attained, but is to be thought of merely as an *absolute* task, i.e. one which simply remains a task" (*PS* 368). Yet, one must *at the same time* think that this task is actualizable, as is expressed in the formula "you should, therefore you can," so that the moral view of the world is lost in "the contradiction of a task which is to remain a task and yet ought to be fulfilled" (*PS* 369), a contradiction that this view can, if not resolve, at least blur only "in the dim remoteness of infinity, to which for that very reason the attainment of the goal has to be postponed" (*PS* 369).[11]

So to overcome this contradiction, we must conceive of the possibility of reconciling the moral will with a reality that is not indefinitely postponed. Here, Hegel literally reverses Fichte's point of view: far from its being the real world that is transformed by the subject's moral activity and that hence approaches and eventually coincides with the ideal (a coincidence that from the moral point of view can never "really" take place), it is the representation of the ideal that will gradually coincide with the real, which is already perfect in itself:

> All unsatisfied endeavor ceases, when we recognize that the final purpose of the world is accomplished no less, as it ever accomplishes itself. Generally speaking, this is the adult's way of looking; while the young person imagines that the world is utterly sunk in wickedness and that the first thing needful is a thorough transformation. The religious mind, on the other hand, views the world as ruled by Divine Providence, and therefore correspondent with what ought to be.

Hegel thus concludes that there is a "harmony between the 'is' and the 'ought to be'" (*E*, addendum to §234, p. 291).[12] Contrasting the position of the "young person" with that of the "adult," Hegel is merely interpreting his own philosophical development from his stay in Tübingen—which was dominated by an ethical conception of history—to Frankfurt where he reconciled the ideal with the real. Thus it is clear that Hegel's philosophy of history was formed through a refutation of the Fichtean point of view.[13]

We see that this criticism claims to take the form of an integration or *Aufhebung*, and not simply a "refutation" [disproof]: this means it represents an internal criticism of Fichte's positions. Later, when Hegel intends to go beyond "the moral view of the world," it is in the direction in which the Hegelian common consciousness is also overcome through philosophical speculation (see *E*, introduction,

§6), that is, by a *more rational* point of view, so that the lingering of an ethical and practical position stems from a misunderstanding of the nature of knowledge or, in other words, from a certain form of irrationalism. Moreover, in showing how this lack of reason could give rise to unacceptable political positions, Hegel makes a connection between Fichte's politics and the Reign of Terror, making his criticisms more persuasive by winning the approval of the enemies of political oppression. Thus, it has often been admitted as self-evident that the condemnation of the moral view of the world was an agreed-upon cause and that its characteristic opposition between the "is" and the "ought" should be judged definitively formal and untenable,[14] so that, of all Hegel's philosophy, this criticism may be the most widely endorsed, even by declared opponents of Hegel's system.[15] In what follows we shall return to the question of its validity. For now, it is important to stress that for Hegel the criticism has real significance and application only against the background of the theory of the cunning of reason. It would be utterly absurd to try to repeat Hegel's criticism of Fichte without also repeating the implications that Hegel himself judged inescapable: Hegel can criticize the "terrorism" of Kant and Fichte only on the basis of a theory of the cunning of reason and hence an idealist ontology (the definition of the real as consistent with the principles of identity and of sufficient reason); without these two references, this criticism would lose all its force and inevitably dissolve into triviality. Conversely, of course, if we "use" Kant or Fichte to criticize the cunning of reason (to open the system closed by Hegel), we must also admit their arguments' consequences, that is, their implications from the ethical point of view. Consequently, nothing would be more vacuous than this unproductive game of "pitting" a "good Hegel" against a "bad Fichte" (Hegel condemns the Reign of Terror), and a "good Fichte" against the "bad Hegel" (Fichte criticizes the cunning of reason and argues for "the opening of the system"). We can reconcile the "good parts" of these two philosophies only if we naïvely nullify the systematic linking and internal cohesion of all their features and thereby rob them of all their significance and force.

(5) If the idea of praxis is wholly illusory, and as a result history is not 'really' created by human action—"for what the individual figures out for himself in his apartness cannot be law for the universal reality" (*VG* 76; *RH*)—if men are merely "a means . . . serving world history, Reason does not attain the Idea in the will of the subject, but only in the action of God" (*VG* 76; *RH*), we must admit that history is

made by and for something else: "Divine Providence may be said to stand to the world and its process in the capacity of absolute cunning. God lets men do as they please with their particular passions and interests; but the result is the accomplishment of—not their plans, but his, and they differ decidedly from the ends primarily sought by those whom he employs" (E, addendum to §209).[16] Surely, God here is not a being that transcends the historical process, but the Reason immanent in this process, or the point of view from which, through the chaotic multiplicity of clashes of particular self-interests, one perceives the rationality emerging as a *resultant:* it remains true—and this is a feature of that theological view of history—that the true meaning of the historical process escapes individuals, not that this meaning escapes all grasp by reason, but because, being fully rational, the meaning goes beyond the sphere of intelligibility of any agent in history. It is on this exact point that Hegel's thought echoes the essential themes of Leibniz's *Theodicy,* that is, basically, the idea that "considering world history, Reason is not subjective whim, but the work of God" (VG 78; RH). If "the justification [of God] consists in making the presence of evil comprehensible in view of the absolute power of Reason" (VG 48; RH), it follows that this theodicy is the very form of any theory of the cunning of reason—the latter aiming to show that from a finite point of view, which is biased and incomplete, what seems evil in the world (war, clashes of particular interests—contradictions and antagonisms of all kinds) is in reality, from a more general point of view (God's), the element necessary for a greater good, an indispensable element for the perfect actualization of reason, so that if we did away with what seems evil in the world, the world would be actually less rational, less perfect. The basis of this argument is the Leibnizian idea that the world proceeds in perfect accord with the "principle of the best," meaning that everything in it has every reason for being. Thus the very idea of the *Theodicy* could not be more radically opposed to that of praxis, for any plan to improve the world is inherently absurd if we admit the perfection and rationality of the universe and its history.

(6) This idea of history must inevitably be somehow naturalistic; by this I mean that, despite Hegel's well-known distinction between the "sciences of the Spirit" and those of nature,[17] the philosophy of history must inevitably lead one to consider only the natural aspect of man: clearly, man enters into history as merely an unconscious component *force,* and Hegel adopts the "physical" image of the composition of the resultant.[18] Therefore, if "*universal* history does not

begin with any conscious end," but if "the end with which history begins ... exists only in itself, that is, *as nature*" or as "unconscious desire," it is evident that in this history, "man makes his appearance as a *natural being* manifesting itself as *natural will:* we have called this the subjective side, need, desire, passion, self-interest, subjective opinion and representation" (*VG* 86–87; *RH*). In short, everything in which and through which man participates in history is not properly human, but natural. Thus, as Fichte emphasized, in every theory of providence, man must be fetishized or reified, integrated as he is in a system that determines him in every respect.

(7) Both "naturalistic" and theological, the theory of the cunning of reason implies a certain conceptionof the *end of history,* referring itself to a *tripartite* idea of the whole of humanity's historical evolution. Furthermore, these two related points[19] can also be easily inferred from the need for the total subjection of the real to the principle of sufficient reason: indeed, if historical events are inescapably interconnected by a "chain" of reasons, it must be admitted that they are in a certain sense already virtually included at the very beginning of history; or, to use Hegel's vocabulary, when something "develops" in history, that is because something was "at the start" first merely "enveloped," merely "in the bud": "What comes before us immediately when we look at development, is that something must be at hand that develops, therefore something en-veloped—the germ, disposition, potential: it is that which Aristotle calls *dynamis;* that is, possibility ... or, it is called, the in itself."[20] Thus history has three elements: (1) the element of the "in itself" in which the whole of evolution is contained in an enveloped or embryonic form; (2) the element of deployment, which Hegel calls "being there," that is, historical evolution strictly speaking, in which events are really deployed in time; and (3) the element of the return to unity, of recollection, which reproduces the origin, the "in itself," but after explaining and deploying everything that was in it only embryonically (which Hegel calls the "for itself"). This final stage then marks the end of universal history—in Hegel's case, the emergence of the modern state.

2. The Political Implications of This Philosophy of History: Hegel's Reading of the French Revolution

The foregoing are, I believe, the seven characteristic features of Hegel's idea of history as the cunning of reason. What are their philosophical presuppositions and political implications? Does this theory succeed in *effectively* eliminating the practical point of view and the ethical dimension? Obviously, we can no longer defer these two questions.

Taking up the first one, I shall, consistent with what I said earlier, use the privileged example of the French Revolution to determine the political attitude of the German idealists. Privileged for analyzing, *in general,* the political implications of a philosophy, the Revolution is especially privileged when it comes to Hegel's conception of history: the Revolution clearly presents the problem of valorizing practice as a tool for changing the world—and from this point of view, Hegel, because of his criticism of the idea of praxis, can only rise in protest against the very spirit of the Revolution; within a conception of history that sees every event as rational and necessary, however, it is plainly impossible to "rise in protest" against some episode in history: this would be to fall back into the illusion (according to which not everything is necessary) on which the practical point of view and hence the spirit of revolution are based. Hegel thus must be both *for* and *against* the French Revolution, the problem (and hence the interest of his interpretation of the Revolution) being the attempt to articulate the two components of this attitude. Thus we see from the start how important it is to examine Hegel's political positions when we refer them to the philosophy of history serving as their theoretical underpinnings, and this way we can judge what political consequences such a philosophy has when it attempts to eliminate Fichte's point of view. Once we have determined the consequences of this elimination, we can pose the problem of its radicality.

In large part, Hegel's attitude toward the French Revolution changed along with his philosophy of history (consistent with the hypothesis suggested here that it is the philosophy of history that connects the speculative and political dimensions of a line of thought): his full allegiance to the ideas of 1789 ended at the same time as he abandoned the basic principles of his initial version of the moral view of the world, when his thinking was strongly influenced by the spreading thought of Fichte. One must not deny the influence on Hegel, as on all the German thinkers, of the realization that the French Revolution was turning into the Reign of Terror. As Bernard Bourgeois rightly stresses, however, this merely illustrated the failure of Hegel's attempt to transform Christianity philosophically into a religion of a free people by applying Kant's ethical principles: "Didn't the French Revolution, in which the particularity jealous of the universal did not tolerate any particularity, show that the actualization of Kantian principles ended in the ugliness of the Terror, the antithesis of freedom and *polis?*"[21] At Berne, Hegel still associated the idea of the French Revolution with that of a restoration of the Greek ideal, and, by explicitly adopting the Fichtean standpoint, he sought to "strengthen" the political revolution through a revolution in ideas; when we learn that this revolution was to involve a return to Kant, we cannot help but be struck by the "Fichtean" character of the connection Hegel makes between the French Revolution and the Copernican revolution, as shown in his letter to Schelling of 16 April 1795: "Out of the Kantian system and its highest achievement I expect a revolution in Germany."[22] Speaking of the "highest achievement" of the Kantian system, Hegel must be referring to Fichte (whom he knew through Schelling),[23] who had already partly carried out Hegel's plan (to rid Christianity of its positivity) by taking the path shown by Kant in his *Religion within the Limits of Reason Alone.* So it is not at all surprising to see Hegel hail the French Revolution in which "humanity is represented as so worthy of esteem in itself," and appeal to the ethical view of the "ought" to criticize politics and religion: "Religion and politics have been hand in glove, the first having taught what despotism wished: contempt of the human race, its incapacity to achieve any kind of good, to be something on its own. With the spread of ideas about how something *should* be, the indolence of staid people, always ready to accept everything as it is, shall disappear. This stimulating force of ideas . . . will elevate spirits, who shall learn to sacrifice themselves to it."[24]

Whatever the many interpretations possible,[25] there is no doubt that Hegel had changed his mind on this point, going from an adherence to the ideas of the Revolution to a critique of them, even if it is stressed, as Joachim Ritter has, that this critique was not at all reactionary in the sense of any sort of restoration of the ancien régime. And we also cannot doubt that this condemnation of the Revolution was made in accordance with Hegel's final philosophy of history when we see just how Hegel related the Revolution to the spirit of Catholicism by contrasting it with the Reformation dominant in Protestant Germany: indeed, if only the Protestant church manages to "reconcile religion with law,"[26] that is because only the Protestant world had managed through thinking to "come to the consciousness of the absolute apex of self-consciousness,"[27] that is, the consciousness of the unity of the rational and the real, thus as §552 of the *Encyclopedia* stresses, a proper understanding of historicity: if "in

Catholicism this spirit of all truth is in actuality set in rigid opposition to the self-conscious spirit," "only in the [Protestant] principle of spirit . . . does the absolute possibility and necessity exist for political power, religion, and the principles of philosophy coinciding in one, and for accomplishing the reconciliation of actuality in general with the spirit, of the state with the religious conscience as well as with the philosophical consciousness."[28] Thus, it is uniquely in the authentic understanding of historicity as the movement by which the real and the rational, which are identical 'in itself,' become so 'for itself' in the state, *that the spirit of revolution disappears in favor of the spirit of reform,* so that it seems legitimate to concur with this conclusion by Jürgen Habermas: "[I]n order not to sacrifice philosophy to the challenge posed by the revolution, Hegel elevated revolution to the primary principle of his philosophy. Only after he had fastened the revolution firmly to the beating heart of the world spirit did he feel secure from it. Hegel did not *curse* the French Revolution and its children into oblivion; he *celebrated* them into oblivion."[29] Even if, as Ritter has correctly argued against Haym, Hegel continued all his life to applaud the "glorious sunrise" of the Revolution,[30] it was at the cost of a radical distinction between the content or result of the events, on the one hand, and the subjective *form* of its *process,*[31] that is, revolutionary consciousness, on the other. Clearly, this development can be fully thought out only in relation to the development of the philosophy of history: although, as we have seen, in 1795 Hegel could justify the revolutionary process,[32] his philosophy of history, starting with the *Phenomenology,* obliged him, as Habermas notably showed, to legitimize the consequences of the French Revolution at the cost of a radical criticism of all revolutionary acts necessarily animated by the spirit of the Terror:[33] he had to "legitimize the revolutionizing of reality without legitimizing the revolutionaries themselves," and so had to undertake "the magnificent attempt to understand the actualization of abstract Right as an objective process."[34] And Hegel had to perform this task because it was imposed on him by the demand to "think of what is" independently of any critical (ethical) gaze on the world, that is, in accordance with his philosophy of history. Thus Hegel had to "legitimize the revolutionary order and still at the same time to criticize revolutionary consciousness,"[35] so that his whole philosophy of the Revolution was a justification of what was unacceptable in the subjective process—that is, in the consciousness of the revolutionaries—at the level of the "objective Spirit," at the level of genuine content.[36] Thus, this was the price of Hegel's criticism of the moral view of the world: if he succeeded in legitimizing the Revolution, or, more exactly, in integrating it into the very movement of the real (= the rational) the way he succeeded in integrating Fichte's ethical point of view, it was by radically attacking the form of individual action and by taking as preeminently dangerous the practical position that radicalizes this point of view. Where the subject's consciousness succeeds in understanding the real, there must action cease, as is shown by the insuperable gulf between the philosopher and the man of action, to which the concluding sentences of *Lectures on the Philosophy of History* are devoted, justifying as though in advance Nietzsche's judgment in *The Birth of Tragedy:* "Knowledge kills action; action requires the veils of illusion."[37] This indeed seems to be the ultimate implication, both philosophical and political, of the Hegelian idea of history.

3. Toward an Internal Criticism of Hegelianism

Before examining the applicability of and problems with this criticism of the very idea of praxis, I would nonetheless like to state that, in my view, its necessary consequences do not *on their own* constitute its refutation: that Hegel's philosophy should leave us a "choice" only between an essentially unintelligent praxis and an essentially inactive contemplation and that these alternatives may seem unsatisfying to the individual are not considerations sufficient to invalidate the line of thinking that contains such implications. Genuine criticism must be internal. So I shall argue that the gulf between action and contemplation produces—in a philosophy that basically aims to be a philosophy of reconciliation—if not a failure, at least a difficulty that creates an opening in the system through which the ethical point of view is reintroduced, and that constitutes the condition of possibility for a post-Hegelian return to critical philosophy. This problem can be picked out at two levels: that of the philosophy of history and that of speculative philosophy properly speaking.

For the philosophy of history, the problem may be summed up concisely: we can get beyond the ethical point of view, whose essence is the distinction between the "is" and the "ought," only by reconciling the ideal and the real, the will and the understanding. It seems that while the Hegelian system manages to think of the reality "in itself" of this reconciliation, it cannot *dialectically* (conceptually) get us to the point at which the reconciliation would also be "for us," such that, for the empirical subject, that which is thought of as reconciled at the level of the theses of the system adopts the figures of scission: scission between two types of activity, even two types of person—the philosopher and the man of action. One of the two following things must be true: either the philosopher efficaciously thinks what is, and then action is purely an illusion; or the man of action produces something "really" new and then the philosopher's understanding never completely coincides with the real. The first hypothesis sends us back to Spinoza, the second to Fichte, and here the problem is that Hegel's system, as a theory of the cunning of reason, must dialectically synthesize the two points of view: it cannot simply consign the ethical view to the realm of illusion, for it is a necessary element of the system (that of the "being-there"), nor can it give action priority over understanding—the solution of making the two viewpoints agree *in succession,* as though action had to occur first and only later to have its intelligibility understood—being plainly unsatisfying since, instead of reconciling the will and the understanding, it amounts to positing a "bad" infinity in which the two never coincide. Habermas partially summed up this difficulty when he showed how Hegel had to have the particular subjective will intervene at the same time as he was forced to deny it, which in the case of the French Revolution amounts to justifying the objective and "natural" element of the Revolution at the expense of its subjective and ethical side:

> The contradiction contained in the construction of the world spirit, which is by no means a dialectical one, thus consists in the following: on the one hand, in order to guarantee the realization of the revolutionary demand in history, a subject must be substituted for this history, which invents the ultimate aim of history as an abstract universal, in order then to actualize it. On the other hand, this universal must not have the character of a theoretically predesigned plan; it is therefore degraded to a self-subsistent being of natural origin, which only "comes to itself"—is realized—after it has objectified itself in the course of history. . . . In the world spirit as the revolutionary who is not yet allowed to be a revolutionary, Hegel's ambivalent relation to the French Revolution is once again brought into focus; Hegel desires the revolutionizing of reality, without any revolutionaries. . . . The hypothesis of the world spirit underlies the paradoxical character of an objective spirit which nevertheless has borrowed its knowledge from the Absolute. Onto it alone is projected what the old Hegel strictly prohibited for politicians as well as for philosophers: at the same time and to act *and* to know.[38]

Thus, if the will and the understanding are reconciled—a reconciliation needed for getting beyond the ethical point of view—it takes place, however, only "in itself," for the objective Spirit, and not "for us" who continue to perceive in succession what, in itself, seems to be necessarily simultaneous: "Only after the spirit has revolutionized reality practically and has made reason actual, can philosophy attain consciousness of the revolutionized world, the world become reason. A communication between philosophers . . . and politically active subjects . . . simply cannot exist."[39] Habermas thus sees this nondialectical contradiction as the stumbling block in Hegel's final philosophy of history, the final philosophy that, according to him, the young Hegel had himself rightly "accused this reconstitution of theory of the same resignation . . . of which he had accused the Christian expectation of salvation, internalized back into contemplation and turned over to an external transcendent authority."[40] And we understand what in some sense justifies Habermas's judgment, since the promised reconciliation of the will and the understanding takes place only in itself and not for us, and so remains *transcendent* for the real individual. "Getting beyond" the Fichtean point of view would thus in reality lead us back to a point short of the critical viewpoint, to a "Spinozistic" philosophy unacceptable to Hegel, at least when he claims to reconcile the particular and the universal by definitively tearing us from the image of the unhappy consciousness. Habermas's analysis, which is persuasive on more than one score, also runs into a problem, however: the aporia thus uncovered is so glaring that it would be presumptuous to think it escaped Hegel's notice. Thus Hegel repeatedly attacked the misrepresentation of his thinking according to which he asserts that the identity of the finite and the infinite, the will and the understanding, is a stable and quasi-transcendental unity: "Such an expression for the Absolute as *unity* of thought and being, of finite and infinite, etc., is false; for unity expresses an abstract and merely quiescent identity" (*E* 279).

Thus we should again examine how, at the level of speculative philosophy, Hegel tries to get beyond the interpretation which would reduce his system to a new form of Spinozism.

Hegel's solution is essentially sketched in the last three paragraphs of the *Encyclopedia,* notably in the 1830 edition whose additions were, as Theodore Geraets has shown, a reply to this sort of objection.[41] Clearly, if we make a *static* unity of the will and the understanding, the point of view of action can only appear illusorily (since, in reality, everything is already played out), just as the understanding, correspondingly, can never coincide with the real other than abstractly in the content-free assertion of their identity. So the attempt must be made to overcome the opposition—which for Hegel is once again that between Fichte and Spinoza—by thinking of the identity as a *process*. Hence the well-known but enigmatic formulas according to which the "unsatisfied endeavor" characteristic of Fichte's ethical point of view "ceases when we recognize" not the stable identity of the real and the rational, but the fact that the "final purpose of the world is accomplished no less than ever accomplishing itself" (*E*, addendum to §234, p. 291). Thus, Hegel, in the paragraph in the *Encyclopedia* about the theory of history, again states that "the Good, the absolutely Good, is eternally accomplishing itself in the world; and the result is that it need not wait upon us, but is already by implication, as well as in full actuality, accomplished" (*E*, addendum to §212, p. 274). It would be easy to produce many quotations in this vein. The problem, we see, is to understand how a process that goes on forever can be completed. Though the solution is not easy because, since even for Hegel it is a matter of the "hardest opposition," the most difficult to think through, the problem, however, can be set out rather simply: the identity of the rational and the real, thus of the will and the understanding, must be thought of both as a *process* (or else we simply come back to a Spinozistic position from which the finite point of view, i.e., the point of view of action, must be regarded as an illusion and not as a real element of the Absolute, which, however, it must be) and as an already completed *result* (without which it would be impossible to reconcile the understanding with the real).

The problem thus set forth, let us see how in §577 of the *Encyclopedia* Hegel suggests a solution: in this paragraph the totality of the system is thought of as the unity of the "first two syllogisms"; according to the first syllogism (§575)—Logic, Nature, Spirit—this system has been objectively realized from the beginnings of time. This is at bottom the most naïve "reading" of philosophy, for it corresponds to the attitude of the subject that, arbitrarily deciding to take up the study of philosophy, believes it should look for *a truth that exists prior to and independently of its own activity*. As Geraets writes: "The first syllogism expresses the actualization of philosophy's concept in its most immediate, most appearance-bound form, that in which philosophy appears as a *thought-object* for a subject separated from and exterior to it, subject which, faced with the objective unfolding of the system, forgets itself in a bad forgetting."[42] This view, which isn't false but simply incomplete, is thus the one that Hegel thought Spinoza's philosophy could not get beyond. In relation to our question, the bracketing of the subject's activity, at the level of the philosophy of history, corresponds to the condemnation of the ethical point of view as wholly illusory, for the former posits that the real and the rational are identical in themselves (*objectively*) in eternity.

In the second syllogism (see §576), which takes the form: Nature—Spirit—Logic, the truth is thought of as *the result of the subject's activity* (which corresponds to the *Phenomenology* interpreted from the point of view of the "naïve consciousness"). In the second syllogism the subject recognizes the universal, the logical, as the product of its subjective activity, which implies that from this second standpoint the identity of the real and the rational is itself a *process*, and not an objective reality closed on itself and always already inscribed in things. Thus here we take the standpoint of "spiritual reflection" for which "knowledge appears as a subjective knowledge whose goal is freedom and which is itself the way to produce it for itself" (*E*, addendum §576). Here, consequently, the truth is conceived as the result of some *indefinite* work to understand the spiritual, that is, the historical. Thus, "if the first reading reveals an achieved totality of thought, one in closure, the second reading, made from the viewpoint of the philosophizing subject himself . . . should . . . necessarily remain an open thinking, someone's effort to understand his time," since "the process of understanding could only be achieved together with the series of figurations which is not the case in the realm of the philosophy of Spirit." [43]

The third syllogism thus must reconcile the two viewpoints, but (here we see the main difficulty arise) in such a way that *this synthesis has the significance of a return to the first syllogism*. Thus the solution, particularly in the third edition of the *Encyclopedia,* stresses the processal character of the third syllogism: logic is the movement of the primordial scission between Nature (where logic is objectively "set down" from the beginnings of time) and Spirit (where logic is constructed by the subject's activity), as much as the getting beyond this scission: thus there is the constant division and reunification of these two aspects, the logical idea (the middle term of the final syllogism) itself being this perpetual process of the splitting and reunification of the first two syllogisms. [44] It thus seems that Hegel gets beyond the aporia that Habermas spotted in his thinking about the Revolution, and he manages to conceive of this identity between the subjective consciousness and the objective Spirit without sacrificing one term to the other, and thereby even manages to reconcile the understanding and the will at the level of this opposition/reunion of the first two syllogisms in the third one. The question, however, remains: what is the status of this reconciliation within the absolute syllogism in relation to the finite individual? The reference to Aristotle at the conclusion of the *Encyclopedia* may be a clue: it definitely suggests that the finite subject must posit the necessity of the third point of view, that of the absolute syllogism, without ever being able to coincide with it: thus it is at least with contemplation for Aristotle because contemplation cannot be practiced throughout existence and is accessible for only a few brief and privileged moments. More precisely, it certainly seems that Hegel posits the third point of view as a simple *condition of possibility for unity*—and hence for intelligibility—of the first two. As Geraets writes, the third syllogism is "the point of view of the speculative idea—point of view which we, individual subjects, could never appropriate—but whose legitimacy we understand, given that without that neither the totality nor any of its moments would be understandable." [45] And, hoping to give the solution to the problems mentioned, Geraets adds what in my opinion, far from providing a solution, is actually the best formulation of the central aporia of Hegel's system: "the very idea of philosophy . . . contains within it 'the toughest opposition': that between the objective system, necessary and complete, and personal reflection aiming at freedom within a total understanding which is never really reached by me as a concrete individual," [46] because, as Hegel himself wrote, "the finitude of the spirit consists . . . in this, that knowledge does not grasp the thing in and by itself in its reason" (*E*, §441).

We are consequently forced to recognize that if Hegel's system goes beyond the ethical point of view and reconciles the will and the understanding, it effects this reconciliation, to repeat the formula that Fichte applied to Spinoza, "at a level where one cannot follow him": for the identity, if just processal, is not "for us" but uniquely "in itself," then what reason is there for positing it? We can express this difficulty in the form of an alternative:

—*Either* the processal unity of the first two syllogisms (of the understanding and of the will) in the third is posited as an ultimate *condition of possibility* for the intelligibility of the system, and in this case we face three problems: (1) the point of view that makes the system intelligible is posited *nondialectically,* for Hegel criticizes the very notion of a condition of possibility for experience as "external reflection," a "'quibbling' formal basis"[47] that the logic of the concept must get beyond; (2) hence this point of view must be a condition of possibility for the *meaning* and not the *truth*[48] of the first two syllogisms and is comparable to the archetypical Kantian understanding and the role it plays in relation to experience in the *Critique of Judgment;*[49] (3) this point of view, which is external to the thing itself, would also be external to the particular subject positing it, so that the reconciliation of the will and the understanding would have to appear more like a *task,* an ideal in Kant's sense, than a reality, hence—to say it all—like an "ought."

—*Or,* to get around these three problems, we admit that the third syllogism is not outside the system: in this case, however, it has to be demonstrable that it is posited *dialectically* (i.e., according to the *logic of the concept,* as *produced* by the very movement of the first two syllogisms, and not according to the *logic of essence,* as their condition of possibility) and is as such accessible to the finite subject.

We should admit that it is the first member of this alternative that seems to correspond most closely to Hegel's thinking. Indeed, in the addition to §234, consistent with the scheme we saw at work in the third syllogism, Hegel emphasizes the processal character of the identity of the "is" and the "ought": "This harmony between the 'is' and the 'ought to be' is not inert and rigidly stationary. The Good, the final end of the world, has being only while it constantly produces itself. And the world of spirit and the world of nature continue to have this distinction, that the latter only moves in a recurring cycle, while the former certainly also makes progress" (*E* 291). This confirms the reading according to which the speculative *model* for getting beyond Fichte's point of view is found to be the absolute syllogism as formulated in §577. But let's look at the way in which this ethical standpoint is "gotten beyond," "superseded": "Nullity and transitoriness constitute merely the superficial features and not the real *essence* of the world" (*E* 291; emphasis added). Thus, the third syllogism tries to posit the identity between the "ought" and the "is" as the *essence* of the world and hence—according to a formulation referring back to the logic of essence—to *external reflection* and not the logic of the concept. What's more, Hegel defines this "essence" of the world as being "the concept that is in and for itself." He clearly means the processal identity between the "ought" and the "is" that characterizes the *concept* is itself thought of as *essence,* that is, as a *condition of possibility* for the *intelligibility of the real* and hence—according to the very criteria of Hegel's thinking—in a way that is

reflexive, "quibbling," and external to the thing itself. Here is, I believe, a problem that Bernard Bourgeois [in his introduction] has expressed perfectly: referring (*E* 107–9) to many writings in which, paradoxically, the logical (the concept, supreme rationality) is presented
as the *essence of the real* (thus, it will again be noticed, according to
a formulation of the *Understanding* and not of *Reason*), he sheds
light on the paradox of presenting the relation between logic and the
real the way Kant and Fichte's critical philosophy does, that is, as a
relation of *foundation* or *condition of possibility:* "This temptation
to explain the (rational) concrete category of concept by the abstract
category (representing the Understanding) of foundation that we
saw in Hegel when he speaks *essentially* of the *concept,* perhaps expresses the difficulty, if not the impossibility, of grasping *as concept*
the relation of logic to the real, of thought and being" (*E* 109). To see
the relation between logic and the real "as a concept" the way Hegel's
system in other respects seems to demand would be to think that
logic *produces* its other (the real) from itself,[50] and is not satisfied, as
in the critical philosophy, simply to be its condition of possibility for
intelligibility (*essence*). Hence Bourgeois's conclusion: "[H]ere we
touch . . . a major problem—perhaps *the* problem—posed by Hegelianism. If for *reality, real being* as such, logic or the concept can be
presented as its *concept* (in the Hegelian sense), if the *status*—the
form—of the irrational or of the nonconceptual can be called rational or conceptual: for the *real,* on the other hand, for *that which* is
real, isn't logic or the real, merely its *essence:* isn't the *content* of the
irrational or of the nonconceptual—this seems to be a tautology—
nonrational or nonconceptual?" (*E* 109).

Hence the relevance of this problem to our question: adequately
conceiving only of the identity between the rational and *reality* (as a
category, not its content) and hence not the identity of the rational
and *the real* (the relation between these terms classically remaining
a relation of essence or foundation), Hegel also cannot fully reconcile the "ought" and the "is." More exactly, he reconciles them only at
an *objectively* and *subjectively transcendent* level: objectively because this reconciliation occurs only at an *essential* or *fundamental*
level that leaves the contingent real external to it; subjectively because it is done from a point of view that the finite individual subject
can never take. Therefore, to use critical terms,we can say that for
Hegel the reconciliation of the "is" and the "ought," which was necessary to enable him to get beyond the Fichtean standpoint, is paradoxically only "a thought" and not "something known," only *assumed*

as a condition for intelligibility with which it is impossible to coincide "really," that is, if you will, as an *Idea*.[51] To specify further the level at which this reconciliation takes place, we could say that if the absolute is the identity between the finite and the infinite, then in this identity the finite means merely a *formal category,* that is, it is not the finite individual, the contingent, that is reconciled with the absolute, but, if you will, finitude as such, so that the individual never seems able to leave the figure of the "unhappy consciousness."

I do not mean that this problem causes Hegel's system to "miscarry,"[52] for Hegel clearly recognizes the existence of a radical contingency of being,[53] which as such can never be fully reconciled with the absolute. I have merely tried to show that *from this fact:* (1) the absolute point of view that the third syllogism represents could not be posited *dialectically* or *conceptually* (which, as Bourgeois has shown, here presents an undeniable problem for Hegel), for it is formulated only in essentialist and reflexive terms, and that consequently (2) the ethical point of view must recover *all its prerogatives* at the level of the contingent, that is, in common consciousness: recovering all its prerogatives means of course that it cannot be relativized or condemned as *illusory,* if the basis for positing it as such (the third syllogism) is itself only a reflexive point of view and not a dialectically posited element in the system; in this case, the standpoint from which one "gets beyond" the Fichtean position is on no account valid for getting beyond it and the two parts contrast as two subjectivities or, I would say, as two interests: a practical interest and a speculative interest, with the speculative interest never managing, it seems to me, to take priority over the practical interest. The only evidence I need is the indication of the "return" of Hegel's ethical point of view where it seemingly should have been most absent: in the philosophy of the state. As Eric Weil has shown,[54] at the end of his study *Hegel and the State:* "We know what the state lacks for it truly to be what it claims to be: it *should* be moral in the interplay of international forces, it *should* provide satisfaction for all in recognition, security, and honor; it *should,* therefore it does not do so. Reconciliation is not achieved among nations, it is not achieved within states."[55] Because the will and the understanding are dialectically reconciled neither at the level of the philosophy of history nor at the speculative level, it was indeed inevitable that the standpoint of the "ought" would also be reintroduced, in whatever small degree,[56] into the sphere of law and politics.

Thus, the best-known and surely most powerful criticism of the ethical view of the world does not, by its *own criteria,* manage to eliminate this point of view, and this in two ways: first, at the level of the contingent, of the particular, the ethical view inevitably continues to keep all its prerogatives. (And isn't this really all that was claimed in the *Critique of Practical Reason* and the *Doctrine of Science?* Did these works ever try to be something other than philosophies of common consciousness, thus of the finite individual?) Then, and this seems to me harder to concede from Hegel's point of view, neither is the ethical dimension eliminated from the philosophical domain of *effectiveness,* for the third syllogism is posited reflexively and nondialectically, so that the moral view (the standpoint of reflection) seems to keep all its prerogatives—and everything happens as though the choice between the ethical viewpoint and the speculative viewpoint could be decided only from an ethical ("self-interested") point of view, speculation (the third syllogism), strictly speaking, having lost all power of constraint from the very fact of its metaphilosophical status as quibbling, ratiocinative discourse about the system.

What are we to conclude from these observations? First, Hegel's criticism, which claims to get beyond, eliminate, or relativize the ethical standpoint or moral view of the world, seems indeed to fail to come off—for he reintroduces the ethical dimension at two points in the system, particularly in its speculative coronation. As a theory of the ethical and practical point of view, Fichteanism cannot be integrated as an element of the system. Correspondingly, neither can the philosophy of history and the philosophy of politics inherent in the moral view of the world be definitively extirpated. Thus, the main stumbling block for Hegel's system appears to be Fichteanism: consequently, within the framework of an attempt to surpass historicism and the groundwork laid for it by Hegel, the idea of a "return to Fichte" seems to make some sense.

The foregoing discussion does not prove that a return to Fichte is the only way to avoid the problems inherent in a theory of history as the cunning of reason; in view of the observation that the assertion that the principle of reason applied without limitation to history leads to these aporias, it is indeed seemingly *also* possible simply to deny the principle of reason, and then to form an *irrationalist* conception of history (in the exact sense of a radical questioning of all legitimacy of the principle of reason). In this possibility we recognize the Heideggerian undertaking, renewed by Hannah Arendt, to conceive of the "History of Being" by removing it from the "realm where the very powerful principle of reason exercises its power";[57]

to think of the event on the model of the spontaneous blossoming of the rose whose flowering is "without a why"—and thus to think of history as a "free consequence" (*freie Folge*), that is, as a process whose "cohesion" (*Zussammenhang*) does not have "the sense of the necessity of a dialectical process."[58] Heidegger's conception of history is sharply antithetical to Hegel's: the problems inherent in the theory of the cunning of reason could thus *theoretically* lead us in this direction, and in that case a "return to Fichte" would definitely not be the only possible outcome. The whole problem, however, is to determine to what extent the ethical dimension (the moral view of the world) is also eliminated in this Heideggerian orientation: if, perchance, even while trying to avoid Hegelianism by entirely rejecting the principle of reason and leaving the framework of the metaphysics of subjectivity, we saw some ethical dimension reintroduced, it would mean that the moral view (the practical, i.e., *Fichtean* standpoint) of the world is definitely uncircumventable—whether in the metaphysics of the subject (whose pinnacle is Hegel's system) or in its supposed "outside" (for from *Being and Time* to his final writings, Heidegger never ceased working to constitute this "outside"). That is why, brought momentarily back as we are *into the context of thought of subjectivity* from Hegel to Fichte (from the elimination of the ethical standpoint to its necessary taking into account), we should also attempt—the better to indicate its significance—to see how far this ethical dimension may be reintroduced in the way Heidegger himself tried to avoid subjectivity and the principle of reason. Symmetrical to this first chapter in which I have tried to show that Hegel's completion of rationality and subjectivity does not succeed in overcoming or eliminating the Fichtean position, the following pages argue that this "superscission" or this going beyond does not work any better when done through an attempted break with reason and the idea of the subject. This further underscores the importance of an exploration of the Fichtean point of view.

Heidegger's Phenomenology and the Irrationalist Negation of Praxis

1. Heidegger's Criticism of Humanism

It is paradoxical to look for an "ethical dimension" in Heidegger's thinking.[1] Since his 1946 "Letter on Humanism," we know that Heidegger insisted on setting his work apart from ethical concerns. To Jean Beaufret's question about "the relation of ontology to a possible ethics" (BH 183; LH 231), Heidegger first replied, as he customarily did, by questioning the question itself—and this at two levels:

—At the terminological level: just as the term "ontology" is inadequate for designating what *Being and Time* initiated in 1927,[2] the term "ethics" belongs to the vocabulary of academic and even scholastic philosophy; in any case it appears "only when original thinking comes to an end" (BH 147; LH 195), and before that era (that of Plato's Academy) thinkers were no more acquainted with "ethics" than they were with "logic" or "physics" (BH 184; LH 232). So if the "question of Being" "cannot be adequately asked in the realm of traditional metaphysics,"[3] and if metaphysics began with Platonism,[4] thinking about Being and its question cannot be adapted to a contemporary terminology of the advent of metaphysics, that is, of "a thinking that is shattered" (BH 171; LH 223). Thus, Heidegger's thinking does not, strictly speaking, concern either "ethics" or "ontology": in this sense Beaufret's question "no longer has any basis" (BH 188; LH 236). Nevertheless, Heidegger immediately says that, though the question was terminologically inadequate, it still had "an essential sense and weight," if we think "more originally" (*ursprünglicher*).

—At the level of its content, the question does indeed deserve examination and possibly ought to be called into question, this time more radically. Understood "more originally," its content then is: does thinking that is directed toward the "memory of Being" provide "directives that can be reality applied to our active lives?" (BH 188;

LH 236). In other words, does it offer the "shepherd of Being" (BH 162; LH 210) material for finding his bearings within *beings?* Can the relation to Being that is to be made possible be normative for the relation to beings? Heidegger gave this question (the one, if you will, of practical applicability) a definite answer: thinking of Being is "neither theoretical nor practical"; it is "recollection of Being and nothing else"; "this thinking has no result" (BH 188; LH 236), and to suppose that it may be normative for our relation to beings is again to ascribe some "result" to it—which cannot be: even understood "more originally," the question of "ethical" extensions of "fundamental ontology" has no grounds for being. And Hannah Arendt, following Heidegger's lead, uses the concept of "releasement" against any voluntarism.

Again, Heidegger's answer needs to be interpreted, and to do this we can go some pages further on in his "Letter on Humanism." He explains how his thinking is an "antihumanism" and "against values": "by the assessment of something as a value what is valued is admitted only as an object for man's estimation "(BH 179; LH 228),[5] that is, "every valuing . . . is a subjectivizing"; in other words, instead of leaving (*lassen*) beings be and deploying itself in its Being, valuing merely makes beings an object for a subject; the point of view of values and the point of view of subjectivity are one, and in this sense "thinking in values is the greatest blasphemy imaginable against Being." It is clear that ethics is thinking that makes the conditions and exigencies of a truly human existence "have value": thus essentially belonging to the metaphysics of subjectivity, ethics can only be alien to thinking of Being. This is how Heidegger can get beyond the question of the ethical extensions of his thinking and show that he is thinking much more "against subjectivizing beings into mere objects" (BH 179; LH 228), hence against values, hence—I would add—against ethics (thus, against Fichte). This is also why Heidegger cannot take the ethical viewpoint thus located into account, if it happened to reappear in his thinking: for him, it would be a sign that this thinking was still captive to what it was attempting to escape, that is, that metaphysics of subjectivity whose moral view of the world, in Fichte, appeared to him merely one of the ultimate moments.

Heidegger versus ethics (versus Fichte): unless meaning by "ethics" not the establishment of values for guiding the subject's mores (*to ethe*), but (in a forceful blow to language that the "Letter on Humanism" attempts) the thinking that "ponders the abode of man" (*to ēthos*). In this and only this sense, the "thinking which thinks the truth of Being as the primordial element of man, as one who eksists, is in itself the original ethics" (BH 187; LH 235).[6] In *this* ethics, however, there is no question—as in the "epigonic" ethics of metaphysics—of producing or reflecting the normative values of practice: here, thinking remains at the threshold of the distinction between theory and practice, namely, at the "level" (which is not a level) or in the "place" (which is not a place)[7] where it does without the presence in which theorists and practitioners, concerned solely with that through which the subject can ensure its value, move with no concern for this doing without.

I must nevertheless call attention to an ethical dimension of Heidegger's thinking that seems not easily reduced to a "primordial ethics," but rather calls to mind the thinking that valorizes. The demonstration of such an—epigonically and not primordially—ethical dimension would quite obviously bring in a series of questions: What is its origin? Is it introduced in the endeavor from the outside, or is it a constitutive dimension? What significance should it be given? What does this reappearance of ethics in thinking that is meant to free itself of it tell us about the thinking itself and its productiveness? If the desacralization of a thinker—a preliminary condition for a genuine dialogue with his thinking—entails the right to suspect that he or she could also display ambiguities or tensions or even contradictions or dead ends, the analysis of what would thus lead Heidegger into an area of ethics that he otherwise vigorously attacked forms part of this process of desacralization—too long and sometimes too facilely held back by the simple, exclusive, and jealous exercise of repetition.

2. Heidegger and the Moral View of the World

To bring out the ethical dimension that I propose to analyze in Heidegger, the 1929 lecture "What Is Metaphysics?" and its related texts[8] constitute, through Heidegger's successive returns to his text of 1929, a valuable document on the shifts and dislocations, or conversely, on the continuity of the Heideggerian journey. From the viewpoint of our concerns (the presence of an ethical dimension), what do we notice?

I will merely mention the state of the problem in 1929: in this regard the ambiguity of the lecture is well known, often emphasized, and gives value to the text as a turning point between an earlier version of Heidegger's thinking (*Being and Time,* 1927) and a later version that the lecture distantly foreshadowed and only gradually developed into what is called the "later Heidegger." Ambiguity because on the one hand everything he said about man (his relation to beings, his mode of existence) is said to proceed from the revelation of Nothingness, the "Other" whose difference from beings proves to be the specific sign of Being,[9] while on the other hand the manifestation of this Nothingness seems to be connected with a choice or decision belonging to the initiative not of the Nothingness itself but of Dasein: for "the nothing[ness] is at first and for the most part distorted with respect to its originality" (this veiling of the Nothing heralds his later thinking about the "withdrawal" or "forgetfulness of Being")—and this because "we usually lose ourselves altogether among beings in a certain way. The more we turn toward beings in our preoccupations, the less we let beings as a whole slip away as such and the more we turn away from the [N]othing[ness]."[10] Thus, if it is we who turn away from the Nothingness (and not yet the Nothingness that withdraws), then, to truly grasp the possibility that anxiety gives to Dasein of letting Nothingness loom forth, we must confront anxiety without fleeing it: "Anxiety is there. It is only sleeping. Its breath quivers perpetually through Dasein, only slightly in those who are jittery, imperceptibly in the 'Oh, yes,' and the 'Oh, no' of men of affairs; but most readily in the reserved, and most assuredly in those who are basically daring."[11] This time, the manifestation of Nothingness thus seems to proceed from Dasein's mode (busy or daring) of existence—but the lecture retains the ambiguity to the end, for it clearly reaffirms that "we are so finite that we cannot even bring ourselves originally before the nothing through our own decision and will."[12] Which, however, does not prevent "What Is Metaphysics?" from concluding with the statement of the "tasks" of philosophy: "[I]t is of decisive importance, first, that we allow space for beings as a whole; second, that we release ourselves into the nothing, which is to say, that we liberate ourselves from those idols everyone has and to which he is wont to go cringing; and finally, that we let the sweep of our suspense take its full course, so that it swings back into the basic question of metaphysics which the nothing itself compels: Why are there beings at all, and why not rather nothing?"[13] It is clear that in indicating these tasks, the decision and ability not to "go cringing" seem established as *bases* for the manifestation of the Nothingness that would otherwise remain hidden. So it is hard not to speak of an ethical dimension to the endeavor: the decision, the *daring* appear valorized with regard to the posited goal (to realize the fundamental possibilities of Dasein), and if we define ethics by the "point of view of values," ethics here is not absent.

Today's reader of Heidegger cannot, however, be surprised by the presence of this ethical viewpoint in the 1929 book: we know the highly ambiguous situation of *Being and Time* and of the early Heidegger with regard to ideas of subjectivity,[14] if only because the 1927 book set up Dasein as the being "to question first" in carrying out the project of fundamental ontology, as though the reference to man or the question of man still remained privileged;[15] Heidegger himself, moreover, recognized the ambiguity when he later wrote in *Nietzsche,* apropos of ending the endeavor of *Being and Time:* "This interruption is motivated in this, that on the path where this attempt is made, it unwillingly runs the risk of in turn becoming a consolidation of subjectivity and thus of hobbling its essential steps."[16] It is not my purpose here to discuss how *Being and Time* had to appear to risk strengthening subjectivity: a reminder of this problem suffices for the presence of an ethical dimension in the early Heidegger to be not too surprising, and given our plan here (to see to what extent an idea that claims to leave modernity and the doctrines of subjectivity escapes the moral view of the world), for us to set aside these early texts of Heidegger's to consider writings that Heidegger himself recognized as most profoundly disturbing the structures of metaphysical discourse.

What place does ethics have in Heidegger's thought after what is generally called the *Kehre* or "turning"? Continuing to follow the guiding thread of "What Is Metaphysics?" we note that the afterword of 1943—while indicating the will to break with anthropologism (hence with subjectivity and hence, in principle, with ethics) (*W* 103)—Heidegger paradoxically maintains the idea of a *task* with its accompanying ethical connotations: "we must [*müssen wir*] prepare ourselves for the unique readiness to experience in nothingness the wide openness of that which grants every being the warrant to be" (*W* 102), and in this equipment for Being it is important that "we not evade Anxiety [*vor der Angst . . . ausweichen*]," which requires a "clear courage [*Der klare Mut*]" and "valor [*Tapferkeit*]," alone capable of "supporting Nothingness [*das Nichts auszustehen*]" (*W* 103). Thus it is Being, of course, that "calls [*anrufen*]," and not the reverse, but despite everything nothing is possible if "essential thinking" does not "pay attention" to what is eventually a matter of thinking with "authority." Similarly, we read in the introduction of 1949 that

overcoming metaphysics presupposes "the effort [*das Bemühen*] finally to learn to attend to the oblivion of Being" to manage to insert
and to "keep" the test of otherness or difference in the relation of
Being to man (*W* 200). These formulas, of which it would be easy
give many instances, can no longer be elucidated on the basis of an
insufficient realization of the "risks" of subjectivity, for on the very
pages where we read these appeals for effort, attention, and vigilance, Heidegger appears to put great care in "taking away from subjectivity . . . the essential determination of man." How are we then to
interpret a putting in place of *values*[17]—hence an ethical dimension—where the project is explicitly to get beyond what is simulta-
neously diagnosed (the "Letter on Humanism" dates from 1946) as
the base of any ethics, that is, the point of view of subjectivity? It is
even harder to see how the question could be evaded since the idea
of the task and its connotations will remain present up to the final
writings, even when, as in the *Discourse on Thinking* (*Gelassenheit*),
meditative thought rejects any activist foundation for becoming
through the conquering will of man—refuses, we could say, the practical philosophy of history *of the Fichtean kind:* "We should do nothing, merely wait"—hence inactivism, but to do this, we must manage
to "dishabituate ourselves of the will," to "remain watchful, ready
with releasement."[18] If the openness to *ethos,* to the abode in which
beings are present (Being), involves this adjustment of behavior
(*ethe*), how do we not see a falling back into everything that is epigonic late-coming in ethics, that is, the foundation of everything that
is and happens on a capacity of the *subject* (with a correspondingly
implicit conception of history in which human practice—here certainly purely "preparatory," but nevertheless decisive—is what
makes *this* future more possible than *that* other one)?

The problem is so obvious that it could not have escaped Heidegger. We easily see this in his constant practice (repeated by his
disciples) of *denegation* or *denial:* for, in all rigor, man's relation to
Being and history (which comes to the same thing since Being is
History) cannot be thought of starting with some foundation on the
subject's initiative; therefore, when making utterances that seem to
bear the stamp of a moral view of the world (for, it seems, we cannot
do without it), we must *deny* that this is what we are doing and constantly take back what was nonetheless stated. Here are just two examples of this practice of denial.

—In his "Letter on Humanism," Heidegger comes back to the
notion of "fallenness" or "ensnarement" (*Verfall*) which in *Being*

and Time he had used to characterize the mode of being of inauthentic Dasein that is exclusively absorbed in beings and forgetful of Being. We then read: "This word does not signify the Fall of Man understood in a 'moral-philosophical' and at the same time secularized way; rather, it designates an essential relationship of man to Being within Being's relation to the essence of man" (*W* 163). This is a double fallenness that is not fallenness: first, because this fallenness is not accidental in the sense of a fault but belongs to the very essence of Dasein; second, because man is not responsible for this fallenness (the forgetfulness of Being is to be thought of as withdrawal). One will thus speak (why?) of fallenness outside of "any moralizing criticism of everyday Dasein,"[19] which will allow for the division of humanity, right down to the last writings, into "authentic" and "inauthentic."

—Apropos of the forgetfulness of being (a "basis," that is not a basis, of this "fallenness," which is not fallenness), the 1937 introduction to "What Is Metaphysics?" definitely indicates that it is certainly a matter, on the part of metaphysics, of a "permanent confusion of beings with Being but this confusion is to be thought as event [*Ereignis*], not as an error. It can in no way be grounded in a mere negligence of thinking or a fleetingness of saying" (*W* 200). The forgetfulness is thus not strictly forgetfulness (otherwise subjectivity is reintroduced as the basis of the direction of all human history), and, correspondingly, if we think of history as "the decline of thought,"[20] this decline is not a decline, for it "still remains, despite everything, completely at the level of the heights and does not sink to the inferior": decline, but not decadence.

The goal of this practice of denial is thus quite clear: to expunge all moralistic connotations incompatible with the aim of the endeavor. If so, however, why resort to a vocabulary with such heightened ethical coloring? Why give such remarks an ethical dimension only immediately to deny it? Why this return to the *Sollen,* to the "ought," to a *Fichteanism denied?*

3. For an Internal Criticism of Heidegger's Phenomenology

I shall resist the temptation of a simple external criticism of the procedure, of seeing it only as a way to reintroduce valorization, the judging point of view, in a procedure that otherwise seems to exclude it. This explanation is surely not off target, especially in reference to Heidegger's disciples and their strong emphasis on value judgments (about the age, the human sciences, technicity, and so on) and of the thereby expedited establishment of a whole romantic pathos (the solitary thinker, martyr to modernity, confronted with the task of maintaining the boundary line for Western thought in the face of the general collapse of humanity into American-style business-ism). The interest of this external interpretation is very limited, so limited is the interest of what it concerns.

It seems to me much more rewarding to relate the practice of these denials to a real and internal problem of the Heideggerian endeavor—a problem about language. We see something of this when we recall how the very practice of denial already appears at the "theoretical" level of talk about Being: indeed we know how Heidegger presents the question of Being as that of the "ground" or "basis" in which all philosophy is rooted[21]—for, here again, the constant denial of these terms whose use (like that of "fundamental ontology") is "dangerous": this usage makes it possible to believe that thinking of Being may still be armed with the principle of reason, when "reason is the fiercest enemy of thinking" and that it is a matter of thinking, for example (against Hegel), of history as a "free consequence" of ceasing to apply the "very powerful principle of reason." If Being is called the basis (*Grund*), it thus cannot be taken in the metaphysical sense of basis: this "ground" is "groundless," this *Grund* is *Abgrund*.[22] All this is well known, but there again why come so near to the language of metaphysics and make necessary this infinite process of denial? We see that external explanation is difficult in this register. In fact, the whole problem comes from the fact that speech forces one to resort to the essentially inadequate language of metaphysics; there can be no question of creating a new language—an imperious gesture through which the subject would fully dominate the language and that shares too much of the authority of subjectivity and its plan of mastery; thus thinking of Being must use the language of metaphysics in a different way.[23] We can effectively "use the same names both within and outside metaphysics"[24] by taking them not in the literal sense, but in a metaphorical or analogous sense. In *Zur Sache des Denkens,* in the protocol of the seminar on *Zeit und Sein,* Heidegger very clearly explains that when we speak of Being as a "gift," as an "offering," that is, starting with "ontic models," "A model is that from which thinking must necessarily take off in such a way that that from which it takes off is what gives it an impetus":[25] one could not more clearly define the analogical use of language, its very deficiency (hence the denials) indicating the otherness and difference in which Being is cut off from these appellations.[26] The practice of denial thus fits into an analogical use of the language of metaphysics, a use that concerns two registers of metaphysical discourse in particular:

—The ontological register of the language of metaphysicians (foundation, root, principle, consequence, cause . . .) is to be analogically transposed into the framework of thinking of Being (Being as *Grund-Abgrund*, as *logos*, but not as *ratio*; as *Ur-sache*, primordial question, but not as *Ursache* in the sense of a cause, and so forth).

—In parallel, the ethical register will be analogically retained to refer to a relation of man to Being that is "scarcely thinkable"[27] and cannot be said in another language other than the one, immediately denied, of ethics *as if* Dasein was that on which the appearance or withdrawal of Being depends. This *ethical analogy* allows us to speak of "decline," of "authenticity," of "daring," which allows asking whether man will be "capable" of anxiety, and so on.

Nevertheless, even if there really is a problem creating the appearance of an analogical discourse and an ethical dimension *denied,* the resort to analogy seems open to two objections:

(1) Isn't the analogy radically empty and pointless? For in speaking of Being what must be expressed is the difference between beings and Being; in the analogy this difference is precisely the one that is left unsaid; when we say of Being that it is a Lighting (*Lichtung*), what escapes discourse is what makes the Lighting of Being different from what in the sky follows the darkness of the storm; thus the difference is always *to be said,* as translators flag it by using a capital letter: Lighting is not lighting. But what is it?

(2) Why therefore insistently resort to a pointless procedure? The answer to this question reveals the incoherence of the resort to analogy: one uses this procedure, seeking, despite everything (despite the withdrawal), to speak of Being, to display the difference where, in all rigor, it is impossible to overcome the withdrawal, where the closure of the endeavor in silence would be called for (Heidegger thinks of it sometimes), except for thereby calling for the recognition of its sterility. The use of analogy thus again involves a will to Parousia (presencing), a desire for increased consciousness and mastery (since, grasping the "basis" of all bases, Heideggerian discourse would indeed be the *strongest*). At bottom, this will to parousia is the old ideal of special metaphysics (to produce the intelligibility of everything that exists by going back to its foundation, and unveiling this foundation by bringing it to the transparency of some

discourse) which paradoxically continues to inspire thinking of Being even when this thinking of Being at the same time clearly must repel this ideal: hence the continual expression of the outside/exterior to the concept (Being) in terms of concepts, and the "bad infinity" of the endlessly reiterated denial.

The resort to a procedure as useless as analogy is thus explained by the presence, at the very heart of Heidegger's thinking, of a will to parousia and mastery inseparable from the various modern metaphysics of subjectivity. We still need to understand, however, how this will to parousia and mastery then can be reintroduced (with an "epigonic" ethical dimension).

Here we encounter a second problem (the first being that of language) in Heidegger's thinking: this problem concerns the idea of history and thus brings us back to the very sphere of our concerns. For Heidegger, history is the history of Being in the sense of the oblivion or forgetfulness of Being. The forgetfulness of Being, however, "belongs to Being itself."[28] Being as withdrawal is its own forgetfulness—these claims of the later Heidegger are too well known to need further elaboration here. The result in any case is that if history is the forgetfulness of Being and Being is its own forgetfulness, "we think of history as Being"[29]—and this thought excludes any founding of history on human *praxis:* this thinking is thus established as resolutely *anti-Fichtean*—at the same time as it claims to be *anti-Hegelian* (in its refusal to apply the principle of reason to history). Therefore here we ought to find the model of a non-Fichtean alternative to the theory of the cunning of reason in the non-Fichtean conception of history (the practical philosophy of history).

Heidegger accurately spots and attacks one first possible reintroduction of the practical foundation of history—the foundation that interprets the forgetfulness of Being as an event and hence thinks of forgetfulness as having "begun" and imputes the responsibility for it to thinkers: if history is decline, this decline is in fact a *structure* and not a movement that could be located and dated; thus the withdrawal from Being in no way followed its "being given," because this "gift" itself is withdrawal, for "as it reveals itself in beings, Being withdraws."[30] Thus, only if thought of this way will the History of Being have no pejorative connotation (meaning decadence), and, correspondingly, the origin of this history cannot be valorized in the sense of a pre-Socratic paradise: any nonradically structural interpretation of the forgetfulness would make Heideggerian thinking of history fall back into the mythology of the origin and fall, that is, into a Rousseauism whose presuppositions were deconstructed by Fichte.[31]

We see the problem take shape: if the decline and forgetfulness were radically thought of as structural, Heideggerian thinking about history would lack any ethical dimension; as we have seen, this is not the case and yet Heidegger, unlike some of his interpreters, definitely thinks of the forgetfulness as a structure and not as an event. How then can the ethical dimension be reintroduced? It is plausible to think that it reappears insofar as the foundation of history on human initiative is reintroduced at a second level, where neither Heidegger nor his interpreters avoid imputing a *responsibility* to man. The introduction to the 1943 "What Is Metaphysics?" presents the way in which metaphysics thinks of beings (in other words, the forgetfulness of Being) as the "obstacle" that prevents man from fully realizing his essence, that is, from accepting the relation of Being to his essence. If Being is its own forgetfulness, how can we think of the forgetfulness of Being as an obstacle? From the *structure* of Being, forgetfulness here seems to become external to Being, as though it were *to be overcome* like an obstacle: if so, we see how a "practical" foundation of history would be reintroduced and, with it, ethics. But how is it with this "obstacle"? Heidegger then explains that metaphysics forms an obstacle to vigilance toward Being in that it *seems* to ask the question of Being—of which, as an ontology, metaphysics claims to be the repository, when in reality it is merely asking the question of the Being of beings [*l'être de l'étant*]: "[Metaphysics] intends [*Sie meint*] beings in their totality and speaks of Being. It names Being and means beings as beings" (*W* 199). So much so that owing to the confusion of beings and Being, the forgetfulness of Being goes unnoticed: "The forgetfulness settles into forgetfulness," says Heidegger, "Being's abandonment of man (= the withdrawal) remains veiled" (*W* 200). *Forgetting the forgetting,* then, which doubles and radicalizes the forgetfulness of Being, for thinking Being would be thinking of its forgetfulness as withdrawal (difference), and the forgetfulness at least would have to be noticed and be discussible. Thus, history as decline is a double forgetfulness, a forgetfulness that doubles from its own forgetfulness. But how are we to interpret the forgetfulness of forgetfulness? Most curiously, this time Heidegger seems to think of it less as structure than as *event,* in the sense in which it is up to man to overcome it: he says that it is important to "bring thinking to a confrontation with the oblivion of Being [*um erst das Denken an die Seinvergessenheit zum Austrag zu bringen*], but it remains to be seen "whether a thinking is capable of this [*Ob jedoch ein Denken dies vermüchte*] "(*W* 200). Inevitably, with human responsibility, the ethical view reemerges and everything happens as though the practical foundation of history (dodged by Heidegger, not by his disciples, at the level of the forgetfulness of Being) reappeared at the level of the forgetfulness of the forgetfulness. The future consequently seems to depend on our effort to overcome our inattention to the forgetfulness; a minimum of practical foundation for future becoming is thereby safeguarded—a minimal amount that then allows for the ethical view, with its division of humanity into the capable and the incapable, the attentive and the inattentive, and so forth.

Let's summarize what we just noted: as an attempt to think of history according to a model that circumvents the theory of the cunning of reason (for "reason is the fiercest enemy of thinking") as well as a foundation of the future on human practice (since the moral view of the world is identified with the metaphysics of subjectivity that is to be broken off with), Heidegger's philosophy does not escape the return of an ethical dimension; this return certainly involves a problem inherent in the way in which language bears the trace of metaphysical representations, but the *analogical* interpretation of Heideggerian ethics must be completed by bringing to the fore that which makes the return to ethical formulations so tempting: what produces this return is Heidegger's (or anyone's?) inability to eliminate or overcome a minimum of foundation of history on *praxis* (here, effort, attention, vigilance)—this foundation, massively condemned at a first level as implying an activism seen as the mark of modern subjectivity's plan of mastery, is later surreptitiously reintroduced at a second level (the forgetfulness of forgetfulness of Being), and hence the judging point of view is allowed back in.

Though Hegel's theory of the cunning of reason does not manage to overcome the ethical (Fichtean) point of view, the Heideggerian *will* to make a radical break with the principle of reason, the plan of mastery, and the category of subjectivity does not make the ethical dimension disappear, nor the only thing that can explain it: a foundation of history on human practice. For Heidegger, this return to ethics clearly does not, *as such,* constitute a "negative" element. What, however, seems dubious to me is the reappearance of ethics under circumstances in which even if the event is accompanied (which it inevitably is) by a minimum of foundation of becoming on man's practical initiative, the path of thinking in which this ethics returns is by definition unable to take it genuinely into account and fully to work out its foundation coherently. Of the theoretical conditions of possibility, this would require that it be possible fully to *thematize* this foundation; but when one lumps together the ethical point of view, practical foundation of history, metaphysics of subjectivity, plan of mastery, domination of reason, and reason thought of as "the fiercest enemy of thinking," it is *out of the question* to grant a status to this foundation of historical development on human initiative (at the level of the forgetfulness of forgetfulness): this foundation can enter only surreptitiously, residually, and if one had to say anything whatever about it, the discourse produced would consist of a pure and simple denial. It is, we could say, "unofficially" that the practical point of view finds a place here—and it couldn't be otherwise. Thus, on the one hand Heidegger does not eliminate the practical point of view, and on the other hand he is not in a theoretical situation such that, given the principles of his thinking, he could thematize it and truly ground it. In other words, Heidegger leads back to Fichte in two ways: (1) because the conceptual model of history that he would have to construct, which is neither Hegelian nor Fichtean, still does not truly circumvent the Fichtean model of a history that depends on human intervention (even though, in Heidegger, this interventionism could not be more thoroughly disguised); (2) because Heidegger cannot really assemble such an interventionist model, given all the dislocations and reinterrogations with his theoretical rigging that that would demand: thus, whoever wishes fully to build this model—which, as we have seen, is not so easy to go beyond, whether within or outside of metaphysics—will surely find it necessary to turn to the work done in this direction by the young Fichte.

When we get back to Leo Strauss's project (to make a political philosophy in the strict sense possible by abandoning historicism, an indispensable condition for liberating the ideal), we may then better understand how we can both recognize the validity of this project and contest its modalities of application: the realization of this project, while indeed implying the criticism of Hegel's preparation for historicism (the criticism of the theory of the cunning of reason—the *Hegelian model* for conceiving of history and the real) does not, however, involve any global condemnation of German idealism as a whole, short of improperly reducing it to its Hegelian completion. On the contrary, within idealism, at least on an ethical level, Fichte provides what is arguably the most vigorous criticism of all theories of the cunning of reason.

Rationalism and irrationalism thus paradoxically agree in rejecting the moral view of the world without managing, however, to expunge it legitimately from representations of the common consciousness. Before I proceed to analyze the works of the young Fichte, we still need to see how Hegelianism and phenomenology succeed no better in resolving the theoretical question of the status of the principle of reason in history.

Toward a Critical Solution of the Antinomy of Historical Reason: Kant's Deconstruction of Metaphysics and the Critique of Historical Reason

1. The Meaning of the Antinomy

The term "antinomy" is understood here just the way Kant used it in the "Transcendental Dialectic" of his *Critique of Pure Reason:* first, an antinomy consists of two opposed theses about the totality of the real; in this case, the totality of the historically real is considered subject, or not, to the principle of reason. Second—and this is essential for solving it—an antinomy is a conflict that *appears* to be a contradiction, that is, an opposition governed by the law of the excluded middle so that one of the propositions must be true and the other false ("either . . . or" says the antinomy). Actually, however, the contradiction is merely apparent, for both the thesis and the antithesis are quite possibly false, which I believe to be the case here: the historically real is neither perfectly rational, nor absolutely contrary to the principle of identity and reason, but merely (at least this is what I argue here) *a nonrational to be rationalized as much as possible.*

The better to see the purely philosophical roots of this antinomy of historical reason, we need to spell out the "ontological" meaning of the thesis and the antithesis.

(1) The thesis can be expressed as follows: "Everything real is, at least in itself if not for us, rational, that is, identifiable and explicable"; I have at some length gone into the implications of this statement for the idea of historicity. It is important to note, however, that expressed this way, the rationalistic idea of history links up, whether it is intended to or not, with a certain theology and one of its best-known arguments, the Ontological Argument. Indeed, if the rationalistic philosophy of history presupposes as established the existence of a viewpoint from which thinking and the real are one—the viewpoint of omniscience or complete knowledge—and when we posit that this viewpoint exists only "in itself," but not "for us," we

thereby mean that it is the viewpoint of a higher or "supreme" being—God's viewpoint. In other words, the rationalistic philosophy of history postulates a place for thought from which it is possible to *deduce* existence, that is, to have a perfectly clear understanding of the reason for being [*raison d'être*] of every event. The underlying structure of this conception of history is what philosophers and theologians call the Ontological Argument, by which the existence of God is inferred from the concept of God (from his essence, which is to have all attributes or qualities), for if he did not exist, he would be lacking one quality or attribute: existence.

Despite appearances, these scholastic-sounding remarks lead to the heart of the rationalist conception of history, for the deduction of existence from the concept has a clear equivalent at the historical level: this equivalent—and all of us will understand that in this sense, the Ontological Argument, oddly, has not completely disappeared from the contemporary concerns of political theory and the social sciences—claims to deduce the existence of particular events in the future from the concept of historicity or, in more modern terms, from the laws of history. In short, we could say that in historical rationalism the Ontological Argument is transposed into the will to deduce (or to predict, which comes to the same thing) the future: for this is indeed a case of deducing the existence of something from the concept of that thing, a deduction that presupposes that the deducer assumes a viewpoint like that of the God of traditional theology, a viewpoint from which existence is perceived as identical with the concept (clearly, one could not claim with certainty to predict the end of history if one did not in some way assume the rationality of the real).

(2) For its part, the antithesis absolutely rules out any possibility of this deduction, preferring to leave the future *totally indeterminate* (Hannah Arendt, following Heidegger, said *all* events are mysterious and *always* surprise us). The phenomenological criticism of rationalistic metaphysics thus becomes radical, for it too makes this assertion about the *totality* of the real, and also because it means to leave nothing *legitimate* in rationalistic metaphysics. Here again, this "radicalism" needs some explanation. Transposed almost word for word by Arendt to the realm of politics (it is but a short step to take from the deconstruction of metaphysics as a totalizing system to the deconstruction of Stalinism as a totalitarian system), Heidegger's criticism of metaphysics, when faced with the Hegelian model's metaphysical use of ontology, tries to show how the idealism thus

produced leaves out one dimension of the real that escapes the principles of identity and reason. What escapes this "identitarian" idea and what Heidegger calls the "ontological difference" is the very fact that *there is the real,* which is what Heidegger calls "Being." Though the reality of the real, the objectivity of the object, can be defined by reference to the two "powerful principles," it is still true that one dimension of the real or of beings slips through their grasp—precisely the "there is": the fact that there are beings with this or that particular determination (the "categories") for "beingness" (for ontological definition): thus existence, Being, is undeducible: "the rose is without a why, it blooms because it blooms." If Being refers to the dimension of the real that escapes the application of the principles of rationality, metaphysical discourse as the search for an ultimate basis for each thing—as the affirmation of God's viewpoint from which it would be possible to have a complete grasp of the universe as intelligible—must by definition miss this dimension. Thus, metaphysics is essentially oblivious to the "miracle of Being" and is inevitably the "forgetfulness of Being," for it is and always will be unaware of what must be thought. Metaphysics thinks the presence of something, the "there is," the fact that being is present, its "presencing," again Being. Hence the *radicalness* of the phenomenological criticism of metaphysics: because metaphysics itself forms an obstacle to what is to be thought of (Being), it behooves us to challenge the principle that every dimension of the real can and must be subject to the principles of identity and reason, and thus *it seems* (but in my opinion it is at just this point that the dialectical illusion proper to phenomenology comes in) to break with *rationality,* with the reason that is essentially forgetful of Being and therefore, according to Heidegger's formula, is "the fiercest enemy of thinking." Hence the irrationalism characteristic of the phenomenological criticism of reason.

To avoid a misunderstanding, one specification is called for: the irrationalism of Heidegger's or Arendt's phenomenological thinking should not be located at the same level at which scientistic thinkers have accused Heidegger of irrationalism, meaning his analysis of the metaphysical presuppositions of science or reason; on the contrary, this whole aspect of the criticism of metaphysics (the criticism of the thesis) and its extensions to various scientific disciplines seems to me a quite "reasonable" undertaking. Here, I mean by irrationalism the fact that this criticism goes "too far," becomes "hyperbolic," the "deconstruction" of metaphysics becoming a genuine "destruction," that is, a criticism "without remainder" that leaves no legitimate use for the concept and demands of reason. (The same goes for the concept of causality in Arendt, which she claimed had *no* application in the social sciences, or the concept of value in Heidegger, which is altogether beset with illegitimacy: "all valorization" being "subjectification" and hence "inauthentic" thinking.) By forbidding itself any appeal to these concepts and demands of reason—which metaphysics has surely failed by dogmatically hypostatizing (but which still permeate it)—phenomenology founders in the indefinitely denied contradiction of referring, despite everything, to these concepts or demands, but in an "unofficial" and unthematizable way.

Kant says in the *Critique of Pure Reason* that there is an antinomy when one of two opposite judgments "does not simply contradict the other, but says something more than is necessary for the contradiction." Thus the thesis not only posits that the real is rationalizable, but also that it is absolutely rational "in itself," while the antithesis defines existence as not only *other* than thinking, as merely *different* from the structures of reason, but it also goes on to consider existence "in itself" and its basis *contrary* to these structures (hence the radical inability of these structures to think of Being and their fate to "forget" it). Hence we have the antinomy of radical rationalism, for which mystery is sheer illusion, versus radical irrationalism, which considers reason essentially "inauthentic": we must seek the solution to this antinomy in the plan for a non-irrational criticism of reason, the "criticist" critique of reason, the model for which was first produced by Kant in the "Appendix to the Transcendental Dialectic" as well as in the *Critique of Judgment*. What seems to me especially interesting in the criticist critique of metaphysics is that it allows for perfectly rigorous thinking about the legitimate uses possible for metaphysical reason *after its critique*. In other words, criticism expounds a critique of metaphysics as vigilant at every point as the phenomenological deconstruction of it; as we shall see, it even precisely analyzes the mechanisms by which the illusion of a perfect rationality of the real is produced in the three preferred domains of classical metaphysics: rational psychology (which produces the illusion of a subject that is perfectly transparent to itself), rational cosmology (which posits a world whose science is completed), rational theology (which asserts the real existence of a viewpoint, God's, from which the two preceding rationalities are visible and deducible); but unlike what is contained in the antithesis of our antinomy, the criticism, once the metaphysical illusion has been condemned, aims to show how the content of the metaphysical theses (the idea of a Subject, the idea of a World, the idea of God) can be preserved as a *requirement* of *meaning* (and not of dogmatic *truth*) by the subject who *reflects* about the real (about itself and about the world).

2. The Four Basic Elements of the Criticist Critique of Metaphysics

I now propose to show that this synthesis represents not a resort to "common sense" or a refined eclecticism, but that it applies to the question of historicity, through an analysis of the four elements that in my opinion make up the genuine powerful moments of this non-irrationalist critique of reason.

For readers unfamiliar with Kant's thinking, it may be helpful to indicate straightaway that these four basic elements are already inscribed into the very plan of the *Critique of Pure Reason* and notably in Kant's distinction between the "concept" (an act of the understanding discussed in the "Transcendental Analytic"), "intuition" (which is the fact of "sensibility" discussed in the "Transcendental Aesthetic"), and the "Idea" (an operation of "Reason," the critique of which is found in the "Transcendental Dialectic"). The definitions of these three terms directly lead us to the heart of our concerns.

Kant gives a classic description of the concept as having two features: "understanding" and "extension." In this regard, this is comparable to the set in mathematics. The "understanding" is the classificatory property or, if you like, the *definition* around which the elements are grouped, and extension corresponds to the elements themselves. Although the concept expresses a property common to a number of elements, we can see that it never gives us a true grasp of *particular* or *real existence* but merely the *general,* that is, what connects this real multiplicity when we abstract the differences that are nonsignificant in relation to the understanding. In other words— which we shall see that, despite appearances, are not trivial—the understanding of a concept does not provide access to its extension; the definition of a class of objects, however perfect it may be, does not "give" us the objects themselves, in short, it does not give us the particular existence, the *individual.*

Kant says that to grasp the particular, the individual, I must have recourse to an "intuition," a representation that is not general but a "particular" that comes within the province not of the understanding, but of the senses (the "sensibility"). For Kant intuition is always sensory, and to grasp some particular existence, it is always necessary to have recourse to what we now call a current empirical *perception,* that is, a perception here and now, located in a completely particular way in space and time (hence the reason why the doctrine of sensibility, the "Transcendental Aesthetic," is largely devoted to an analysis of space and time). The stakes of these seemingly quite obvious assertions are clear: without lingering right now on the underlying arguments, Kant's purpose is, beginning with the study of sensibility to reject any form of the Ontological Argument, any attempt to deduce existence from thought: the real can never be anything but "given" and not *deduced* from the concept that, according to a well-known formula, without intuition remains "empty." Thus there exists—this is the deep meaning of these assertions—the "nonconceptual," the "outside of concept," or, if you will, the "nonrational." Thus, Kant's theory of sensibility expresses what could be called, despite the anachronism, Kant's "anti-Hegelianism."

On the other hand, the Idea constitutes the metaphysical operation par excellence, one aiming to deduce the particular from the concept (of the general) by grasping it through Reason and not through intuition. The idea, which corresponds to the way God would perceive the world, would be the concept that, as it were, has become capable (we shall see by what devices) of deducing its *extension* from its *comprehension.* Strictly speaking, we would have an Idea if we could draw from a general property the real individuals corresponding to it. If such an operation were possible, we could then directly *know* individual existence instead of being constrained only to "perceive" it (to "intuit" it), and we could do without what Kant calls "sensibility." In this regard we could say that "intuition" and "Idea" are competitive, aiming at the same goal but using different means: both of them seek to grasp this spatiotemporal existence that the concept leaves outside of itself as its extension, but intuition reaches this goal through sense perception while the Idea claims the goal is reachable through Reason alone. If we could have an Idea, there would be no intuition, and everything would be wholly thinkable or rational; conversely, if, as "common sense" already believes, it turned out that intuition is irreplaceable for grasping spatiotemporal existence, the idea would be a mere metaphysical illusion whose critique and exact status remain to be spelled out.

The competition between the Idea and the intuition *seems* almost unfair, for the aim of the idea *seems* absurd; one can scarcely see how, in defining a table or a tree even with the greatest care, it would be possible to make the table and the tree themselves exist, any more than at first sight we understand what meaning this plan of deducing the real from Reason could have.

It would be wrong, however, to underestimate the opponent: in claiming to have these Ideas, the metaphysician does not mean he has a mysterious faculty of producing or deducing the real from his own reason (thus, Krug, a well-known contemporary critic of Hegel, was surely wrong to demand of Hegel that he deduce the feather from the quill with which he asserted the rationality of the real). Hegel means, more subtly surely, that if "for us" the real is perceived in sensory representations in space and time, there *exists* a point of view, that of God or of complete science, from which this real that "for us" seems sensory is "in itself" or in fact rational. And applied to history, this metaphysics effectively yields a thesis that, it will be agreed, could have some plausibility: the thesis that historical reality is in itself rational and hence deducible from the viewpoint of the one who possesses the laws of this historical rationality. Thus we are, with these three Kantian definitions, at the heart of our concerns.

We can now understand why Kant's critique of metaphysics (the plan represented by the Idea) must necessarily go though four fundamental stages: (*a*) to develop a theory of finitude so as to settle the conflict between intuition and Idea. Why a theory of finitude? Because, obviously, we have to know if the fact that existence "for us" is given in space and time from the outside by an intuition (which means a *finitude*, a *limitation,* if you will) is the sign of an *imperfection* (compared with the infinite understanding of a God) or if, on the contrary, the assertion of the real existence of an infinite point of view (the point of view of the Idea) is illusory: this is the essential task of the first part of the *Critique of Pure Reason,* the "Transcendental Aesthetic". (*b*) Once this question is resolved, we need to analyze the mechanisms that produce the *Idea* according to which the real is by definition rational, (*c*) to carry out the critique of this illusion/ Idea before (*d*) inquiring about the status the Idea/illusion may still have *after this critique.* (On this last point, as I have suggested, Kant's critique of metaphysics essentially differs from Heidegger's deconstruction, for it leads, as I shall try to show, to granting reason a *certain* legitimacy beyond its metaphysical claims.) It is in the analysis of this final stage that the solution to our antinomy should begin to appear.

Since it is clearly not my aim here to analyze Kant's critique of metaphysics for its own sake, I shall merely adumbrate the general significance of these four stages for answering our question: that of the antinomy of historical reason.

(a) Kant's Theory of Finitude and the A Priori Nonrationality of the Real

To get a better understanding of the scope of Kant's doctrine of finitude in the "Transcendental Aesthetic," we should perhaps recall how it diverges from the traditional conception.

In Cartesian metaphysics, man's finitude—the fact that he is limited, that is, receives the external objects that affect him *from the outside,* and is thereby a sensory being—is always thought of *relative* to an absolute whose existence was previously posited and in the face of which man sees himself as a limited being. This absolute is that of the divine understanding—an infinite understanding because, from the point of view of God (or omniscience), the real and the rational are one, the idea is not limited by an object corresponding to it. Finitude is then experienced as an essential imperfection in man, a lack, and the "sensibility" (the fact of being *passive, receptive* with regard to objects that are only *given* to us in space and time) is, as a mark of this finitude, devalorized (from the viewpoint of God, to whom nothing is sensory, but everything is intelligible).

We see a complete reversal of this metaphysical idea of finitude in the "Transcendental Aesthetic": the subject's passivity or receptivity is first posited, a priori, as a condition of possibility for all knowledge or representation, and it is, on the contrary, in relation to this *first assertion which raises the sensibility = passivity (spatiotemporal receptivity) to the level of an ontological feature (without it, no object)*[1] that the absolute itself will be *relativized,* that is, thought of as a simple subjective viewpoint (meaning) and not as a reality in itself (truth).

This reversal—which could be shown to be contained in the notion of "pure intuition," that is, basically, an a priori passivity that Kant uses to designate those frameworks for any offering up of the object that space and time are—has a consequence of immediate interest to us here: in positing receptivity as an ontological necessity, an indispensable element for the apprehension of beings (objects), and thereby making the idea of completed science (included in the notion of an infinite divine understanding) a simple subjective ideal, a pure idea and not a reality in itself, *Kant opens up an irreducible space for the nonconceptual or nonrational:* science will never succeed, any more than metaphysics, in wholly rationalizing the world, for all objective knowledge implies a contribution by the senses and hence an element of the nonconceptual. The scientific ideal of rationalizing the real will thus necessarily take the form of an infinite process that nothing can guarantee beforehand, for the real is not thought of as in itself and a priori rational.

At this point in elaborating the critique of metaphysics, we are merely at the stage of the initial claims. To confirm them, we clearly need to carry out their deconstruction and to begin the analysis of the mechanisms produced by the illusion of the perfect rationality of the real.

(b) The Mechanisms Producing Ideas as Illusions about the Rationality of the Real

Here again, my discussion is confined to the main point: metaphysics in general (and hence the metaphysics of history expressed by the thesis of our antinomy) does not represent—or, in any case, does not *only* represent—an arbitrary choice in favor of an unlimited extension of the principle of reason. On the contrary, it should be stressed—and this observation becomes important when we see the naïveté of certain thinkers who believe they can now "get beyond" the rationalistic philosophies of history by simply doing without philosophical thinking—that the principle of sufficient reason (which we don't see who could do without) includes its own metaphysical evolution: to seek to explain an event or fact is, like it or not, already virtually to aim at the ideal of an explanation of the totality of what is: for the principle of reason has no reason to cease operating, and when we have found the reason [*raison d'être*] for an event, this principle leads us to seek the reason for *that* reason, the cause of *that* cause until we find, if possible, an ultimate cause. It is precisely this metaphysical potentiality of the principle of reason that makes it so hard to *limit,* and in certain respects we understand that it is easier— as Arendt did—to pretend to be able to do without this principle and to declare it absolutely illegitimate in the domain of history. (Besides, why would it be less illegitimate in another domain if being, whether human or not, is fundamentally mysterious, open to Being, and not closed on some ultimate foundation?)

In the "Transcendental Dialectic," Kant meticulously explains the mechanisms by which this indefinite repetition of the principle of reason (of the hypothetical syllogism) must inevitably produce the idea of a science that is complete "in itself" (from God's point of view, if not man's), that is, the idea of a perfect subjection of the totality of the real to this powerful logical principle. Without going into the details of this mechanism, one can indicate that it has three primary aspects:

—First, the aim of perfect rationality necessarily takes the form of a quest for the *unconditioned:* to engage in an indefinite search for the reason for the reason, the cause of the cause, is in the final analysis to seek an ultimate cause, a cause that would itself be unconditioned by another antecedent cause—in short, an *unconditioned beginning:* only if we had this ultimate basis could we assert the perfect rationality of the *totality* of the real. Applied to history, this metaphysical ideal leads to positing a beginning and an end of history, these two end terms embracing the *totality* of historical development.

—We next observe that this quest for the unconditioned must necessarily proceed in three directions or, if you will, give rise to three metaphysical Ideas, three illusory forms of the perfect rationality of the real: first the quest can take the way of the *subject* and seek to think of what a subject that was transparent to itself would be, that is, a subject that was not the predicate of another reality, but that was perfectly *self-grounded;* the quest can then take the side of the *object,* of the World, and seek to think of what a universe would be if the knowledge of it were complete down to the last detail; finally, synthesizing these two elements, the absolute subject and the rational world, the quest can attempt to produce the point of view from which these two realities, *subject and object,* would be one, united in a perfect rationality. The first quest is that of rational psychology, the second that of rational cosmology, and the third that of rational theology, the culminating point of these three elements of "special metaphysics." [2]

—Third, it is still necessary to indicate that the infinitely reduplicated functioning of the principle of reason, a mechanism that culminates in the idea of a God for whom reality and rationality, objectivity and subjectivity, are one, displays the articulation that metaphysically unites the principle of reason and the ontological argument taken in its widest sense, that is, as the deduction of existence from the idea: through the principle of reason we arrive at the idea of a first cause—of a cause in itself—and hence the idea of a point of view for which every rational being, concept and intuition, idea and existence become identical. In the rationalistic philosophy of history, as has been suggested, the metaphysical use of the principle of reason thus leads to a secularized form of the Ontological Argument, for it allows for thinking of the future as predictable, as deducible from the concept (the laws of history) at least in itself or, which comes to the same thing, from the viewpoint of someone who, after the fashion of the God of metaphysics, has a perfect knowledge of history.

If the principle of reason embryonically contains these three metaphysical implications, what criticism of it is called for if we want not only to get out of the thesis of our antinomy, but also to avoid the irrationalism of the antithesis?

(c) The Critique of the Metaphysical Illusion and Getting beyond the Thesis

Critical philosophy rejects metaphysics—and hence the rationalist philosophy of history that is only a particular application of it— on three counts: because it is sophistical, it is not true, and it is devoid of meaning. Because the first two points are relatively simple and familiar, I shall merely review them briefly before going on to analyze in more detail the theory of meaning on the basis of which metaphysical discourse can be accused of meaninglessness.

(1) Metaphysics is sophistical for one basic reason: because it hypostatizes the idea of the unconditioned (obtained through the indefinite repetition of the principle of reason), it goes illegitimately from the idea to existence to the effective reality of this unconditioned. It is in this sense that Kant wrote, in a phrasing that is often read and often quoted, but whose true significance is rarely noted: "general logic considered as an organon is always a logic of appearance, that is, it is dialectical": it is through a simply logical use of a simply formal principle, the principle of reason that, by endlessly seeking the reason for the reason, one arrives at the cause of a cause, the Idea of an ultimate cause; and the fact that this Idea thus appears *necessary,* that is, as automatically produced by the internal logic of the working of the principle of reason, in no way justifies (here is the "dialectical," the "sophistical") using this idea as an "organon," that is, reifying it by granting it real content, in short, deducing from it the effective existence of a God (or a science complete in itself). This is the first metaphysical illusion, that in which a logically or subjectively necessary Idea is confounded with an objective Idea that effectively possesses a real correlate. Metaphysics can thus be described as a form of intellectual fetishism, for it forgets the mental *activity* leading to the Idea of the unconditioned, in favor of the *product,* the (falsely) objective content of the Idea.

(2) Besides being sophistical, dogmatic rationalism is also devoid of any scientific truth, for its propositions cannot be either verified or disconfirmed by experience. In the language of Karl Popper—whose neopositivism explicitly owes a great deal here to Kantianism—we could say that metaphysical propositions (particularly their chief principle, the assertion of the perfect rationality of the real) are not "falsifiable," that they fall into a domain that, located beyond space and time, lies outside all check by experience.

(3) Metaphysics also proves devoid of meaning. For a full understanding of this assertion, we should recall Kant's theory of meaning as expounded in the doctrine of what he calls the "Schematism." For it is at this level that we find the hard core of the critical criticism of metaphysics, also where we can get around the thesis and the antithesis of our antinomy in a direction different from that suggested by positivistic critics (who are happy enough with the first two objections). Following Cohen and Cassirer,[3] Alexis Philonenko has shown that Kant's theory of the Schematism is essentially designed to resolve the classic empiricist objections to the Cartesians concerning the "representability" of general concepts. According to the empiricists, innate ideas and general concepts have no meaning for the simple reason that it is impossible to represent a general concept from a psychological point of view. Each time I think of the idea of a triangle, for example, it is obvious that I represent to myself not a universal and abstract notion, but a particular triangle (a particular image) with a particular shape and size. Hence the empiricists' conclusion that general concepts are merely empty, meaningless abstractions, every representation being particular from the viewpoint of the empirical subject (but there is no other viewpoint!). Kant inevitably had to deal with this objection for at least two reasons: first, because he always recognized its validity at a psychological level; second, because he nevertheless admitted the existence of necessary and a priori universal concepts, the categories—of which we've pointed out how they defined ontology (the criteria of objecthood in general)—as well as the scientific concepts (for example, mathematical concepts like the concept of the triangle). For Kant, the problem posed by empiricism thus became the following: how can general concepts be particularized, represented by the finite subject through an empirical consciousness in time, without ceasing to have that generality without which they could not be said to have objective (universal) validity? This is the question that the theory of schematism attempts to resolve. The solution is as follows: concepts are not uni-

versal images (which, Kant grants the empiricists, makes no sense psychologically) but merely "schemata," that is, universal methods (valid for every time and place) for the construction of objects. The concept of triangle, for example, is not a "general representation" but a set of rules defining the way to proceed *in time,* with a rule and compass, to trace a *particular* image of a triangle that, despite its particularity, shares a certain number of properties (three angles, three sides, 180 degrees, and so forth) with all other triangles. Kant calls this operation of the "schematization" of concepts by the term "presentation" (*Darstellung*). We can now see how this theory of schematization or presentation helps resolve the antinomy of the Cartesians and the empiricists: as a schema, the general concept may be *both* particularized and grasped in time (by the "internal sense," says Kant) through the empirical consciousness that concretizes the rules for construction without a loss in universality (since whoever draws the triangle and whatever its size and shape, the procedures of construction will remain the same). In the same way we could show how all universal concepts can be taken as schemata: the concept of causality, for example, does not mean some "creation in general" but merely a procedure—that of the experimental method—by which one isolates a variable in order to test a hypothesis for explaining some phenomenon, and so on. The important thing here, however, is to see that the theory of schematism presupposes a theory of meaning: a concept has meaning for a concrete empirical subject only if it can be schematized, represented in time (the internal sense) proper to the consciousness of this subject; a discourse can make sense only if it can be in some way related to experience, "present" in an "intuition." "How can we obtain some meaning, some significance in our concepts if some intuition—always having in the final analysis to be the example of some experience possible—was not subject to them?"[4]

Kant, then, made a break with Cartesianism: the concept ceased being thought of as a general image in the understanding and became the *activity* of constructing objects or objective (scientific) laws; it ceased being a passive representation, but work: a *Begreifen.* Hence the third objection to metaphysics: metaphysical discourse is by definition unschematizable, unrepresentable by the empirical human consciousness: I can certainly define God's omniscience as "the knowledge of everything," and can very well assert that, from his point of view, the totality of the real is rational, but I can attribute no *meaning* to these statements, for I can never represent them to myself concretely: for me, a finite being, the real always remains at least partially opaque or impenetrable, sensory, and the idea of omniscience can never be "presented" in my consciousness. Metaphysical discourse thus appears as discourse that, although conceptually coherent, occupies a sphere from which I as a finite being am excluded. In other words, metaphysical discourse is tenable only by someone who forswears meaning, who forswears representing to himself what he says, and thus negates himself behind his own statements.

Considering the three objections to the thesis of our antinomy from a criticist point of view, we thus seem to be led irrevocably toward the antithesis, which holds that because the discourse of reason is neither true nor meaningful, we must renounce reason and take it to be "the fiercest enemy of thinking." Haven't we, without even realizing it, made this radical criticism that we were attacking? Suggesting that the difference between the phenomenological and the criticist attacks on metaphysics lay in the fact that the latter granted a certain legitimate use for metaphysical discourse *after* its deconstruction, this use could be located at the level of meaning. How would this use be possible if, not being true, metaphysics (hence the thesis of our antinomy) is also devoid of meaning? This question can be answered by examining the fourth and final element of this criticist criticism of dogmatic rationalism.

(d) The Status of Ideas after Their Criticism: Reason as a Requirement of Meaning or the Overcoming of the Antithesis

Though criticist criticism essentially takes the form of a *defetishization* expressing the intellectual mechanisms that produce the Idea of the perfect rationality of the real (of the subject, the World, and their unity in God or a complete and systematic science) and specifying how, once engendered, this Idea is reified, hypostatized, in a discourse that then escapes the subject that makes it (an unschematizable, unrepresentable discourse), we still must ask under what circumstances can metaphysics be defetishized and what is left after this "defetishization."

Metaphysical discourse culminates in the Idea of God understood as not only the ultimate term in which the quest for causes and reasons must end, but also as the point of view from which the totality of the universe forms a coherent, transparent, and rational whole—a system.

Abstracting from the question of its meaning or truth, this Idea of a system has some noteworthy properties: looked at from the viewpoint of a God the Idea of which is produced through the mechanical repetition of the principle of reason, the World (and thereby the history of the world and its human inhabitants) must have a certain number of features that make it a proper *system*. It must (1) group under one single law (2) the greatest possible plurality of different beings (3) with no gap or hiatus between these beings that would shatter systematic rationality (the principle of continuity); thus, (4) to the possessor of completed science, this systematic unity of the totality of diversity could appear fully rational, so that intuition and concept, existence and thought would be one.[5] Obviously, the philosophy of history expressed by the thesis of our antinomy has these very features and is merely the application of this Idea of a system to historicity (hence the eminently theological character of attempts that, even in the guise of a secularization of this representation of the system, claim to hold the key to the whole course of history).

I have said how this notion of system in its fetishized or reified form—in that it was posited as objective and valid in itself—was neither true nor meaningful. I have also stressed, however, that this Idea of reason was still *necessary,* being inevitably produced by the functioning of an ontological principle (the principle of reason) that it seems impossible to claim to do without. Hence the project of "defetishizing" this Idea to give it back, if not a truth, at least a meaning:

- defetishizing the notion of a system amounts to restoring its status as an Idea, that is, a subjective but still necessary requirement of human reason;
- giving it some meaning: if we refer to the theory of meaning just sketched, this is the attempt to schematize it, to make it fall into consciousness.

Although in its fetishized form the Idea of a system is unschematizable or unrepresentable, it can be schematized and hence have some meaning as a *requirement:* since to schematize a concept is to transform it into a set of rules for constructing an object in time, to schematize the Idea of a system amounts to conceiving of it as an imperative addressed to the human understanding to work to form our scientific knowledge as much as possible into a system. In other words, as a reified metaphysical Idea, the notion of a system *asserts* the rationality of the real in itself, while as a *schema* it merely requires that we seek to produce a maximum of systematicity in our knowledge. Defetishized and transformed into a requirement on a horizon of expectation and not posited as a dogmatic assertion, the Idea of a system may thus be schematized, not in its totality and not in one fell swoop, but in the course of that partial and indefinite process characteristic of all truly scientific activity. Each bit of scientific progress then functions as an illustration of this Idea, reminding us of its demand on us to work at the rationality of the real, if it is true that "truths are grouped in a system while error is lost in a shapeless magma."[6] In this sense, once deconstructed, the Ideas of reason still preserve a certain legitimacy, a "regulative use, which is indispensably necessary for directing the understanding toward a certain aim. With that aim in prospect, the directional lines of all rules of the understanding meet in one point, which serves to give them the greatest unity together with their greatest spread, although that point is only an idea (*focus imaginarius*) from which concepts of the understanding do not actually emanate, as it lies completely outside the boundaries of possible experience."[7]

Because the Idea of a system (of perfect rationality) is purely subjective, nothing guarantees that it will find the least exemplification in reality; but nothing stands in the way of finding the "beginnings of presentation" in it—and, by recalling this Idea, of giving it a concrete meaning as a requirement. Kant calls the beginnings of presentation or schematization "symbols," and the process by which the real by itself evokes the Idea of a system has a meaning for subjective "reflection" (in what Kant calls "reflective judgment"), but not an objective truth. The regulative use of the Idea of a system (or, if you like, the thesis of our antinomy) thus makes it possible to give a meaning to certain phenomena and, if truth be told, to all phenomena such as scientific progress and the beautiful object, that provide a beginnings of realization to our requirement of systematicity and thus create an "esthetic" satisfaction.[8]

Thus we should perhaps seek the ultimate solution to our antinomy following the model of what Kant calls the process of 'reflection.' The term "reflection" (which is perfectly univocal in Kant) refers to an intellectual activity that, whatever the object it applies to, includes five elements. An example, the formation of empirical concepts (borrowed from Kant's *logic*), may serve as an illustration and more concrete explanation of how we may find the solution to our antinomy in this paradigm of the reflective process. To form the empirical concept of a set of unfamiliar objects (for example, a variety of trees not yet classified), one should go through what we would now call an operation of "classification": by comparing resemblances and by abstracting out nonessential differences, we group objects together in a common class; we thus form the empirical concept. This simple operation contains the five elements making up the reflection (of "reflective judgment"):

(1) The reflecting activity goes from the particular to the universal, from the individuals to the class.

(2) The general (or the universal) is thus not present before the activity of reflection, but only after it and through it. (This is why a reflective judgment is opposed to a "determinative" judgment which, on the contrary, goes from the universal to the particular and hence constitutes only an *application* of the universal.

(3) Although the general is not given as a concept from the start, there necessarily exists a horizon of implicit expectation that serves as a guiding thread or, as Kant says, a "principle" for this reflection: in this case, this principle is provided by the logic of classes: it consists in the *hope*, the *requirement*, that the real be classifiable and thus conform to logic. The general that is not given as a determinative concept is thus classifiable as an Idea, as a requirement, or to use two synonymous expressions, "regulative principle" and "principle of reflection."

(4) Consequently, it is perfectly *contingent* whether or not the real corresponds to this requirement of logical rationality *that we do not impose on it but merely submit it to:* it is possible that the real does not correspond to our subjective requirement of logical systematicity so that we do not manage to form either genus or species. In short, in terms that are now familiar, it could be that the real is "illogical," that it is not rational—a possibility quite explicitly envisaged in the *Critique of Pure Reason.*[9] So on just this point the criticism of metaphysics links up with the Idea of reflection: if the real is contingent in relation to our requirement of logical systematicity, the reason is that, having broken the circle of metaphysics, we have clearly posited the nonrationality of the real: the notion of reflection is possible because systematicity and rationality are not longer *assertions,* but *requirements.*

(5) The activity of reflection thus proves to be the source of a satisfaction that Kant in the third *Critique* calls "esthetic" (the term here expresses, unlike its use in the first *Critique,* the notion of beauty): because the real is contingent in relation to the principle of our reflection (to our demand for logical rationality), because this principle is not a certainty but a requirement, there can be pleasure of an esthetic kind in it, a satisfaction that nothing guarantees a priori.

Hence in the judgment of taste we find the five elements described, this judgment also proceeding (*a*) from the particular to the universal; (*b*) and this without concept; (*c*) the Idea of a system taking the place of the principle of reflection; (*d*) the existence of the beautiful object being contingent in relation to this Idea; (*e*) and agreement/harmony, also contingent, of the particular real with the universal requirement of system creating esthetic pleasure: indeed, the Idea of a system or of the perfect rationality of the real requires that the sensory (the nonrational par excellence) and the intelligible be reconciled (without which, by definition, everything would not be rational). The beautiful object, contingently bringing about a certain harmony between the sensible and the intelligible (painting and music, for example, are both material, but who can deny that they seem to have meaning?), *symbolically* recalls this Idea of a system.

The activity of reflection explained in the five elements just mentioned then provides us with the paradigm of a solution to our antinomy: the thesis can be preserved as a requirement, of the "principle of reflection" or guiding thread without the abolishment of the antithesis, the assertion of contingency; and vice versa, the retention of the antithesis does not eliminate rationality provided it is posited as a requirement of meaning and not as a dogmatic truth.

Armed with this paradigm for a solution, we can now apply it concretely to the question of the status of the principle of reason in conceiving of historicity. To summarize the preceding, it has a twofold status:

- On the one hand, the principle of reason can be used as a *scientific concept* in seeking to explain a phenomenon (the principle of causality);
- on the other hand, when the principle of reason reduplicates itself in an infinite quest for *the* ultimate cause of all causes, it can produce the metaphysical illusion of the perfect rationality of the real (the Idea of God or a system).

To be meaningful, the principle of reason must, consistent with what has been said, be schematizable, representable in the internal sense, in the temporal empirical consciousness.

—This schematization takes place in the scientific use of the principle of reason, when causality does not mean an effect's *creative entity,* but a method (the experimental method) with which hypotheses are put forward, variables are isolated, and so forth, to determine what event invariably follows what other event (see the "second analogy of experience" in the *Critique of Pure Reason*).

—For its part, the metaphysical Idea of a system is schematized when, transformed into a requirement, it too becomes just a method for organizing our knowledge and giving meaning to phenomena that in themselves point to this systematic organization (like the beautiful object).

This twofold schematization of the twofold status of the principle of reason (as a scientific concept and as a defetishized metaphysical Idea) thus lays out the articulation of what could be a *critical historical science* and a *critical philosophy of history:*

—A critical historical science: we too often forget that the expression "science of history" is ambiguous. Owing to the influence of "scientific" Marxism, it now tends to mean a pseudoscience or pseudometaphysics of history that in fact corresponds to the philosophy of history that occupies position number three in the diagram shown in the introduction to this book. As such, the expression has been rightly discredited, notably in studies like those of Karl Popper on historicism. It would be absurd, however, to conclude that every claim to scientificity in the study of history is illusory and that this claim is inevitably confounded with the plan for a science of history as mapped out from the purview of Marxism. In other words, it would be absurd to object, as Arendt did, to the use of the concept of causality in history on the fallacious reason that this use inevitably fosters the plan for some Marxian "science of history." As I have argued elsewhere,[10] there is a possible use of the principle of causality in history that confers a scientific but still nonhistoricist status to this discipline:[11] this was the project of Max Weber, who, in a clearly Kant-inspired tradition, undertook to give a nonhistoricist status to the use of causality in history, one compatible with the indeterminacy and contingency characteristic of the world of the mind. Without going into the details of Weber's idea of historical causality—Raymond Aron did this analysis brilliantly in his writings on Weber and the question of historical objectivity—I shall confine myself to stressing that it applies to historicity the scientific concept of causality taken as a *schema,* and thus elaborates an experimental *historical* method whose hypotheses are tested in the social sciences. For Weber, the point of the famous question What would have happened if the Persians had won the battle of Marathon? a question said to make historians smile, was to show the compatibility between the use of causality and historical indeterminacy (contingency).

—But it is also a *critical* philosophy of history that may be based on the schematization of the second status of the principle of reason. Taken as a requirement of rationality, the idea of a system may—as Kant tried to show in his pamphlets on the philosophy of history, but especially in §83 of the *Critique of Judgment*—serve as a horizon of quasi-esthetic expectation for a philosophical historiography. Without postulating the truth of some "cunning of reason," the idea of a system can use the general structure of this philosophy of history as a guiding principle, as a principle of reflection that provides a meaning to events marking an epoch, or in Kant's terms, to the notion of Progress.

We can now formulate the solution to our antinomy: the principle of reason—in its two uses as a scientific concept and as a regulative Idea, provided in both cases it serves as a schema and is thereby *limited*—is in no way incompatible with the assertion of contingency or, what amounts to the same thing, the nonrationality of the real. Schematized, meaning put in accord with the conditions appropriate to the radical finitude of the human mind, the principle of reason may give rise to a historical science and a philosophy of history, neither of which denies the indeterminacy of historicity but without abandoning (an epistemologically impossible and singularly dangerous attempt at the political level) the demands of rationality.

The critical solution of this antinomy thus justifies two conclusions and, it is true, creates a major difficulty.

The first conclusion concerns the fact that this solution invites us to think schematically (methodically) of both the antithesis and the thesis of our antinomy: to think of the thesis schematically is, as has been explained, to transform it into a requirement and hence a method. To think of the antithesis schematically is—and we can see this only now—to think of contingency or the "ontological difference" not in "objective" terms, as a difference between "Being and being," between the "presence" and "presencing," but in "subjective" but still nonmetaphysical terms, as the surprise or occasional esthetic pleasure experienced by the subject who, demanding rationality without postulating its instantiation in advance, *sometimes* sees his expectation partially satisfied.

The second conclusion concerns the articulation between historical science and the critical philosophy of history. The solution to our antinomy leads to positing two end terms: on the one hand the radical and by definition nonrational contingency of the real, and on the other hand the requirement of perfect and systematic rationality, these two extremes corresponding to the "schematic" idea of the antithesis and the thesis. Taken together in the critical solution of the antinomy, these two moments sketch the framework of a critical philosophy of history. But it is between these two extremes that critical historical science may come to lodge itself, that is to say, the science that with the help of the scientific concept of causality always constructs partial and hypothetical explanations and rejects neither the dimension of contingency nor the dimension of meaning which are also dimensions of history and so avoids the temptations of historicism and irrationalism.

This critical solution to the antinomy in connection with the status of the principle of reason in the field of history, however, despite its soundness in my eyes at the purely theoretical level, seems to me to raise a formidable problem in practical philosophy. It enables us to get out of the aporias inevitably produced by the two dogmatisms of Hegelianism and its phenomenological deconstruction; it noncontradictorily sanctions thinking of history as contingent while maintaining the requirements of speculative reason, but it leaves us quite uncertain about the status of human freedom in history, for it can answer a question about the cause of the historical event only from a purely *theoretical* point of view, by proposing partial explanations that open onto the undetermined and are oriented toward an overall view of progress in which individual freedom is as absent as in Hegelianism. In other words, from a theoretical point of view it is certainly essential that the theory of the cunning of reason —or of the "design of nature"—not have the status of a dogmatic assertion, for the schematization of this idea allows us *at the same time* to introduce contingency and scientificity in the field of history. From a practical (ethical) point of view, however, it seems that this difference has no impact: whether or not the rationalism of the thesis has the status of a "principle of reflection," a simple requirement, doesn't change anything in the fact that it essentially rules out the moral view of history. And it would be utterly fallacious—although this is often done in the phenomenological tradition—to conclude surreptitiously from *contingency* to *moral freedom:* as was suggested in the introduction, it is not because the human world is fundamentally undetermined or because we escape the total hold of dogmatic rationalism that we can without further ado think of ourselves as freedom in action, as the ultimate foundation of our own acts. In short, *limiting* the thesis and antithesis of our antinomy does not yet justify our thinking of *indeterminacy* as moral freedom, and the practical philosophy of history (the "moral view of the world") remains largely problematic at the point we have reached in our search. Hence the question we now take up: under what circumstances can an ethical view of history be compatible with the theoretical solution to the antinomy just set forth?

To explore, if not to eliminate, the aporias to which this question leads, I propose to analyze the young Fichte's philosophy of history, for it constitutes the most vigorous and coherent exposition of the presuppositions and ultimate implications of an ethical view of history.

The Ethical View of History and the Foundation of the Idea of Praxis in the Thought of the Young Fichte

The French Revolution
and the
Copernican Revolution

In his letter of April 1795 to Baggessen,[1] Fichte defines the relation of his philosophy to the French Revolution in these terms:

> Mine will be the first system of liberty. Just as this nation (France) delivers mankind from its material chains, my system will deliver it from the yoke of the thing in itself, from external influences; its first principles make man into an autonomous being. The *Wissenschaftslehre* [*Science of Knowledge*] was born during the years the French nation made political liberty triumph through its energy; it was born following an intimate struggle with myself and with all the prejudices anchored within me, and this conquest of freedom contributed to the birth of the *Science of Knowledge:* I owe it to the value of the French nation to have been raised even higher; it gave birth in me to the energy necessary to the understanding of these ideas. While I was writing the work on the Revolution, the first signs, the first foreshadowings of my system emerged in me as a sort of recompense.[2]

If we are to believe Fichte, the *Science of Knowledge* grew out of his thinking about the concrete history of the French Revolution. When we add that for him the Revolution was just one manifestation (*Darstellung*) of "another, incomparably greater revolution" (*B* 83),[3] we see that Fichte's earliest philosophy, as a completion of the Copernican revolution, was meant to provide a philosophical foundation for the French Revolution.[4] We also see that we will have to look into the 1794 *Science of Knowledge* for the foundation of the idea of history that consistently underlies the criticism of Rehberg in the *Beiträge.*

Fichte's transposition of the Copernican revolution to the level of the philosophy of history is quite clear: it appears in the preface to the *Beiträge:* "we will never find anything in all

99

of world history which we did not lay there ourselves: but through the judgment of actual events, [mankind] may more easily develop out of itself what lies in itself: and so does the French Revolution seem to me a rich painting on the great text of human rights and human worth" (*B* 81). As is often the case in a philosophy whose stated goal is to justify the common consciousness,[5] the thesis is almost banal: it simply means, at least at a first level, that it is mankind, and mankind alone, who creates its history.

This thesis is more complex than it seems, however, when we take account of the parallelism it sets up between actual history (the French Revolution) and philosophical history (the Copernican revolution) and when we try to identify what it excludes: the determination of history by something other than the free and transforming activity of man.

"In the history of the world we never find anything except what we have first put in it ourselves": this proposition is obviously a parody of the preface to the *Critique of Pure Reason:* "We cognize a priori of things only what we have put into them ourselves."[6] Thus the letter to Baggessen suggests a parallelism between the historical domination (of "material chains") and what can be called the "theoretical domination" exercised by the dogmatism of the fully constituted object that would be reflected in a purely passive subject. So that one is tempted to posit the following equation, which Fichte would surely have accepted: if the Copernican revolution is the essence of criticism and frees us from subservience to the dogmatism of the object (which clearly puts an external limitation on the subject's spontaneity or freedom), it follows that any dogmatic or even insufficiently critical philosophy (the retention of the thing in itself in Kantianism displaying such a critical insufficiency) must lead to a denial of man's total freedom in the face of his history: realism—the thesis that the subject's representations are causally produced by an external object in itself—implies a conception of consciousness as a simple passive "reflection," and, as such, realism (we would now say "materialism") implies determinism. Consequently, to think radically of the idea that history is throughout the doing of man must also be to think radically of criticism, that is, to eliminate the thing in itself. Therefore, only the *Science of Knowledge,* as the completion of Kantianism, can allow for the full legitimization of

PREAMBLE

the philosophy of history of the *Beiträge:*[7] it alone will succeed in completely eliminating the idea of a determination of history that is not fully the result of the free activity of men.

It is on this exact point in the *Beiträge* that Fichte's thinking diverges from Kant's. Although not explicit in this form (that happened only in the writings of 1794), the idea appears that there is a taint of dogmatism in Kant's thesis of a "design of nature" and hence a determination of history by some element foreign to the free activity of man. For the Fichte of 1794 this idea of history is the exact counterpart to the dogmatic residue of the thing in itself in transcendental philosophy. In 1793, Fichte seems to link the valorization of political activism (here, the Revolution) to the rejection of any philosophy of history pivoting on the idea of a "design of nature," an idea expressed by Kant in his 1784 "Idea for a Universal History with a Cosmopolitan Purpose"—where he characterizes the constitution of a just state as a "pathologically extorted agreement" (and not freely produced, as Fichte wished). Fichte expresses this rejection in a note to the *Beiträge:*

> Since we are not here writing a treatise against history, let us note down what follows: "We need history, among other things, to admire the wisdom of Providence in working out its great plan"— but that is not true. You only wish to admire you own sagacity. You have a nation that goes something like: you would do it *this* way if you were Providence. One could show, with incomparably greater probability, in the march heretofore of mankind's destinies the plan of an evil, misanthropic being, who had arranged everything toward man's greatest possible moral corruption and misery. But that would not be true either. The only truth is: that an infinite manifold is given, in itself neither good nor evil, but first becoming one or the other through the free application of reasoning beings, and that it will not, in fact, become better before *we* have done so. (*B* 105)

Echoing the fundamental themes of Fichte's ideas in 1793 about history, this text immediately suggests two observations, which will be discussed in detail in the next chapter:

—Clearly, this text is addressed to Kant's Idea of a providential design of nature mentioned at the end of the fourth proposition of his "Idea of a Universal History": "[T]he sources of the very unsociableness and continual resistance which cause so many evils, at the same time encourage man towards

101

new exertions of his powers and thus towards further development of his natural capacities. They would thus seem to indicate the design of a wise creator—not, as it might seem, the hand of a malicious spirit who had meddled in the creator's glorious work or spoiled it out of envy" (IUH 45). Thus we can conclude that the *Beiträge* opposes—at the source of such thinking—any application of a theodicy to the theory of history, and—regarding consequences—any theory of the "cunning of reason." The difference here between Kant and Fichte, often covered over (notably by Hegel), needs to be clarified, for it is a paradigm of the rejection by the young Fichte of any deterministic and rationalist visions of history (be they only, like Kant's, considered as simple points of view).

Kant's criticism is inserted in the antinomy of providence and the malicious spirit. Rejecting both thesis and antithesis, Fichte asserts—as he should in any critical solution of an antinomy—a position of *neutrality,* with seemingly important consequences. The obvious result is the assertion that the historical diverse or manifold is given,[8] that is, that manifoldness is in itself neutral and insignificant and that it is man—and man alone—who freely gives meaning to it by transforming it. Thus Fichte reaffirms the initial thesis of the preface, almost certainly against Kant.

One may, however, allow oneself to think that this prefigures Fichte's criticism of Rousseau in his 1794 "Lectures on the Vocation of the Scholar." For this note in the *Beiträge* asks questions about not only the motor of history, but also its starting point—that is, the state of nature. We should recall that the *Beiträge* is primarily a polemic against Rehberg. We should also recall that the reactionary argument for authoritarian despotism focuses on human weakness: people are wicked and selfish, and so, to preclude anarchy, need a powerful ruler. Fichte rejected Kant's solution of the providential cunning of nature and hence was led to deny that state of nature. The 1793 reference to Rousseau thus proves essentially strategic. We should note, however, that in the *Beiträge,* and contrary to the opinion of most exegetes,[9] Fichte saw the state of nature not as good, but as neutral: only a neutral state of nature (meaning a starting point for history in which the pure freedom of man faces only a neutral diverseness) is compatible with the radical assertion of the absoluteness of human freedom as the motor of the historical process. Conversely, as soon as the starting point of history is thought of as good, history can only be romantic and nostalgic: the end of history must be the future restoration of a state that held in the past. This is the basis of the argumentation elaborated in the 1794 "Lectures on the Vocation of the Scholar." For reasons to be discussed, Fichte could not have made this criticism in 1793. It is still true, however, that even in the *Beiträge* the assertion of man's absolute freedom is accompanied by a determinate representation of history's starting point as neutral.

To grasp the meaning and implications of the philosophy of history in the *Beiträge,* we need to examine (chap. 4): (1) Fichte's 1793 criticism of Kant's philosophy of history as a criticism of any theory of the cunning of reason, (2) his 1794 criticism of Rousseau's philosophy of history as a criticism of any "romantic" theory of history.

Through these two criticisms, the exigencies of a pure theory of praxis gradually took form in Fichte's thinking, and he was then able to undertake to ground them in transcendental philosophy (chap. 5). Then, with full knowledge of the case, we can come back to the problems incurred by this moral view of the world (chap. 6).

The Criticisms of Kant and Rousseau: Fichte's Development from 1793 to 1794

1. Ambiguities in Kant's Philosophy of History

Fichte saw Kant's retention of the thing in itself as the sign of a crucial shortcoming, a lack of radicalness in carrying out the Copernican revolution, with the resulting persistence of a certain heteronomy at the level of the idea of history: we are forced to note that Kant's first important writing on this subject, "Idea for a Universal History with a Cosmopolitan Purpose," displays a certain ambiguity in determining what the motor element of the historical process is, for it is hard to see whether it should be imputed, if only partially, to human free will or just to the hypothetical "design of nature." I am bringing up this problem with Kant's thinking because I believe that it is precisely through criticism of it that Fichte argued most radically against any philosophy of the cunning of reason. Thus, it is by determining his difference from Kant here that we can also see how, to repeat a formula of K. Schumann, the "actually post-Hegelian" [1] Fichte could not be truly converted to a pure theory of the "cunning of reason," even when his final philosophy would almost have had to lead him to it. [2]

The ambiguity in Kant's 1784 text seems to me to lie in the tension between a mechanistic and a voluntarist conception of history. In the first five propositions of the "Idea for a Universal History," Kant attempts to lend weight to the thesis of a belief in progress, to apply a physical model inherited from Leibniz to history: that of the resultant of the composition of forces in a parallelogram. [3] Taken in isolation, human wills are little more than a tissue of "folly" and "childish vanity" (IUH 42), for they separately pursue their own selfish ends which as such are necessarily particular. This is the 1784 sketch of the answer Kant was to give in 1793–95 to Rehberg's objections (see my introduction). The relative optimism attending the belief in progress cannot be based on men's good will (on their morality), but only on the observation of a natural necessity contained in the resultant of this infinity of forces of particular wills: "since [the philosopher] cannot assume that mankind follows any rational *purpose of its own* in its collective actions ... the only way out ... is ... to attempt to discover a *purpose in nature*" (IUH 42). Thus, through the play of the hypothesis of providence, Kant's philosophy of history begins to look like a theory of the cunning of nature in which human action is not *consciously* and *voluntarily* the motor element of history. To repeat: it is this element, but only as a component force, and as such blind. It is important to stress that for Kant—unlike Schelling and Hegel—this vision of history is merely an "Idea," merely a simple "guiding principle of reason" (IUH 42) for the philosopher's *reflection,* and in no way an objective or scientific interpretation of history. It is still true that even at the level of what is just a subjective "thought" and not a piece of "knowledge," human freedom seems to be eliminated from the "phenomenal" course of historical events.

I have already stated how in 1793–95 Kant reiterated this general thesis in defense of the French Revolution. Backed up in the fourth proposition of the "Idea for a Universal History" by the introduction of the concept of "unsociable sociableness"—that is, by the already "dialectical" (in the Hegelian sense) thesis that their unsociableness (through conflict owing to selfishness) forces people to enter into society and to construct a legal order (sociableness)—the thesis is expressed in the fifth proposition by a metaphor that seems to me to foreshadow the central problem of the text of 1784:

> Man, who is otherwise so enamored with unrestrained freedom, is forced to enter this state of restriction by sheer necessity. And this is indeed the most stringent of all forms of necessity, for it is imposed by men upon themselves, in that their inclinations make it impossible for them to exist side by side for long in a state of wild freedom. But once enclosed within a precinct like that of civil union, the same inclinations have the most beneficial effect. In the same way, trees in a forest, by seeking to deprive each other of air and sunlight, compel each other to find these by upward growth, so that they grow beautiful and straight—whereas those which put out branches at will, in freedom and in isolation from others, grow stunted, bent and twisted. (IUH 46)

What can we conclude from this fifth proposition?

First, this clearly confirms the idea of a mechanistic and naturalistic history in which man has an influence only as a physical force and not as a moral being.[4] *Naturally* forced to enter the "precinct of civil union," man is, once inside this precinct, also forced to move toward a just constitution.[5] No mention is made of any intervention by practical reason in history, and if we must reckon *with* human freedom (with man's selfish will), we must definitely not rely *on* it (on his moral will).

At the end of the fifth proposition, the attainment of the law does not seem to be in question, inscribed as it is in the design of nature according to a dialectical schema: "the finest social order"—and we know that, in Kant's mind, that can only be a republican constitution—cannot be hindered by man's wickedness, for it itself is merely the "fruit of his unsociability" (its resultant) (IUH 46).

We note that in this metaphor, the "wood man is made of" seems quite capable of going from "twisted" to "straight," provided it is located in a "precinct" that symbolizes the *closed* system in which only the physical schema of the composition of forces can function.[6]

It is on this point that I believe the ambiguity in Kant's thinking about history becomes fully apparent, for the sixth proposition of 1784 contradicts the fifth almost word for word. Here we find the assertion that human freedom makes it "impossible" to actualize the just society, since "nothing straight can be constructed from such warped wood as that which man is made of" (IUH 46)![7] Kant immediately suggests the reason for this failure in terms that come as a surprise to the reader: what is required for the actualization of the republican constitution is "above all else . . . a good will prepared to accept the [constitution]" (IUH 47). Taking up Kant's metaphor, we may legitimately wonder how the same "wood" that in the fifth proposition was supposed to straighten out simply by the natural mechanism to the point of "growing beautiful and straight," can in the sixth proposition be hopelessly "twisted."[8] The answer is provided by the resort to the concept of "good will"; abandoning the physical and mechanistic vision of history, Kant suddenly adopts, in the sixth proposition, an ethical point of view. From that point on, according to the logic exposed by Rehberg in connection with the French Revolution, the human wickedness inscribed into the very conception of the state of nature inevitably becomes an insuperable obstacle to the actualization of the rule of law, since the rule of law depends on a moral will that is lacking.

To my knowledge, Alexis Philonenko is the only interpreter of Kant to have noticed this problem. Despite its interest, however, the solution Philonenko proposes in *Théorie et praxis* does not seem to me fully satisfactory. He argues that in 1784 Kant was still confusing morality and politics, the "reign of ends" and the republican constitution, and that this confusion prevented Kant from solving the political problem. In 1795, however, "clearly separating the ethical problem and the political problem that he confounded in 1784,"[9] Kant could finally judge that the question of the actualization of a republican constitution could be solved "even for a race of devils," since it does not "require the moral betterment of men," according to the formulas of his "Perpetual Peace" already quoted. This interpretation, which certainly has the virtue of relating the problem of Kant's texts to the central question of the relations between morality and politics, seems to me, however, to be open to two objections. It rests on the hypothesis of a *change* in Kant's thinking, a change that can be summed up as follows: in 1784 Kant based the actualization of law on human good will and since this is absent, the problem proved insoluble; in 1795, however, morality and politics are clearly separated, the actualization of the law could proceed from the interplay of selfish urges. We should note that (1) the idea of making the actualization of law depend on a natural mechanism is already largely developed in the first five propositions of the "Idea" and hence is not at all new in 1795, so that the contradiction spotted by Philonenko (now the political problem is said to be insoluble, now it seems to be solvable) is to be found not so much between the two texts of Kant (1784/1795) than already *within* the text of 1784 itself. (2) On the other hand, if Kant's thinking truly changed on this point, it is unclear how, in the writings after 1795, he could go on maintaining that the political problem is insoluble, as he explicitly does in the *Contest of Faculties* (1798): "It is a pleasant dream to hope that a political product of the sort we here have in mind will one day be brought to perfection, at however remote a date." This is why I think we need to look for the solution to this difficulty in the *Critique of Judgment,* which attempts to reconcile the theoretical viewpoint with the ethical viewpoint, which are diametrically opposed here.

Whatever this solution (to which I shall return), it seems that Kant's doctrine can provide a coherent answer to the objection of reactionary thinking only if it looks at history from a purely theoretical and hence necessarily naturalistic and deterministic viewpoint: the introduction of the ethical viewpoint—of freedom as practical reason—immediately making the political question aporetic.[10] Despite the ambiguity we have seen, this can justify considering the theoretical aspect of Kant's philosophy of history and rejecting any interpretation that would make it *exclusively* a moral idealism comparable to the young Fichte's.

We can thus see how Fichte could find Kant's conception of history unsatisfactory, for it presents the following alternative: either history is thought of theoretically (in terms of natural causality and the "design of nature") and hence is insufficiently critical or "revolutionary"; or history is conceived on an ethical terrain, and, starting not from the hypothesis but from the genuine assertion of the radical "twistedness" of man, it necessarily becomes pessimistic and thus links up, at least in its conclusions, with reactionary thought, where Fichte's thinking, which begins with a neutral state of nature, can claim to be located midway between optimism and pessimism.

Fichte is not mistaken about this; from the opening chapters of the *Beiträge,* he argues against two essential points in the philosophy of the "design of nature": the question of the role of war in cultural progress, and that of the starting point (the state of nature) and the end point of history (retention or elimination of the state).

We see how important the question of war is when we see that it is inevitably at stake in the conflict between philosophies of the cunning of reason—which, by their very essence, cannot help justifying war—and the properly ethical view of history. Every philosophy of the cunning of reason or design of nature (the difference is here unimportant) is necessarily dialectical in the sense that peace must always be realized through its opposite, war (sociability through unsociability). Thus to some extent we find Kant himself, despite the *ethical* repugnance that this idea clearly provoked in him,[11] justifying war at the level of the philosophy of history, a justification reminiscent of certain theses of Hegel,[12] and we can see this at three levels: anthropological, legal, and metaphysical:[13]

—In his "Idea for a Universal History," Kant presents war from an anthropological viewpoint as a factor in cultural progress or perfectibility, as a means for making man's "natural inclinations" go from potential to action: "Nature should thus be thanked for fostering social incompatibility, enviously competitive vanity, and insatiable desires for possession or even power. Without these desires, all man's excellent natural capacities would never be roused to develop. Man wishes concord, but nature, knowing better what is good for his species, wishes discord" (IUH 45, fourth proposition). Many quotations could be presented to the effect that nature, essentially conflictual,[14] becomes a means for cultivating[15] natural inclinations, thus attesting to the first basic function of war in Kant's thinking.

—From a legal point of view, war contributes to straightening man's natural "twistedness" and, as paradoxical as it seems, Kant's thesis is as follows: as the first supplement to "Perpetual Peace" stresses, war provides the surest guarantee of peace to come. Kant's thinking is especially rigorous on this point: after excluding every possibility of basing hope for peace on people's good will,[16] all that remains is, once again, only their natural antagonism to constrain them to form a state and eventually a republic.[17] Peace in the republic becomes a real possibility by virtue of the "First Definitive Article of a Perpetual Peace,"[18] and thus war proves to be the chief means nature uses to force man, if not to morality, at least to legality and peace, as the seventh proposition of the "Idea for a Universal History" already asserts: "Nature has thus again employed the unsociableness of men, and even of the large societies and states which human beings construct, as a means of arriving at a condition of calm and security through their inevitable *antagonism*. Wars . . . are the means by which nature drives nations to . . . [abandon] a lawless state of savagery and entering a federation of peoples" (IUH 47).[19]

—From a metaphysical viewpoint, finally war is based, as paradoxical as it may at first seem, on the Idea of divine wisdom,[20] the notion of the "design of nature" being explained by the intention of providence, since no intention can be ascribed to purely physical nature (see IUH 45):

> War is inevitable. Sometimes this results in states splitting up and resolving themselves into lesser states, sometimes one state absorbs other smaller states and endeavors to build up a larger unit. But if on the part of man war is a thoughtless undertaking, being stirred up by unbridled passions, it is nevertheless a deep-seated, perhaps farsighted, attempt on the part of supreme wisdom, if not to ground, to prepare the way for a rule of law governing the freedom of states and thus to bring about their unity in a system established on a moral basis. And in spite of the terrible calamities which it inflicts on the human race, and the possibly even greater hardships imposed by the constant preparation for it in time of peace, yet—as the prospect of the dawn of a lasting reign of national happiness keeps ever retreating farther into the distance—it is one more spur to developing to the highest pitch all talents that minister to culture.[21]

I have quoted nearly all of this passage because I believe it contains the main points bringing together Kant's and Hegel's ideas of history and also reveals how fundamentally different they are. It is plausible to think that what the young Fichte was criticizing in Kant is precisely what I call Hegelian. So it is important to clarify this rapprochement: it is shown in the idea that war is necessary (inevitable) and even useful,[22] that is, by the "idea" that what seems to be irrational (antagonism) is actually rational—that is, to adopt the Hegelian formulation, through the identity of the rational and the real. In this deeply metaphysical sense, Kant's conception of history finds its ultimate anchoring point in the idea of divine wisdom and harmony.[23]

This similarity of thinking in Kant and Hegel should not, however, make us overlook the profound differences between them. We easily see this in the quotation, and it bears essentially on two points:

—First, war is referred to the idea of a divine intention only in the hypothetical mode of the "perhaps." That is, in Kantian terms, divine wisdom here is merely a "point of view," without any objective value—in short, it is a "reflective" judgment and not a "determinative judgment" and hence a simply subjective judgment expressed in the mode of "as if." This first observation thus considerably relativizes the "idea" of the identity of the rational and the real implied by Kant's conception of war. For us, for our "faculty of judging," there is the *supposition* of the identity of the real and the rational.[24]

—We next note that the movement of nature (which from a higher point of view is called providence) aims only to "prepare for" and not to "establish" a moral system. As the text directly following the one quoted from the *Critique of Judgment*, §83, clearly asserts: "We see nature striving [through the conflicts it uses to reach its goal] on purposive lines to give us that education [*Ausbildung*] that opens the door to higher ends than it can itself afford." What Kant means to reveal is the chasm separating the world of history (and, correspondingly, politics) from that of ethics: just because history *as such* is "natural," it can at most lead us to *legality* (external conformity to the laws of reason) but in no way to *morality* (external *and* internal conformity to reason, that is, the conformity of the intention itself).[25] Thus, history can only *prepare*[26] for morality by establishing a legal world in which actions necessarily (through the mechanism of nature itself) become consistent with duty. The shift to morality proper, however, presupposes a leap: producing the intention's conformity to the law cannot be done mechanically, since this conformity comes under the jurisdiction of the legislation of freedom. It is the mediating function of history (bringing about the necessary but not sufficient connection between nature and freedom) that justifies its position in the third *Critique,* the reflecting judgment being itself a middle term between the two parts of the philosophy.[27]

2. The Rejection of Determinism

What was Fichte's reaction to this idea of history and war? Judging Kant's thinking insufficiently critical, the young Fichte probably must have "doubted" the truth of Kant's philosophy of history and couched the question of war and peace in new terms.[28]

It is not my intention here to discuss the circumstances in which Fichte wrote the *Beiträge,* nor to present a systematic analysis of its content. Besides, that would be superfluous after Philonenko's masterly interpretation of this difficult work.[29] I thus set aside the analysis of the various commentaries on the *Beiträge,* since Philonenko seems to explain its essential problems quite clearly. I shall simply show how in the first three chapters of the *Beiträge* the young Fichte is arguing almost point for point against the ideas he claims to be extending[30] and thus proves perhaps the most radical ethical critic of the theories of the cunning of reason. Because the *Beiträge* was not meant as a philosophy of history and the question is not taken up thematically, it seems better to identify some of the characteristic features of the idea of history consistently underlying this work so as to bring out their interconnectedness.

(1) What becomes apparent in the opening pages of the *Beiträge* is the idea that history cannot be its own court of judgment. This is the deeper meaning of the echoing of Rousseau's theme of the separation of right and fact that Fichte introduces in the text of 1793 (see *B* 88, 89, 93), and this distinction not only has the value of a foundation for the autonomy of the sphere of rights, but also signifies the refusal to apply any project of "theodicy" to history, even if only by way of a supposition of "reflection" as in Kant: "The question of Ought and Can, which is, as will soon become apparent, another expression for the question of rights, does not belong before the tribunal of history. . . . It belongs before another tribunal which we shall search for" (*B* 97). The tribunal is in fact that of the Self "pure and initial form" (*B* 97), that is, that of the "moral law" (*B* 98). No doubt Fichte's thinking is rather unoriginal here compared to that of Kant, who also distinguished fact from right and hence did not fall into the vicious circle of judging the historical event in relation to a law and the law in relation to the historical event. What distinguishes Fichte from Kant here, however, and opposes him (in advance) to Hegel's idea of a universal history/universal tribunal is his rigorous application of the distinction between right and fact to the philosophy of history: "Do we want to say: is right, what has happened most

often, and determine the ethical good by way of the majority of acts, like church dogma in councils, through the majority of votes? Do we want to say: is wise, what succeeds? Or would we rather take both questions together, look to success as the touchstone of both justice and wisdom and then, once arrived, call the robber a hero or a criminal, and Socrates an offender or a virtuous sage?" (*B* 89). There is no doubt that Kant easily escapes these questions on the *ethical* level. From what seems to be his view in "Perpetual Peace,"[31] however, how can he not make success the criterion, if not of moral goodness, then at least of the progress of culture and freedom in history?[32]

(2) What is at bottom in question here is the definition of man as both a phenomenal and an intelligible being. It appears that Kant's solution to the third antinomy must lead to applying a rigorous determinism to the course of phenomena and hence thus to history as a series of events in the world. In this vision of history, as Fichte well realized, at the level of phenomena it is hard to differentiate between man and animal, for the criterion of finality (intentional action) is inadequate (see chap. 3). Every deterministic idea of man as a sensitive creature reduces him to a mere plaything of some natural mechanism. Thus Fichte attacks those who "renounce their spirituality and reasonable nature, and make themselves into animals, determined by external impressions through their senses; into machines, irresistibly moved by the intermeshing of gears; into trees, in which the circulation and distillation of sap brings forth the fruit of thought";[33] thus "they immediately make themselves through such assertions into all these things, provided only that their thinking machine be correctly assembled" (*B* 89). In short, the immediate result of any dogmatism in the idea of history is to reify man, and if the text just quoted is not explicitly and uniquely directed against Kant, it does involve a criticism of what still reflects a residual dogmatism in Kant,[34] at least to Fichte's mind, or, if you will, a sign of his being insufficiently "revolutionary." It is in just this sense that, elaborating the profound idea of reification sketched in the *Beiträge,* the second introduction to the *Science of Knowledge* can maintain that Kant "was not convinced" (§9) when he wrote the *Critique of Pure Reason:* he who does not fully coincide with his own humanity cannot be convinced. As early as the *Beiträge,* Fichte uses this conception of reification to elaborate a criticism of political prejudices which foretells at many points the criticism of the transcendental illusion in the *Science of Knowledge* of 1794 (see chap. 5), and which is surely the most original element in his reflection on history in 1793.

(3) In the *Beiträge* we find, next to a classic attack on "ideologies" as both erroneous and self-interestedly biased (see, e.g., *B* 93), a "deconstruction" of political prejudice as a factor of reification. What Fichte is essentially criticizing, for example, in Rehberg's dogmatism is the creation of a discourse in which (*a*) man does not appear as a free being, and (b) the subject is, as such, inevitably eliminated. This is why in the *Beiträge* Fichte carefully specifies the *status* of different types of discourse, clearly distinguishing between the subjective element of certainty and the objective moment of truth: "Due to the authority of our fathers or teachers we accept, without proof, certain propositions as principles, that which they are not, their truth depending on the possibility of their derivation from yet higher principles. We go into the world and find our 'principles' again among everybody we get to now, because they also have taken them up on the authority of their parents and teachers. *No one makes us aware, through contradiction, of our lack of conviction, and of our need to examine those principles once again*" (*B* 91, emphasis added). Prejudice is in the final analysis only an opinion that is not contradicted and is even perfectly coherent in itself,[35] but that proves unthinkable "for us," for a very simple reason: its very content eliminates the subject thinking it. This is why the intervention of a *person* is needed for the prejudice to become problematic "for us." This is dogmatic discourse about history: in all its forms—whether the discourse of chance, providence, or necessity—it denies freedom; even when fully coherent, as in Spinoza, its fundamental defect is its *unrepresentability* by the subject producing it. How indeed could a being who—as author of his own discourse must necessarily think of himself as free—speak in a "machinelike" way of himself as a thing? It is noteworthy that under these circumstances, Fichte's constant argument against the dogmatics is expressed this way: "They have not correctly understood themselves" (*B* 94). There is no remedy for this attitude, for such discourse is the sign of not only an error but primarily a moral failing: man's rejection of his own humanity, namely, his freedom. Thus the dogmatist cannot be forced to reconsider his error: "It is not at all my purpose here to protect their humanity against themselves, and prove to them that they really are not unreasoning animals but pure spirit. If the clockwork that is their spirit is working properly, they cannot come upon our questions nor take part in our researches" (*B* 89).[36] Far from being purely rhetorical, the warning in the preface is to be taken seriously, and the difference it introduces between certainty and truth has a genuine critical

value:[37] it suggests the idea of a "metaphysics of politics" and a corresponding "criticism of politics."

As we have seen in connection with the dogmatic idea of history, political prejudice eliminates the point of view of subjectivity (conviction). It is a sort of "fetishized" discourse that forgets the activity in favor of the product. This is just where Fichte's 1794 critique, repeating Kant's theory of schematism, applies to metaphysics: being about the absolute, it necessarily eliminates the philosophizing subject. Correspondingly, criticism is the philosophy that reminds man of his limits and hence restores him to himself.[38] We can say that in this sense, critique of dogmatic politics is essentially "defetishization." It shows that the content of dogmatic discourse (the "in itself") implies certain philosophical representations ("for itself") in the person making it and hence that this discourse is not neutral, but profoundly, that is, intrinsically, self-interested.[39] Thus, for example, the very person who denies philosophy the capacity to think of "life" is implicitly presupposing a conception of the relations between theory and praxis that is eminently philosophical: "You have been most unfair to yourselves; you are philosophers more than you could have believed. It is with you as with Monsieur Jourdain in [Molière's] comedy: you have philosophized all your lives without hearing a thing about it" (*B* 106). As we shall see, Fichte essentially characterizes this implicit philosophy of dogmatic and reactionary thought as the philosophy of the past.

(4) What Fichte primarily means to valorize against dogmatism about the philosophy of history is the idea of the future, the idea that the future *totally* eludes the hold of the past. For Fichte, dogmatic discourse about history is summed up in the old saw that "there's nothing new under the sun,"[40] the dogmatic imagination then finding its highest form in "imitation."[41] Thus Fichte criticizes the "empiricists," those whose only guide is "routine," for being unable to judge the future by any yardstick other than the past. This conception of time not only involves a logical circle (*B* 96), but also reveals the same dogmatic desire to reject, along with the idea of the future, the idea of human freedom: "You keep saying: our philosophical principles won't allow themselves to be introduced into life ... but by that you mean, of course, on condition *that everything remain as it now is.* ... You want everything to stay quite as of old, and the injunction 'propose us what is doable' really means 'propose to us what we do'" (*B* 107–8), that is to say in reality what is already done: "History, history, they cry out, is the guardian of all epochs, the teacher of

peoples, the infallible prophet of the future" (*B* 100). And what is at stake in this sacralization of the past is the negation of the future. The significance of this attack on dogmatism is clear: any theory that applies the principle of causality to history (and hence denies freedom as a principle of human action) can imagine temporality only on the basis of the past and must necessarily ignore the idea of a history temporalized based on the future, on a project.[42] It is in this sense that Fichte wrote to Achelis in 1790: "It has become clear to me that the most disastrous consequences for society would follow from accepting the proposition of the necessity of all human action,"[43] one of the most disastrous being the consequent inability of the dogmatist to think the new, in this case, the French Revolution.[44] What the *Beiträge* provides here is the assertion of the fundamental identity of theories of chance, necessity, and providence: an identity positive in that the only criterion of historical progress in the three theories is "success," negative in that all three equally deny freedom: "But I beg of you, how do you conduct your affairs in life? Do you leave them to the blind winds of chance, or, since you usually speak so piously, to the direction of providence, or do you also conduct yourself according to rules? If it's the first case—why then your verbose warnings to the peoples not to let themselves be dazzled by the delusions of philosophers? Be quiet then, and let your chance rule. If the philosophers win, they will have been right; if they do not win, they will have been wrong" (*B* 106). We cannot help but note that, here again, this is indirectly aimed at Kant, for his philosophy of history represents a theodicy in which man has little choice but to satisfy the ends of providence.[45]

(5) Thus the court of judgment for history can only be the categorical imperative, the law of freedom: "We desire to judge facts according to a law which neither derives from nor is contained in any fact. So where do we think we shall take this law? Where do we think to find it? No doubt in our Self, since it is not to be met outside us" (*B* 97). It is here, and only here, that the Copernican revolution is completed at the level of history: to admit that the moral law is the principle of every historical judgment is necessarily to posit that human acts are free in the sphere of phenomena, since we are dealing here with empirical man; for the imperative can evidently only be meaningful "for actions that depend on *reason alone* and not from natural necessity, that is, only for free actions" (*B* 98, emphasis added). That is to say that the French Revolution must be judged exclusively as a free action,[46] there where in Kant, it appears—as a con-

sequence of the solution to the third antinomy—*both* as free and as causally (naturally) determined.[47]

(6) As a consequence of points (4) and (5)—history is not determined by the past, that is, by natural causality, but by the future, that is, by the freedom of projects—the real, the empirically given that freedom transforms and fashions according to its ends, should be regarded as absolutely inert and devoid of positive significance. In other words, experience (here meaning nature, the real, the "not-I"), far from determining the direction of history, gets meaning only from the free projects that man conceives for it. This is the sense of the quotation at the very beginning of part 2 of this book,[48] where Fichte repudiates any idea of providence.[49] He adds emphasis to this in adding the following observation: "In itself experience is a box strewn about with the letters of the alphabet; it is only the human spirit which brings a sense to this chaos, putting together here an Iliad, there a historical drama à la Schlenkert" (*B* 107). We can see how far away we have gotten from Kant's conception of a chaos, of a merely apparent chance that conceals a providential wisdom. The completion of the Copernican revolution has this price: the assumption that in front of history man finds himself the sole possessor of meaning.[50]

(7) These premises inevitably lead Fichte to cast doubt on Kant's justification of war, particularly on the idea that war could have any positive role whatever in cultural progress. Contrary to the theses defended in the third *Critique*, Fichte clearly asserts a radical break between nature and culture, culture proceeding not at all from nature: "To begin with: no one is 'made' cultured, each has to *cultivate himself*. Any purely passive attitude is the very opposite of culture [*Kultur*]; personal culture [*Bildung*] comes about through self-activity and aims at self-activity. No plan for culture can be established so that its achievement be a necessity; any such plan acts upon freedom and depends on the use of freedom" (*B* 125). It could not be said more clearly that culture cannot be imputed to some design of nature. And it is with valid logic that Fichte argues against any educational value in war: "War lifts to heroism only such souls as already have such a force in them; the ignoble ones it excites to pillage and oppression of the feeble without defenses" (*B* 125).[51] In short, it is not nature that, in the guise of the futile chaos of war, conceals the harmonious design of culture, but here as elsewhere only freedom cultivates. In connecting the issue of culture with that of war (see also *B* 130), Fichte clearly indicates his desire to break with any the-

ology of history. Thus in the pages directly following this text, he again argues against the idea of any kind of educational value to political oppression.[52] No doubt the monarchy had the "merit" of fostering culture by disciplining sensibility and establishing a certain form of order and legality (*B* 126, 131, 132). There again, however, we should see no more cunning of nature or design of providence than we should feel any gratitude to tyrants. For cultural progress is in reality due to human freedom, and any "cunning" we might speak of would be more a "cunning of freedom": "If we have won culture over to the idea of freedom not only *under* your political constitutions but also through them, we have nothing to thank you for, since such was not your goal and was in fact its contrary. You aimed to annihilate in mankind all freedom of will except your own; we fought you for it, and if in the process we become stronger, we surely owe you nothing for that" (*B* 131).[53] And Fichte's whole discussion of the state of nature (the description of society "in the first sense of the term")[54] indicates that man would have been quite capable of freely cultivating himself in peace, without the intervention of that providence whose only deed would be to set traps along the path of his existence.

(8) I shall not discuss in detail here Fichte's complex theories on the state of nature and the social contract. I would merely like to conclude this simple description of the basic elements of his 1793 philosophy of history by mentioning that it also implies a certain conception of the state. In this respect, it can be looked at from three angles: strategic, historical, and metaphysical.

—Strategically, as we have seen (in the introduction), his philosophy is intended to meet the objections of reactionary thinking against the Enlightenment. Thus he attacks the logic of the reasoning that posits the following equation: human weakness = a solution of continuity between the general will and the will of all = necessity = necessity for an authoritarian state. It will be recalled that within the framework of philosophy of history (thus, if we set aside the *legal* solution sketched in 1796) there seem to be only two possible solutions for the philosophers: Kant's, which admits the premise (human weakness) but denies the conclusion[55] through a theory of history in which selfishness is not an obstacle to the actualization of rights; and Fichte's, adopted in the *Beiträge,* which simply denies both the premise and the conclusion; thus he rejects the thesis of human wickedness, and in the sphere of political reflection this leads him to discard Kant's representation of the state of nature in favor of a *neutral* conception of it: "Responsible for this is that false notion of human beings' state of nature; the war of all against all about who should be law; the right of the stronger, who should rule on this land" (*B* 158). Fichte rejects this thesis because he clearly sees its political implications, which appeal to man's "original wickedness" by justifying the state and "its law of constraint" (*B* 185). Conversely, in Fichte's view—and we are momentarily placing ourselves only at the level of the logic of the argumentation, not at that of the arguments themselves—one consequence is inevitable: the state is basically superfluous, for it can never be more than a transitional institution, a means and not an end: "If the final goal could ever be perfectly achieved, there would no longer be any need for a political constitution" (*B* 135).[56]

—Historically, this is certainly the point at which the difference between Kant and Fichte emerges most clearly: everything happens as though history necessarily had to be represented in two ways, depending on the point of view adopted, with three obligatory and systematically opposed stages in each of its representations:

In Kant: the state of nature is bad, history is "natural," and the end of history is the state as an end in itself.

In Fichte: The state of nature is neutral, history is that of freedom (it can be good or bad), and the end of history is the suppression of the state which is merely a means, "whatever one very great man says."[57]

—Metaphysically, what differentiates the two philosophers is (1) their different conceptions of the relation between ethics and politics, and (2) their divergent applications of the solution to the third antinomy. Kant admits a very clear distinction between the spheres of history and of ethics—this distinction alone permitting him to escape the aporias of the sixth proposition of the 1784 text—so that politics sometimes seems to lie more in the domain of natural causality than that of free causality. No doubt ethics and politics are in agreement in the final analysis,[58] since legality is the condition of possibility for the actualization of morality. Throughout history, however, the two do not coincide, and this is precisely what to some extent justifies a reasonable belief in progress. In 1793 Fichte, on the other hand, did not distinguish between ethics and history; moreover, he made history the unique place for the exercise of moral action. For Fichte, the distinction between phenomena and noumena, between causality and freedom, does not insert itself between ethics as the domain of intention and history as that of the real evolution, but in a certain sense, already in 1793, between ethics and positive law, natural law being still confused by Fichte with morality.[59] This is clearly indicated by Fichte's distinction between the "domain of contracts"—that of the phenomenal world, of what he calls society "in the second sense of the term," that is, the society of fact that constitutes the domain of alienable rights (*B* 118, 119, 161)— and the purely ethical sphere of inalienable rights (the intelligible world). And it is this distinction that in 1793 allows for lowering the state to the rank of a means: considered the result of a quite ordinary contract, the state is part of the phenomenal world of alienable rights; only that which is located at the level of an intelligible world can be said to be an end in itself: "This culture toward freedom is the sole possible final goal of man, *insofar as he is a part of the sensible world;* this highest sensible goal is not the final goal of man as such but the last means of achieving his higher spiritual goal: the complete concordance of his will with the law of reason. Everything that men do and pursue must permit itself to be regarded as a means for this final goal in the sensible world, or it is a pursuance without purpose, an irrational pursuit" (*B* 124). No doubt here Fichte is merely following the *Critique of Judgment,* which also makes culture into a simple means toward morality. What is radically new in relation to Kant, however, is Fichte's use of Kant's theory to devalorize the state and from this to infer that, being only of the cultural order, the state may be modified or eliminated at will: "No state's constitution is unchangeable; it is in their nature to change. A bad one, which hinders the necessary purpose of all political associations, must be changed; a good one, which promotes it, changes itself. The first is a bit of fire in rotting stubble, making smoke without light or warmth; the latter a candle, which consumes itself even as it gives light, and would go out if day came" (*B* 136). Here again, Fichte's conclusion is diametrically opposed to the letter of Kant's philosophy and, denying that the state is an end in itself and that the social pact itself can be revoked, he once again proves a disciple more of Rousseau than of Kant.[60]

The simple description of Fichte's 1793 philosophy of history seems enough to understand how his attachment to the French Revolution and his criticism of the monarchical state are legitimized at this level of his philosophy. For it is very much the philosophy of history that, applying the distinction between the sensory world and the intelligible world to society, leads to the devalorization of the state in favor of the individual, the sole possessor of ethical value.

Under these circumstances, the philosophy of history makes it imperative that the individual *act* against every form of political oppression.

It is on just this point, however, that the *Beiträge's* achievement—the justification of the Revolution against reactionary thinking—is also its failure, and the basic aporia of Fichte's thinking in 1793 becomes blatant: once the revolutionary process is justified, how does this purely negative philosophy of limits to the state, and how does the anarchistic individualism that shines through on every page of the "treatise against the state" that the *Beiträge* is,[61] manage to take responsibility for the *result* of this process?[62]

It is not my plan here to examine the political and legal aporias (notably concerning the idea of the contract and the definition of the *people*) of the *Beiträge,* but merely to underscore in the sole sphere of philosophy of history, the considerable problems created by Fichte's purely ethical and individualistic positions. These can be summed up concisely: all of Fichte's thinking in 1793 about history being thinking about freedom and project, can be regarded as a philosophy of the future. Can this philosophy be fully compatible with the *Beiträge's* central thesis that the Revolution is primarily justified by a criticism of the state that operates from a *pre*political position and that, as such, must rely *methodologically* on the idea of a *return* to the ethical individualism of natural right? A prisoner of a prepolitical idea of right, which itself results from a confusion between natural right and ethics,[63] Fichte's 1793 criticism of the state does not get beyond the idea that, in the face of political oppression by the ancien régime, the Revolution was bound to result in a return to ethical individualism. The ultimate reason for the aporia can be formulated in these terms: in 1793, Fichte attempted to justify the French Revolution by constructing a philosophy of history that frees itself of orthodox Kantianism only to fall back into a romantic "Rousseauean" vision of the starting point of history. It did not take Fichte long to spot this problem. This supposes, as we see, that the present be no longer criticized on the basis of the *past,* but of the future, which is impossible from the viewpoint of the *Beiträge.*[64] Fichte's thinking about history became fully coherent only in 1794 with his criticism of Rousseau in the "Lectures on the Vocation of the Scholar." This critique also illuminates the transition from the *Beiträge* to the *Science of Rights,* where the state of nature for man is not found in a prepolitical natural right, but in the actualization of rational right in the future (see chap. 5, this vol.). Thus, by analyzing the critique of Rousseau we can see how the persistence of a reference to the *past* is contrary to the spirit of Fichte's philosophy of history in 1793, and arrive at a coherent idea of this definitive philosophy of the future Fichte settled on in the *Science of Knowledge* of 1794.[65]

3. The Rejection of Rousseauean Romanticism

From Fichte's perspective in 1793—to defend the unity of theory and praxis against reactionary thinking—Rousseau, far from being the "idealist" and "utopian" thinker that Burke or Rehberg took him for, appeared as one whose "dreams are fulfilling themselves,"[66] and even one who had finally "awakened the human spirit"[67] and is at the origin of a veritable "new creation of human thinking."[68] Thus it is not without a certain surprise that we read Fichte, scarcely a year later, writing the words opening the chapter on Rousseau in the "Lectures on the Vocation of the Scholar": "For the discovery of truth, the disputation of opposing errors is of no observable profit. . . . But the citation of opposed opinions is of great profit for the *understandable and clear presentation* of truth once found" (FL 335). The contribution of the man who could play such an essential role for Fichte in 1793 is singularly reduced: all told, the study of Rousseau would serve merely to clarify negatively the exposition of the truth, an illustration of errors to avoid. The difference from his statement of 1793 is so great that this criticism could be summed up as follows:

> Rousseau separates fact and right by an uncrossable ditch; the second *Discourse* shows us fact and all the disorders it contains, while the *Social Contract* shows us right, society as it should have been. No doubt he is correct in Fichte's eyes in envisioning the conditions of possibility for good social institutions, but he depicts them as a dream and shows men an ideal without indicating any way to achieve it. On the other hand, Fichte sees in history the slow and difficult penetration of fact by right, and the role of the philosopher is to further this labor.[69]

How could Rousseau's "image" get so tarnished as to become that of a romantic dreamer who "had the energy, but more that of suffering than of activity"?

No doubt it did not escape Fichte's notice that Rousseau's criticism of the "arts and sciences" ran counter to a defense of the Enlightenment.[70] Why, however, has what was not a problem for Fichte in 1793 become one in 1794? If we are right in thinking that Fichte and Rousseau here differ in their philosophies of history,[71] what change occurred between 1793 and 1794 to justify such an about-face on Fichte's part?

We will briefly recall the main points of this famous criticism: it is directed mainly at Rousseau's idea of the state of nature, which Fichte saw as determining the rate of speed of a history essentially in decline: "For him regression is advancement; for him the abandoned state of nature is the final goal which a now corrupt and miseducated humanity must strive to attain" (FL 336). In this, Fichte is definitely caricaturing Rousseau;[72] but his purpose is to assert more clearly his contrasting conviction that nature is deeply bad (i.e., inert or lazy) and that only history, as the terrain for the exercise of free action, is the site of meaning and value. Thus he endeavors to refute the idea that progress, in giving rise to artificial needs in man, "denatures" him. What's more, if it is true that nature is bad in itself, progress as a factor of "denaturing" must be positive: "Man is by nature lazy and inert, of a kind with matter, out of which he arose. . . . It is not need which is the source of vice; it is the impulse to activity and to virtue: laziness is the source of all vices. To enjoy as much as possible and to do as little as possible—that's corrupted nature's task" (FL 343).[73] And, Fichte adds: "There is no well-being for man if he has not successfully fought this natural inertia, and if he does not find his delight and all his enjoyment in activity and in activity alone" (FL 343).

Thus the hypothesis is here confirmed that what essentially distinguishes Fichte from Rousseau stems from their conceptions of history: if in Rousseau, at least as Fichte interprets him, "what we should become is depicted as something we have already been, and that which we have to achieve is presented as something lost" (FL 343), for Fichte, on the other hand, "in the perspective on the future lies the true character of humanity" (FL 340). Here we find the thesis, already central in 1793, that the philosophy of history that thinks of the present on the basis of the past must inevitably lead to man's reification; paradoxically, however, it does not apply to either Burke or Rehberg, but to the very person who in 1793 appeared to Fichte as the thinker of the future: "*Before* us lies what Rousseau, with the name state of nature, and various poets under the appellation of the golden age, have placed *behind* us" (FL 342) if it is true that "Reason's struggle against passion, the gradual, slow victory, obtained with effort and trouble and work" are "the most interesting and most instructive things we could see" (FL 344; see also 346). The criticism of the romantic "laziness" of someone who "wanted undisturbed tranquility, both internal and external" (FL 341), may therefore conclude with the exclamation: "Action, action! That's what we are here for" (FL 345).

This critique of Rousseau seems to extend the thinking of the *Beiträge* as much as it changes it, and it calls for two observations:

(1) First, Fichte spells out the criticism of the theories of providence that we had seen at work in the text of 1793. He even adds a new and surely more important argument than the earlier ones by dropping Kant's notion of evil as selfishness: if evil is merely natural laziness and nature is itself essentially dead,[74] the idea of a history based on the assumption of the self-rationalization of particular natural inclinations or on the hope for a rationality springing from the free interplay of selfish inclinations becomes in principle absurd. If nature is purely and simply inert, it can neither be "cunning," nor plan some unknown "design." There thus cannot be some "pathologically extorted agreement," to use Kant's phrase, any more than we can admit the idea of a "cunning of reason" in Hegel's sense: nothing can result from natural inertia, and if nature must be "vivified" and transformed, it can only be from the outside, by the free action of men (*SW* 3:363). In short, history must be the history of freedom, and, unlike the views of Kant, Schelling, or Hegel, the rationalization of the world—if achieved, which for Fichte is not *yet* fixed as a necessity—can only come from an *external* term, can happen only *by* and *for* free action: *by* free action because nature lacks the dynamism that enables it to transform itself dialectically into its other; *for* free action because if the "not-I" is conceived of as pure dead inertia, then free action is to be the unique source of meaning and value.

We thus see how, to Fichte, "Rousseau's Platonism"—the origin of history in a lost paradise—may be an error, even a moral failing: for the "temporal life," that is, man's use of his freedom, in time and history, to effect practical change in the world must under these conditions appear as a "fall" or "decline." We must on the contrary assert that if there is history, negation, and vivification of the dead natural element, it is so that there can be the free action of man: "Nature is raw and wild without man's hand, and it had to be so, for man to be forced to come out of the inactive state of nature and work upon it—so that he himself could become, from a mere product of nature, a free reasoning being" (FL 34).[75]

(2) We next note that Fichte extends his criticism of the philosophies of the past to a point that is essentially new compared to 1793: what is at issue here is not just natural historical determinism, but the *critical function* of the state of nature regarding the present in the philosophy of history, with Fichte accusing Rousseau—as he had Rehberg—of at least partially covering over that essence of humanity that consists in having "the future in view": "Rousseau forgets that mankind can and should approach this state only through worry, toil, and work" (FL 343). The break with the 1793 text is undeniable, for there Fichte fully agrees with Rousseau and explicitly refers to the critical function of the state of nature: "In Natural Law, it used to be thought—as I shall recall in passing—that one had to go back to an original state of nature in man; lately people get all worked up about this procedure and find in it the origin of who knows what incongruities. *And yet this way is the only good one:* to discover the grounds for the binding nature of all contracts, one must think of man as not yet bound by any external contracts, standing under the sole laws of his nature, that is, ethical laws; *that is the state of nature*" (*B* 118; first emphasis added). Thus, as Philonenko emphasizes, "in the *Contributions* Fichte manifestly remains caught within in an old viewpoint, the state of original peace corresponding to a Golden Age located in a distant past. . . . In this Fichte remains a disciple of Rousseau."[76] We clearly still have to determine the reason and significance of this evolution. It seems to me to raise two questions:

—In what sense can we say that in 1793 Fichte was still a "prisoner" of the "myth of a Golden Age set in a distant past"? Doesn't this assertion run counter to Fichte's consistently held thesis that the state of nature never actually existed (see *B* 118)? The answer here can be succinct: although Fichte—like Rousseau, moreover[77]—makes the state of nature purely hypothetical, in 1793 the hypothesis still had a position of—if not chronological, then at least logical—anteriority in its critical function with regard to the state: it is quite remarkable that in the very passage in which Fichte denies the reality of the state of nature, he makes it the fundamental term on which he bases the critique of the state and hence of the present: Fichte responds to the dogmatists who point out the nonexistence of the state of nature: "And if that were true—who told you then to look for our ideas in the real world? Do you have to see everything? Too bad it is not there! It *should* be there. In truth, our sagacious teachers of natural law believe that: each person, from his birth, is bound by and bound to the State, because of the latter's concretely realized achievements. Unfortunately this principle was always put into practice before it was theoretically established. The State has asked none of us for his consent, but it should have done so, and we would have been in the state of nature" (*B* 118). So it is plausible to think that Fichte's criticism of Rousseau in the "Fifth Lecture" is at least partially a criticism of his own 1793 conception of the prepolitical state of nature.[78]

If this is Fichte's evolution, if the idea that he essentially argues against in 1794 is indeed that of a restoration of the past, we must turn to his transcendental philosophy to see the deeper reason for this: for we cannot doubt that the issue here is the very conception of the relations between truth and time. How not to notice that, philosophically, the tripartite idea of history connected with the representation of the "Golden Age" (the lost paradise—the fall—the return to paradise) is nothing other, *philosophically* speaking, than a vestige of the Platonic theory of the truth that was contemplated (the Golden Age), then forgotten (the fall), and now being sought back? Therefore, only transcendental philosophy as a philosophy of time and truth (as a theory of finitude) can provide the ultimate foundation for the new conception of temporality emerging in 1794. And in fact, as we shall see, the *Science of Knowledge* eliminates any possibility of representing an atemporal state of nature not wholly thought of as the result of a construction owing to the historical activity of man—and this from the setting up of the first three "principles." With that, Fichte dropped the whole Platonic-Rousseauean doctrine of the Fall in favor of an idea of temporality resolutely oriented to the future. It is thus the ultimate stage that we still need to go through to have a complete grasp of the conception of praxis corresponding to the genuine completion of the Copernican revolution and thereby the accomplishment of the project proper to the philosophy of the young Fichte. Despite its speculative aridity and dryness—everyone agrees with an expression of Pierre-Philippe Druet's,[79] who awards it "first prize for strangeness and obscurity"—Fichte's theoretical philosophy thus always remains faithful to his initial *practical* project about which the young Fichte one day declared to Kant that it would "suffice to take up half his life."[80]

Through a simple analysis of the *method* Fichte used in the *Science of Knowledge,* I shall here limit myself to identifying the new conception of temporality founded by transcendental philosophy. We shall see how this theory of time is actually neither the simple putting into form of the political theory of 1793 (contrary to what M.

126

Buhr has maintained),[81] nor a *radical* inauguration of a new period (Druet's thesis), but all at once the elaboration and the transformation of a political philosophy that, resolutely attempting to be a philosophy of the future, could not make do for long with a nostalgic concept of the state of nature.

The Foundation of the Practical Philosophy of History in the *Science of Knowledge*

1. The Method of the *Science of Knowledge* and the Elimination of the Notion of the Golden Age

Very generally, we can characterize the method of the *Foundations of the Science of Knowledge* as a repetition *in reverse* of the treatment of the *Critique of Pure Reason*.[1] The *Critique of Pure Reason* follows a method that is "natural" in going from the true to the false: the "Transcendental Aesthetic" begins with the assertion of the first and most fundamental truth: the radical finitude of the subject, defined by the a priori receptivity (pure intuition) of its ability to know: the existence of consciousness or subjectivity requires that existence be given. Existence can thus never be dialectically *deduced* from the concept (of the subject) as being its other, for here otherness is irreducible. The "Aesthetic" thus sets up the truth that makes metaphysics, as the ontological argument (the attempt to go from the subject, from the concept, to existence), a logic of appearance (a "dialectics"). This first truth makes it possible in the "Analytic" to take up the study of the structures of objectivity (the deductions of the categories and schematisms) and thus arrive at the second kind of truth: scientific truth. Taken together, the "Aesthetic" and the "Analytic" thus form the totality of the truth insofar as they provide the true theory of existence (of manifestation) and the adequate thought of the essence or quiddity of the object. Only then does it become possible to take up the "Dialectic," that is, the criticism of the metaphysical error of identifying essence and manifestation (existence) by deducing the latter from the former. The *Critique of Pure Reason* thus proceeds from the true to the false, from the categories to the Ideas, from the "Analytic" to the "Dialectic."

We should note, however, that Kant himself seems to suggest the reverse procedure: for him, the "Transcendental Dialectic" (the antinomies in particular) in turn proves the truth of the "Analytic." We recall that the *Critique of Pure Reason* calls on two types of proofs:

- a direct proof, that of the transcendental analytic, which could be called a proof through the consciousness of impossibility: it begins with the notion of possible experience to show that to conceive of experience, such and such *conditions* (intuitions, categories, schemata, principles) must be admitted;
- an indirect proof: provided by the "Transcendental Dialectic": it brings out to someone who does not admit the *conditions* revealed by the "Aesthetic" and the "Analytic," that their negation is a source of error or, more precisely, the very source of the transcendental illusion.

Fichte takes this second route to the exclusion of the first. He thus begins with the false (of the "Dialectic") to go to the true through a deconstruction and gradual reduction of error: Fichte opens the *Science of Knowledge* with a "Transcendental Dialectic" to progress to the schematism, then to a deduction of essence and time and, finally, the very matter of sensation. It is on this point only that the Copernican revolution and the corresponding practical philosophy of history are completed.

We should observe that this treatment, as opposed as it may seem to Kant's, can still be thought of as remaining within the framework of critical philosophy. Fichte never claimed to be doing anything more than giving Kant's philosophy a systematic form. What he meant to replace in Kantianism was only the defects owing to the imperfection of the exposition.[2] Thus we can connect this method to Kant's in two ways:

—We can first bring out (and this argument has some importance when we are inquiring about the systematic form of a philosophy, and hence about the legitimacy of its starting point) that the transcendental illusion is a beginning that is in a certain way not arbitrary for a Kantian, as Kant himself says that this illusion is *necessary.*

—We can think (and this represents a metaphysical deduction of the categories) that if we can go from the categories to the Ideas, we should conversely be able to get the categories from the Ideas through the deconstruction of the latter. Fichte thus starts with the Kantian idea that metaphysics includes everything, even if only in the mode of illusion or, if you will, from negation (negation of temporality, of the difference between essence and existence, and so forth).

The critique of metaphysics thus must be able to bring out the truth of metaphysics. If metaphysics is forgetfulness, abstraction of the difference between the subject and the object, between being and thinking, in short, of finitude, the critique of metaphysics may be presented, to use a borrowed vocabulary, as a "negative dialectics," meaning a reparation, a restoration of what was eliminated in the totalizing process of metaphysics.[3] The advantage of this method is clear: as metaphysics is itself systematic, the critique of it will also be systematic. Therefore, philosophy, at least in its theoretical part, will essentially reduce to a *Dialectics,* meaning, as Kant did, not only a setting up, but also a deconstruction of appearance.[4]

As Philonenko shows (*LH,* chap. 5),[5] Fichte does not start with the absolute self to be reached by intellectual intuition but with the absolute self as a transcendental illusion, that is to say, with what Kant called a "paralogism of pure reason." I shall not go over here Philonenko's many irrefutable arguments for this thesis, but merely focus on the consequences relevant to our concerns.

—The first consequence stems from the fact that because the absolute self is posited as an Idea or illusion and not as a being in itself really attained by an "intellectual intuition," the finite subject is not *really* eliminated by the absolute self, as it necessarily would be if this grasp of the absolute self were veridical. This observation is of the utmost importance for understanding how the *Science of Knowledge* proceeds. It means that the philosopher's (the finite subject's) reflection can continue to exist after the first principle precisely because the first principle, as an *illusion,* does not negate finitude. The whole dialectics rests on this initial split between the philosophizing subject and the absolute self, which, as an absolute, does deny the finite subject, but which, as a merely illusory absolute, lets it subsist despite all. "Reflection is free" (*SK* 12): the philosopher can start and pursue the work of deconstructing the illusion as he sees fit.

—Hegel's reading of Fichte thereby falls apart. Thinking that Fichte starts with the absolute, Hegel criticizes him for the inconsistency[6] of positing a second principle after the first, when reflection should have stopped. For Fichte to continue his "deduction," Hegel suggests, costs him two errors: (*a*) the error of any "philosophy of reflection," which speaks about the "thing itself" *from the outside,* instead of leaving it to its free development; (*b*) the error of starting with the absolute and then introducing the multiple (the finite) not through a deduction but simply empirically because the philosophizing self knows that the external world exists.

This criticism—which would be deserved if Hegel had been correct in thinking that Fichte's philosophy started with the Kantian "intellectual intuition,"[7] that is, a veridical grasp of the absolute—is voided, however, when we realize that this is not a genesis starting from the truth but a dialectics of illusion that by definition leaves the critical—finite—subject to go on existing.

These observations thus cast light on the meaning of the first two principles. When we realize that the first principle positing the absolute self is an illusion or "paralogism," then by reflecting about the conditions of possibility for its positing—reflection that remains fully legitimate when we see that the starting point is not the truth—we must arrive, with the second principle, at the assertion of an absolute not-self. As Philonenko has written: "The transition from the self to the not-self is made *at the level of the presuppositions* that compel the constructions of the first two principles" (*LH* 162). Once posited, the two terms formed by the self and the not-self are absolutely opposed in such a way that we must try to reconcile them by admitting a third synthetic principle: "In the self, the self opposes a divisible not-self to the divisible self."

I do not propose to analyze in detail the structure of Fichte's dialectics, nor the way he systematically articulates the different elements of Kant's "Transcendental Dialectic" (see *LH*, chap. 5). I would simply like (1) to examine the philosophical problem really involved in this antinomy of the self and the not-self, and (2) to show how the solution using the principle of sufficient reason in §3 of the *Science of Knowledge* implies a certain conception of temporality that alone can explain the evolution of the philosophy of history underlying the critique of Rousseau in 1794.

(1) I shall first briefly indicate how the self and the not-self are opposed in an antinomy that can be formulated in two ways:

—From a strictly logical point of view, it is clear that the positing of a not-self is absolutely incompatible with that of an absolute self claiming to be the totality of the real—the problem once again being the impossibility of positing one without positing the other, for the logical constructions establishing them are strictly parallel.

—When, however, we relate this opposition to the history of philosophy, we see that Fichte is posing the classic problem of representation, whose critical formulation we find in Kant (in his letter to Markus Herz of 21 February 1772) and its skeptical formulation in Berkeley: how can I manage to posit something outside myself when this something by definition always remains an in-itself, only *for me*[8] and hence never an in-itself genuinely external to me. Dogmatic realism (asserting the existence of the not-self in itself) always presupposes a moment of self-negation, that is, the positing of an in-itself that is not for me even though it is again the self that posited that this in-itself was not for it. It is thus always *for the self* that the in-itself is asserted to be not *for the self,* the dogmatic assertion necessarily forgetting the first "for me" and thus falling into a contradiction: "[T]he realist hypothesis, that the material of representation might be given to us somehow from without, admittedly made its appearance in the course of our investigation . . . but on closer examination we found that such a hypothesis would contradict the principle proposed, since that to which a material was given from without would be no self at all, as it was required to be, but a not-self" (*SK* 197) since the in-itself cannot be both in itself and for me.[9]

This plainly does not mean that Fichte is accepting the "idealist" solution, that is, the pure and simple negation of the not-self: it should be stressed that both terms posited must be posited necessarily such that in presupposing each other, they reciprocally imply each other[10] in such a way that the simple juxtaposition of the first two principles constitutes an "analytic" opposition, that is, a logical contradiction. But because they are in other respects both "certain" (from the viewpoint of formal logic "used as an organon"), they still must be reconciled, just as (to move from the strictly logical terrain to that of the classic questions of the history of philosophy) a solution has to be found to the problem of representation. The following problem crops up here in Fichte's thinking: as we have seen, the two principles are opposed in a contradictory or analytic way.[11] That is, from the viewpoint of formal logic, they must not be compatible because an absolute contradiction is necessarily governed by the principle of the excluded middle. If Fichte judges that the two principles must be synthetically reconcilable in a third one, this must be because he is implicitly thinking that the analytic contradiction is merely apparent and actually conceals a *synthetic opposition,* which undeniably confirms, if there were any need for it, the correctness of Philonenko's claim that in the first three principles the *Science of Knowledge* sets up a dialectical logic of appearance. To be convinced of this, all we have to do is recall what an "antinomy" is for Kant.

An antinomy (see chap. 3, this vol.) is an opposition between two theses presented in the form of a contradiction—hence an opposition governed by the law of the excluded middle so it seems that one of the two propositions has to be true and the other false—while it is in fact merely an opposition between contraries or subcontraries. Thus, in the *Critique of Pure Reason* the first two antinomies are oppositions between contraries (opposites of the same kind) such that the thesis and the antithesis can both be false, and they only *seem* to fall under the law of the excluded middle: for example, "the world is neither finite nor infinite" and the alternative is not exclusive, for the world can be thought of as indefinite. In the third and fourth antinomies, the converse solution holds, for it is a matter of subcontraries (the subject has a different meaning in the thesis from the one it has in the antithesis); thus, in the third antinomy, for example, where the thesis considers man as noumenon and the antithesis as phenomenon, the two propositions that only apparently contradict each other can both be true provided the sense of the subject is spelled out in each.

The opposition between the first two principles is thus quite precisely presented as an antinomy (that of idealism and realism). Therefore, they need to be "reconciled," that is, as in Kant, transformed into a transcendental opposition that, at the level of illusion, appears to be a logical contradiction such that the transition from the first principle to the second can be interpreted as the "transition from the paralogisms and their synthesis in an absolute self to the antinomy of representation" (*LH* 164), and it is this antithesis that the third principle—which thus corresponds to the statement of the critical solution of an antinomy[12]—is supposed to reconcile synthetically. This combination will thus solve the problem of representation, for it reconciles idealism and realism, the philosophical positions underlying the first two principles. Before considering the significance of this critique of metaphysics, however, we need to see how it sets up at the level of the third principle.

(2) Starting from the illusion of the absolute self (the first principle), we have also had to accept a second principle that, when combined with the first, produces an antinomy (an opposition that seems to be an analytic contradiction) whose real significance is the problem of representation (how can I admit the existence of something outside of myself?). The question whose answer must be indicated by the third principle can thus be expressed as follows: a merely apparent analytic contradiction is to be transformed into a real synthetic opposition. As Philonenko has indicated, this problem presupposes that three requirements be met: "First, the two opposed terms must not be opposed merely *qualitatively* (self and not-self, red and not-red) but also *quantitatively*: the idea of quantity grounds think-

able oppositions. Second, the quantitative opposition must have a qualitative meaning: otherwise, the opposite terms could be considered to have the same sign and thus be additive. Third, if the opposition keeps a qualitative meaning, the two opposites must, reunited, make up one and the same whole" (*LH* 166). Thus, to be thinkable, the opposition must become quantitative: the two terms are no longer absolutely opposed, but only in part. Hence the idea of a "divisible" self and a "divisible" not-self, that is, two terms that divide up reality. What enables us to think of this opposition as having a qualitative sense (such that the two terms continue to be opposed, not being additive) is the introduction of the concept of negative magnitude that grounds the idea of reciprocal action: the self and the not-self divide up the whole of reality, their opposite quantities being reciprocally related, as in a system of forces. This totality is none other than that of the absolute self that still remains the substrate of the division between the finite self and the finite not-self: hence the formulation of the third principle: "In the self I oppose a divisible not-self to the divisible self" (*SK* 110).

Thus the antinomy is formally resolved: the first principle remains in the third as a substrate[13] of the division of the two terms into which the totality of the real is divided (divisible finite self and divisible not-self). Therefore, the not-self is no longer absolutely opposed to the self and the problem of representation now reduces to that of the relations between the finite self and the not-self, relations fraught with a series of antinomies that we cannot analyze here. For now, it is important to make two observations about the method Fichte adopted in this transcendental dialectics, to stress its relevance to our question of temporality and history:

(*a*) Fichte's is a three-term method; as is shown in this passage in which he summarizes the main points of his endeavor: "There have to be syntheses, so from now on our whole procedure will be synthetic. . . . But no synthesis is possible without a preceding antithesis. . . . In every proposition, therefore, we must begin by pointing out opposites which are to be reconciled" (*SK* 113).[14] Translated into the language of Kant, this passage means: one needs to start from an antithesis instead of an antinomy, for an antithesis always precedes a synthesis.[15] Then by reconciling the opposed terms (this reconciliation is possible since, as we have seen, as in any antinomy, we are dealing with merely *apparent* analytic contradictions) one should achieve the synthesis. One must go from the Ideas (antitheses) to the categories (syntheses), from a "Dialectic" to an "Analytic," and reconstruct the *Critique of Pure Reason* starting with its concluding phase.[16] We thus are faced with two terms that correspond to each other or, to use Philonenko's expression, "express each other" [*s'entre-expriment*] (*LH* 255–56), as they in fact did in Kant's *Critique* where the Ideas are deduced from the categories, "The Antithetics of Pure Reason" of the categorical syntheses of the "Analytic." This method would still be incomplete and incomprehensible, however, if we didn't take into account the "reflection" of the philosopher analyzing the synthetic and antithetical acts of the transcendental subject (which in Kant corresponds to the transcendental analysis described in the "Amphibology of the Concepts of Reflection"): "According to §3, all synthetic concepts arise through a unification of opposites. We ought therefore to begin by seeking out such opposed characteristics in the concepts already postulated (the self and the not-self, insofar as they are posited as determining one another); and this is done by reflection, which is a voluntary act of the mind" (*SK* 120).

The three terms of this method can be summed up as follows: the first two principles posited by the philosopher's reflection constitute an antinomy; this antinomy is synthetically combined by a third principle, thus indicating the basis of every synthesis. Reflection begins its analysis again with the third principle and uncovers a new antinomy: as has been said, the third principle is still fraught with a whole series of oppositions. Even a brief analysis of it is sufficient to show that the proposition "the self posits itself as limited by the not-self" yields two seemingly contradictory propositions (the self determines itself, the self is determined) that thus constitute a new antinomy that must be recombined etc., "until we arrive at opposites which can no longer be altogether combined" (*SK* 113).

(*b*) Antinomy, synthesis, analytic reflection—these are the three terms of the method constitutive of Fichte's systematization of Kant's "Transcendental Dialectic." By itself, however, this approach would remain devoid of sense (of meaning and direction) if the search for syntheses was not prompted by some need. Here we see the striking originality of Fichte's method: if the antitheses need to be combined, it is because the first principle, which is merely an illusion, already has a *regulative* value: it is because the self's identity is constantly threatened by the antinomies produced by the positing of the not-self that they need to be reconciled in such a way that if the theoretical part of the *Science of Knowledge* rests essentially on the second and third principles (on the antitheses and syntheses), it is still the first principle that, all together, prompts it: "the theoretical portion of our Science of Knowledge ... will actually be evolved only from the two latter principles, since here *the first has a merely regulative validity*" (*SK* 119, emphasis added). Once again, there is no doubt that this first principle is not a true principle, but a transcendental illusion, since in it the self is thought of in light of the third principle, as the *substratum* of the finite self's and the not-self's divisibility and, for that reason, as the *totality* of the real, which is the very definition of the transcendental illusions on the Subject analyzed by the *Critique of Pure Reason*. So that here it is illusion that possesses the regulative value determining the whole treatment of the *Science of Knowledge:* it is necessary to reconcile the antinomies to preserve this *Idea* of the self's identity (personhood) that is contained in the very illusion of the absolute self: thus, "we could simply not have undertaken all our previous inquiries without a beneficent deception on the part of the imagination, which interposed a substrate unawares beneath these mere opposites; we ought not to have been able to entertain them, for they were nothing at all, and one cannot reflect about nothing. This deception could not have been obviated, nor should it have been; its product needed merely to be cast out and excluded from the sum of our deliberations, and this has now been done" (*SK* 200–201). This noteworthy passage[17] must be understood as follows: thanks to the initial illusion of the absolute self, we could fictively attribute a *substrate* (the absolute self) to the opposition, in truth the only real one, of finite self and not-self. Without this illusion, we could not think of their opposition. Once one has *sifted* the truth from error, however, it is necessary to remove the initial illusion, that is to say, we must cease thinking of the absolute self as a *substrate* present at the start of the dialectics, to grasp it in its truth, that is, as a *moral ideal* to be found only in the future.

We can see that this conception of dialectics will have important consequences for the idea of history, since in the structure of the *Science of Knowledge* the Platonic idea of the Fall and its related notions of decline and a return to authenticity become radically unthinkable. We shall be coming back to this. For the moment let's merely note that this regulative meaning of the first principle—a meaning in full accord with its position as Idea—can shed light on two important points in the method of the *Science of Knowledge:*

(1) First, the relation between the three principles is spelled out: while the second principle produces the antinomy whose solution is sketched by the third, the first principle makes the whole *Science of*

Knowledge systematically coherent, for it posits the requirement of identity without which the process of reconciling the antinomies would have neither a starting point nor point of completion:

> Just as there can be no antithesis without synthesis, no synthesis without antithesis, so there can be neither without a thesis—an absolute positing, whereby an *A* (the self) is neither equated nor opposed to any other, but is just absolutely posited. This, as applied to our system, is what gives strength and completeness to the whole; it must be a system, and it must be *one;* the opposites must be united, so long as opposition remains, until absolute unity is effected; a thing, indeed— as will appear in due course—which could be brought about only by a completed approximation to infinity, which in itself is impossible. (*SK* 113–14)

Since the starting point is merely a reified idea, the system will finally be a system open to an infinite approximation of the infinite: thus the very form of the 'ought,' of the future, is inscribed in the theoretical part of the *Science of Knowledge:* "The necessity of opposing and uniting in the manner prescribed rests directly on the third principle; the necessity of combination in general, on the first, highest, absolutely unconditioned principle. The *form* of the system is based on the highest synthesis; *that* there should be a system at all, on the absolute thesis" (*SK* 114). The requirement of identity, which is the truth of the starting point, thus already shows up at the very heart of the illusion primordially surrounding it (an illusion because the self is initially thought of as a *substrate,* not as an ethical requirement), such that the entire dialectic will consist in making appear as the future, as a task to perform in history, what was initially posited as a substrate anterior to the appearance of the world and temporality (of the not-self). Thus the oppositions must finally be combined in "the Idea of a self whose consciousness has been determined by nothing outside itself, it being rather its own mere consciousness which determines everything outside it. Yet this Idea is itself unthinkable, since for us it contains a contradiction. But it is nevertheless imposed upon us as our highest practical goal. Man must approximate, ad infinitum, to a freedom he can never, in principle, attain" (*SK* 115).

(2) Human freedom consequently appears to involve a "thetic judgment" that is impossible to explain, since "for any given thetic judgment, no ground can be supplied" (*SK* 115). To grasp the significance of this assertion, we have to go back to the methodical signifi-

cance taken by the principle of reason in the form Fichte gives it in §3 of the *Science of Knowledge:* "A in part = not-A, and vice versa." This somewhat unusual formulation is explained as follows: "Every opposite is like its opponent in one respect, = X; and every like is opposed to its like in one respect, = X. Such a respect, = X, is called the ground, in the first case of *conjunction* [*Beziehungsgrund*], and in the second of *distinction* [*Unterscheidungsgrund*]" (*SK* 110). The principle of reason then appears as the logical principle of classification into genera and species. For example, "a plant is not an animal: here the ground of distinction we reflect upon is the specific difference between plant and animal, while the ground of conjunction we disregard is the fact of organization in general" (*SK* 114). As opposites, the plant and the animal are united in a higher quality = X (the *Beziehungsgrund*) which is the class of organized beings. As identical terms, on the other hand, they diverge in another term = X (the *Unterscheidungsgrund*) which is the specific difference between a plant and an animal. The principle of reason thus has a double structure that can be represented schematically by a diamond shape (fig. 2).

When we go from A and B to X, we find the *reason* for their difference, and when we go to X', the *reason* for their identity. We see that this structure is to be the ultimate basis for the method of the *Science of Knowledge,* a synthetic method that "seeks out in opposites that quality in which they are the same" (*SK* 113): it will thus be a matter of seeking the *Beziehungsgrund,* as it were, of the opposi-

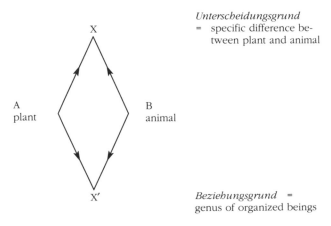

Figure 2.

tion between the self and the not-self that gets its antinomial character from the initial error supplied by the first principle. In this sense, "the logical rules governing all antithesis and synthesis are derived from the third principle" (*SK* 112), hence from the principle of reason underlying it, so that the articulation of the first three principles can be diagramed as follows (fig. 3).

It becomes clear how human freedom represents a thetic judgment and so escapes the principle of reason: the thetic judgment is "one in which something is asserted, not to be like anything else or opposed to anything else, but simply to be identical with itself" and hence presupposes "no ground of conjunction or distinction at all" (*SK* 114). What the thetic judgment presupposes, on the other hand, is just "as a matter of logical form ... simply the *requirement* for a ground or reason [*eine Aufgabe für einen Grund*]" (*SK* 114). The truth of the thetic judgment "man is free" is thus an essentially practical truth since it is thought of only as a task (*Aufgabe*). Here the sense of the regulative function of the first principle becomes explicit.

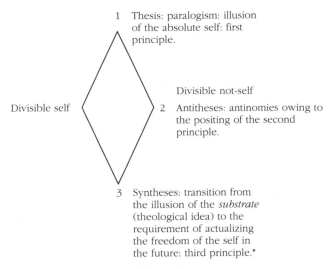

1 Thesis: paralogism: illusion of the absolute self: first principle.

Divisible not-self

Divisible self

2 Antitheses: antinomies owing to the positing of the second principle.

3 Syntheses: transition from the illusion of the *substrate* (theological idea) to the requirement of actualizing the freedom of the self in the future: third principle.*

Figure 3.

*The analysis of the third principle brings to light new antinomies that are in turn recombined according to the same scheme until every antinomy has vanished and the illusion of the substrate has been completely reduced. See *SK* 120. On the relation between this tripartite schema and the three Kantian ideas, see *LH* 255–56.

Thesis, antithesis, synthesis, and reflection—these are the elements constitutive of the dialectical method Fichte adopts in the *Science of Knowledge*. When we think about the nature of the illusion that forms the starting point in the book, we see that it consists essentially in the negation of *finitude* and *temporality,* and that as such it is identical with what Kant describes in the "Transcendental Dialectic" as the "transcendental illusion" of metaphysics. The deconstruction of the illusion will thus aim to restore man to his own truth, which Fichte formulates as follows: "as soon as you come to be clear about your philosophy, [this illusion] falls from your eyes like scales. . . . You will then claim to know no more in life than that you are finite, and finite in *this particular* way, which you are obliged to account for the presence of *that sort of world* outside you; and you will no more be minded to overstep these bounds than you are to cease being yourself" (*SK* 82, second introduction).

Reading this passage, we find it hard to understand how Fichte could so long have been regarded as the champion of "subjective idealism," for his only aim was to remind man of his finitude by connecting his consciousness with that of a world. One can see the reason for this, however, and it is of considerable methodical importance: believing that Fichte was starting with the truth, with an authentic grasp of the absolute self, his interpreters could find only a radical idealism in the *Science of Knowledge*'s deduction not only of forms of sensibility, but also of their content. Conversely, when we realize that Fichte starts with *illusion,* this deduction takes on the opposite meaning: certainly, one can say that in some way the initial absolute self includes all reality, but this must be understood in a purely negative way. The absolute self includes all reality in the sense in which it denies all reality: as Kant's "Transcendental Dialectic" indicates, it is absolute and hence in its claim to eternal self-sufficiency must deny the external world and temporality. Therefore, Fichte's treatment appears essentially "reparative": it represents an attempt, in a purely *negative* dialectics, to deconstruct the illusion in order to restore what the illusion eliminated in its very claim to absoluteness, to wit, the external world and the finite subject situated in time.

2. The Idea of the Future in the *Science of Knowledge*

The traditional interpretation of the *Science of Knowledge* saw the theoretical and practical parts as necessarily opposed: if we assume that the theoretical philosophy is a radical idealism that "deduces everything" from the absolute self, moral action loses all meaning, for want of encountering some reality to which to apply itself. This is Martial Gueroult's opinion:

> In Fichte, the theoretical or genetic point of view not only fails to show the reality of the elements to be affirmed by practical philosophy, but, far from providing a place for them, it (speculative reason) brings a direct demonstration of their unreality. It thereby makes a number of practical assertions impossible. In this case, from two things one: either the genesis must be absolutely valid, and then the practical assertions are invalid; or the practical assertions must be preserved, and then the genesis is illusory.[18]

As we have seen, however, this reading is untenable. In completing the dialectics of the illusion and beginning finally on solid ground what he calls "the pragmatic history of the human mind"—that is, the common consciousness's conquest of the truth uncovered by the philosopher—Fichte himself gives the following summary of the explorations made in the first hundred pages of the *Science of Knowledge*:

> Our task was to investigate whether . . . it was possible to entertain the problematically established principle: the self posits itself as determined by the not-self. We have attempted this under all possible determinations thereof, as exhaustively enumerated though a systematic deduction; by setting aside the illicit and unthinkable, we have confined the thinkable to an ever more restricted circle, and so step by step have approached ever nearer to the truth, till we finally discovered the only possible way of conceiving what we are obliged to conceive. (*SK* 196)

This passage would be clearly nonsensical if Fichte had started from the truth of the absolute self, all the more so as further on he adds: "it follows . . . that from now on we shall no longer be concerned with mere hypotheses, in which the modicum of true content must first be separated from the empty dross" (*SK* 198). Thus in the *Science of Knowledge* the absolute self must be considered a simple "Idea" (*SK*, pts. 3 and 5, *passim*) that proceeds from the status of a dialectical illusion to that of an ideal of practical reason, a path that Philonenko sums up as follows: "The absolute self is thought of . . . as an Ideal. No longer as the substrate that was 'behind us' after §2 of the *Science of Knowledge*, but as the unattainable Idea that proposes itself to all, such is at present the Self" (*LH* 305). Thus, as we have seen, what is at stake in interpreting the *Science of Knowledge* is the very structure of the notion of temporality, and Philonenko's reading makes it possible to understand how, starting with the transcendental philosophy, Fichte's philosophy of history must have changed from 1793 (where the transcendental philosophy had not yet taken form) to 1794. Indeed, if the reference to Rousseau must necessarily have changed from 1793 to 1794, it is clearly because the dialectics of illusion set up in the *Science of Knowledge,* which eliminates the very idea of a "Fall," completely destroys the idea of an original state of peace in the name of which the present is criticized. That is clearly shown by the critique of Rousseau we saw in the "Lectures on the Vocation of the Scholar" and also and especially by Fichte's criticism of Schelling's philosophy of history. I say "especially" because Schelling, quite unlike Fichte, begins his own system (at least, in his earliest writings) with the intellectual intuition of the absolute self (see *LH,* chap. 5), such that he gives us a fairly exact picture of what Fichte's philosophy would have been if it had indeed taken as its starting point the "self = self" as expressing a truth.

In Schelling we see that this initial positing necessarily makes his philosophy a philosophy of the Fall:[19] indeed, if the grasp of the absolute, as in the Platonic myths, *precedes* real existence in time, this existence (hence all history) must be considered a fall from paradise, an inexplicable decline that gets us ever farther from the origin. So it is clear that the starting point of philosophy a priori demands a certain representation of time and hence determines, also a priori, an overall view of the direction of history: if the absolute is prior to temporality (to the appearance of the finite subject situated in the world and in time), history will necessarily be "romantic," centered on the ideal of a restoration; if the reverse is true, and no truth precedes the finite consciousness but must on the contrary be totally constructed by it and consequently the coincidence with the absolute, far from having existed before temporal life, *must be* actualized, history will be essentially oriented to the future, and if not "revolutionary," at least inevitably "progressivist" and activist.

The overall representation of the direction of history thus is inscribed in the very structure of the two philosophical systems such that Fichte, radicalizing in the *Science of Knowledge*'s the project that in the *Beiträge* was still in embryo, inevitably had to eliminate any idea of restoration from his philosophy of history. In other respects, we are easily convinced of the strictly philosophical character of Schelling's conception of history when we see how the structure of the fall is inscribed in it in a wholly a priori way, independently of any search or empirical verification. What's more, for Schelling this structure provided the necessary framework for future historical research:

> There is no barbaric condition which does not proceed from a collapsed culture. It is reserved to the future efforts of earth history to show how those peoples living in a savage state are the only tribes cut off from a connection to the rest of the world and partially scattered through revolutions, and thus robbed of ties and of the already acquired instruments of culture, fell back into their present state. I hold the state of culture absolutely to be the first of the human race, and the founding of the states, sciences, religion, and arts as simultaneous or rather as one thing, so that everything was not truly divided but in the most perfect mutual penetration, as it shall be again in the last completion.[20]

Thus, for Schelling it is certain that before any verification by historical study, history is in decline, civilization comes before barbarism, and the new can be nothing other than the restoration of the old. Schelling's philosophy of history is thus already implied by his speculative philosophy, that is, his conception of the relations between absolute and finite existence, as Fichte saw remarkably well in a text directed against the *System of Identity:* "The starting point can only be that which is most undetermined, least completed; otherwise, we would have no reason to go beyond it and determine it more precisely in thought."[21] In its Platonic character, Schelling's philosophy, like those of Rousseau and Spinoza, which have the same basic structure in Fichte's eyes, reveals an inability to think of action,[22] as is shown a contrario in Schelling's harsh criticism of "Lectures on the Vocation of the Scholar" of 1794.

Already in the 1800 *System of Transcendental Idealism,* in a return to Herder and Leibniz, Schelling elaborated a theory of the cunning of reason according to which the competition of freedoms must necessarily (i.e., unconsciously) lead to the "second nature" that is the rational state. The interplay of particular wills appeared to him secretly imbued by a necessity (Providence) that is the motor of the unconscious action of the species. The apparent chance (freedom) of individual actions is thus opposed to the harmony (necessity) that prevails at the level of the species: "In freedom there must again be necessity; this in turn means: through freedom itself, and while I believe I'm acting freely, what I am not aiming at must arise unconsciously, that is without my doing."[23] Here we meet again a philosophy of history very close to Kant's, save that it does not have the simple status of Idea or guiding principle for reflection but is on the contrary posited objectively. History is thus represented, to use a very Leibnizian metaphor, as a play in which the actors seem, apparently at least, to be making up their parts as they go along, but in reality, what gives the drama meaning and coherence is that a "poet ... has previously established the objective success of the whole with the free playing of everyone in such harmony that in the end in fact something rational must come out." [24]

This philosophy of history, itself derived from the Schellingian conception of the absolute starting point of philosophy, [25] could only be opposed to that of Fichte: if rationalization is immanent in the very process of history and inevitably emerges from the simple interplay of particular inclinations, action with a claim to be transforming, the very notion of a project must be a pure illusion of finitude: "All action is conceivable only through an original union of freedom and necessity. The proof is that every action—the individual's as well as that of the species—must be thought of as action, as free, but as objective result, as subject to natural laws. Subjectively then do we act for internal appearance; objectively, we never act: an Other acts through us." [26] And it is utterly extraordinary that Schelling then sets about ridiculing Fichte's criticism of Rousseau. It is thus to the "Action, action! That's what we are here for," which, as we have seen, concludes that famous criticism, that Schelling replies: "Action! Action! is a call that resounds on many sides, but is uttered most loudly by those who cannot get ahead with knowledge. ... It is supposed that anyone can act, for this depends only on freedom of the will. On the other hand, knowledge, particularly philosophical knowledge, is not within the reach of all even with the best will in the world." [27] The meaning of this passage is clear, beyond the purely polemical aspect: to exhort to action, to the transformation of the real as Fichte does, is to misunderstand the nature of knowledge and to think incorrectly of the Absolute that is the identity of the rational and the real. [28] It thus must be admitted that, conversely, it is because Fichte thinks of the Absolute *first* as a (theoretical) illusion, and later as (practical) Idea, that his early philosophy is essentially opposed not only to any theory of the cunning of reason (which was the case in 1793), but also to any conception of history as "in decline."

In summary, we can say that in 1793 Fichte, still Kantian to the core, conceived of (*a*) the deployment of *philosophy* according to a natural method of the *Critique of Pure Reason,* a method that begins with the truth and proceeds to the criticism of error. On the historical level, (*b*) though he rejects Kant's theory of the design of nature, Fichte remains a prisoner of Rousseau's view of an original state in relation to which only the criticism of the present is thinkable. On the political level, (*c*) the ethical valorization of the state of nature originally generates a total criticism of the state. Starting in 1796, however, (*a*) philosophy's starting point is the absolute as a pure illusion of metaphysical speculation. Correspondingly, (*b*) the notion of a Golden Age is radically eliminated from the philosophy of history, or more exactly, it totally "switches" from the past to the future, here following very exactly the movement of the illusion of "self = self" in the 1794 *Science of Knowledge,* and it manifests itself in the critique of Rousseau and then that of Schelling. Finally, (*c*) on the political level, natural right can become man's future and no longer a mythical past to be restored: the state will no longer be the fall from morality but will become the indispensable condition for its actualization. In this sense, the anti-Rousseauean formula, *"Before* us is located what Rousseau has placed *behind* us under the name of state of nature and the poets under the vocable Golden Age," forms the middle term between what is done at the level of transcendental philosophy and what is done at the level of political reflection, as is shown in this passage from the *Science of Rights:* "[N]o natural right, that is to say no juridical relation between men, is possible outside of a being together under positive laws. . . . But what we lose on the one hand we more than make up for on the other: for the State itself becomes man's state of nature, and its laws should be nothing else than actualized natural right" (*SW* 3:148–49).

Fichte thus understands that if no primordial state of freedom is thinkable, it must be admitted that man can obtain his freedom only from what he himself actualizes in the future, in short, that nothing is given man at the start, but he himself must construct everything through his own work, through the transformation that he effects on the real and, we could say, against himself.

The meaning of history proves thus entirely determined by human activity, because originally subordinate to it: "[T]he endgoal of reason has nothing arbitrary about it; it is necessary, it is our very isness. Here we perceive a project preceded by no thought, but which precedes all thought. This project is what is truly first, originating, necessary." [29] Totally actualized through freedom and not by the cunning of any necessity, history in Fichte's thinking completes the Copernican revolution; it is man who in the face of the real is finally the sole giver of meaning: "What does *being free* mean? Evidently being able to carry out the conceptions of acts I may entertain. But the carrying out always *follows* the conception, and the perception of the desired product of my causality is always—in relation to its first conception—a matter of the *future*. Freedom is therefore always posited in the future . . . as far as the *individual himself* is posited in the future" (*SR* 77; *SW* 3:51–52).

An "Esthetic" Interpretation of the Moral View of the World: Toward a "Critical" Synthesis of the Philosophies of History

1. Freedom and Determinism: The Question of the Third Antinomy and the Problem of the Recognition of Others

Based on a systematic repetition of the plan of Kant's "Transcendental Dialectic," the young Fichte's philosophy of history thus does not represent, as one tenacious legend would have it, an extravagant return to idealist metaphysics: the movement from the deconstruction of dogmatism (whose inevitable correlate is a theory of the cunning of reason) to a mode of thought of history as the effect of freedom is already present at the heart of the very structure of the *Science of Knowledge.* By destroying the illusion of an absolute self—a *theoretical* illusion of a *substrate anterior* to the appearance of the world, temporality, and intersubjectivity—the *Science of Knowledge* transforms this absolute self into a simple *practical Idea* opening humanity to its *future,* and Fichte here finds the same inspiration as Kant's *Critique of Practical Reason.*[1]

Fichte develops, with an unrivaled rigor among Kant's followers, the ultimate "conditions of possibility" of a moral view of the world, that is, lest we forget, of the only philosophy of history in which a historical event is truly thought of as a result of human free will. It will be agreed that under these circumstances it is very difficult not to feel some admiration and even some sympathy for this philosophical project whose "revolutionary" consequences it is possible to doubt in other respects: who indeed could claim to have completely scrapped the *feeling* that at least in certain cases our actions are the effect of our free will? The rationalist or "phenomenological" argument against the idea of will may *theoretically* succeed in persuading the person who devotes himself to it; it can never eliminate the moment of self-reflection in which the "illusion" that one claimed to dispel reasserts itself. As Raymond Aron observed, discussing Max

Weber, "no man of action acts while telling himself that, in any case, 'it's all the same,'"[2] which, I would add, he would however have to do if he *really* thought that historical events are the "effect" of necessity or a "miracle of Being." Banal as the argument may be, it remains irrefutable.

We still, however, have to get beyond the "feeling." As I suggested in the introduction (sec. 5[2]), the first and chief problem encountered by the moral view of the world—and Fichte is not mistaken about this—is the question of its compatibility with mechanism, with the natural law of the principle of causality. Here we come up against the formidable problem posed by the third antinomy in the *Critique of Pure Reason:* we certainly have a sense, at least in certain cases, of acting freely (i.e., voluntarily), but how could this feeling be anything other than simply an illusion as regards mechanism or, if you like, the determinism that asserts the absolute necessity of the interlinking of events in the world?

In Kant, this conflict takes the form of an antinomy, the thesis asserting the necessity of admitting, beyond natural causality, "a free causality for the explanation of phenomena," the antithesis holding that "there is no freedom" but that "everything happens in the world according to the laws of nature." As in every antinomy,[3] the contradiction *appears* absolute, as governed by the law of the excluded middle such that it *seems* (this is appearance, the "dialectics") that one has to choose between one or the other of the two propositions (depending on whether one favors freedom, i.e., the possibility of morality, or on the contrary, rationality, i.e., the possibility of science).

The "critical solution" of this antinomy is well known. I shall limit myself to recalling its principle: it shows how these apparently contradictory judgments are in fact reconcilable, for each takes the subject of their statement in a different sense (they are not "contradictories," but "subcontraries"): thus it is possible to assert, with the antithesis, that mechanism is valid for the *phenomenal* world while freedom, as the thesis has it, remains thinkable (if not knowable) in the *noumenal* world.

This "solution" raises as many problems as it resolves. As Jacques Rivelaygue has shown[4]—and this was one of the principal issues in the quarrel between Heidegger and Ernst Cassirer at Davos—it is very hard to reconcile the idea of freedom (of intelligible and noumenal causality) with Kant's theory of meaning which requires that a concept be temporalized (schematized) to have meaning. It is then

so hard to see how freedom and causality are reconciled in a particular case (the historical event) that one cannot imagine setting forth
the various interpretations proposed by the commentators of Kant,
so great is their number.[5] It is enough for me to indicate how Kant's
own solution to this antinomy in the first *Critique* was bound to leave
the young Fichte dissatisfied.

As Alexis Philonenko—whom the reader should keep in mind
for a proper understanding of what follows the chief discussions of
the question[6]—has shown, Fichte brought to light the fundamental
inconvenience concerning an ethical view of history, of the solution
to this third antinomy: the distinction between the sensory world
(the phenomenal world, which he thought thoroughly dominated by
natural causality) and the intelligible world (the noumenal world, in
which freedom remains possible) appears to imply that (1) being
phenomenal, human acts are wholly subject to determinism, and (2)
at the level of phenomena it is strictly impossible to distinguish between a free action and a determined one. Hence the famous passage
in Kant that Philonenko, following Ernst Cassirer, judges "dialectical"
in the pejorative sense, and which seems wholly to justify Spinozism
at the level of phenomena (but is the object of historical science
other than phenomenal?): "[I]f it were possible for us to have so deep
an insight into a man's character, as shown in both inner and outer
actions, that every, even the least, incentive to these actions and all
external occasions which affect them were so known to us that his
future conduct could be predicted with as great a certainty as the
occurrence of a lunar or solar eclipse."[7]

Philonenko (before later qualifying his judgment—as is proper
in any analysis of Kant) does not hesitate to write that "This debatable
text is terrifying for Kant's doctrine of freedom: I do not know something, that I am transcendentally free . . . and I also know something:
and the reason is that in the sensory world all my acts can be calcu-
lated in advance as exactly as an eclipse of the moon or the sun. If it
is necessary to exist this way, that's awful! Oh, surely the laws of nature are preserved, but freedom?"[8] Debatable, terrifying, and awful,
perhaps, but, as Fichte saw, an inevitable consequence of the assertion of the absolute validity of mechanism at the level of phenomena:
"Where are the boundaries to reasoning beings? The objects of my
actions are, indeed, only ever phenomena in the sensible world;
among these phenomena, to which shall I apply the concept of reasoning being and to which shall I not apply it? You yourself know it
very well! ought to answer Kant. But if this answer is a just one, it is

also anything but philosophical. I mount upon a horse, without asking its permission and without wishing in turn to be mounted by him; but why do I have greater scruples toward he who rents the horses?"[9] This passage, like the preceding ones, will (one hopes) induce a smile. And yet, starting from the solution to the third antinomy, it is, Fichte adds, "a very serious question to know whether or not, upheld as I am by general opinion, I am mounting and riding a horse as unjustly as the Russian lord who, also upheld by general opinion, hunts down, sells, and in a joking manner lashes his serfs."[10] And how, from what seems to be Kant's viewpoint (one thinks of the proof, in the "second analogy," of the soundness of the principle of causality as a determinative judgment constitutive of experience), do we answer these questions?

Fichte, surely, judged that this was impossible. In the second chapter of the *Science of Rights* he writes, in a passage that should be quoted in its entirety:

> It is a vexatious question that, so far as I know, philosophy has never yet solved: how do we come to transfer the conception of rationality to some objects in the sensory world and not others? . . . Kant says: "Act so that the principle of your will can be the principle of a universal legislation." . . . But I act every day upon animals and lifeless objects without ever seriously entertaining that rule. I am told that, of course, the rule applies only to beings who are capable of a consciousness of laws, hence rational beings. But who is to tell me what specific objects in nature are rational beings; whether, perhaps, only the white European or also the Negro, whether only the full-grown man or also the child, can claim the protection of that legislation; or whether, perhaps, the faithful house-dog may not likewise claim it? (*SR* 119–20, trans. modified; *SW* 3:80–81)

Fichte surely did not think that this question was of anything but purely *philosophical* importance, confiding (perhaps wrongly!) that it would not occur to anyone to doubt that his fellow man was his fellow man (*SR* 120; *SW* 3:81). But he wanted to stress—and with what perspicacity—that for lack of an answer to this question, the supreme principle of the moral view of history, the categorical imperative itself, "had neither applicability nor reality" in a phenomenal world forever dominated by mechanistic determinism. Requiring that "freedom be present in the sensory world" (*LH* 52), refusing to satisfy himself with the discourse of "these pitiable babblers," the "orthodox" Kantians—who, contemptuous of their own intelligence, always tended to hew the Kantian line to the letter—wasn't Fichte forced to go beyond the limits of criticism, that is, the limits of human finitude? Did he not run the risk of constructing a moral philosophy that is—to use an analogy whose meaning must now be clear—to practical ontology what Hegelianism is to theoretical ontology, in short, the risk of confusing meaning and truth, method and being? A hard question that would require an exhaustive interpretation of the evolution of Fichte's philosophy. Philonenko himself could write that on this path Fichte saw himself "forced to overstep the limits of Kantian phenomenology," here lying in the "great defect in his philosophy, a defect also partially responsible for the ontotheological development of the *Doctrine of Science* after 1801."[11]

2. Mechanism and Finality: The Antinomy of the Teleological Judgment and the Limitation of Mechanism

I shall set this question aside, however, because it clearly falls outside the scope of this book and also because, based on the third *Critique,* it seems to me possible to sketch an "esthetic solution" to the problem, admirably set forth by Fichte, raised by the moral view of the world from the point of view of the third antimony. It will be seen, however, that in this "solution" (which, for reasons that will be understood more exactly in what follows, cannot be more than an analysis of the ultimate aporias created by a finite being's attempt to think of the infinite) Fichte's question and answer link up in essence with the spirit of the third *Critique.*

Before indicating its principle, I should spell out what I take to be the significance and stakes of an "esthetic solution." For the possibility of articulating the different philosophies of history discussed up to now depends on this solution. Because we cannot get round the questions raised by Fichte, we need to determine the possibility and *legitimacy* of distinguishing between mechanism and freedom in the phenomenal world while keeping within the framework of criticism (of finitude). If this distinction proves impossible, just because of what the solution to the third antinomy allows us to suppose, the project of this whole book would fail and it would thus be impossible to articulate the various philosophies of history: we would have to give up granting any legitimacy to the moral view of the world and, with Spinoza, consign it to the terrible domain of "delirium."

So we know the aim of the "solution" to be sketched. What, however, does "esthetic" mean here? As you might have suspected, I understand the term in the sense Kant uses in the third *Critique,* in reference to the quintuple structure of "reflective judgment" (see chap. 3, this vol.). To sketch an "esthetic solution" to the third antinomy thus involves doing for the central idea of practical ontology (the idea of freedom) what was done (chap. 3) for the idea of the perfect rationality of the real. This idea is thus posited not as an idea that is "really presentable" in the phenomenon (the historical event), but as a principle of reflection about history. If this operation proves possible (which, once again, is in no way established when we think of the solution of the third antinomy: how indeed do we make use of freedom, if only as a principle of reflection about phenomena, if phenomena are *wholly* subject to mechanism?), we will have resolved the antinomy of mechanism and freedom in a way perfectly analogous to the solution proposed in chapter 3 for the antinomy of rationalism and phenomenology (where, positing the idea of perfect rationality as a principle of reflection, this idea became compatible with the "ontological difference," with the contingency of the real). All that will then remain is to attempt an articulation of the three philosophies of history, an articulation whose possibility would be made conceivable, with mechanism (rationalism) and freedom (moral view) agreeing at a level (that of the principles of reflection) that, by definition, does not eliminate the contingency of the real (history as a "miracle of Being," if one favors that vocabulary).

Let's get back to our main problem: how can we create a breach in the very world of phenomena, within mechanism, in order to have a thinkable use for the idea of freedom, if only as a simple principle giving *meaning* (and not *truth*)? This is the exact point, I think, the correct interpretation of another Kantian antinomy, the antinomy of the teleological judgment that concludes the *Critique of Judgment,*[12] that makes it possible to correct the seemingly disastrous effects for the moral view of the world apparently created by the solution to the third antinomy as formulated in the first *Critique.* We are not, it goes without saying, about to make Hegel's mistake of confusing this antinomy—which bears on the opposition between mechanism and finality—with the third one, and in seeing merely a straightforward repetition of the latter. As Philonenko has shown, its structure is really quite different from that of the other antinomies and, for that reason, so is also the solution it provides. What's more, far from reducing to the third antimony, the antinomy of teleological judgment adds the idea, central for our concerns, that mechanism does not reign undividedly in the phenomenal world since two points of view coexist on *this world* (the mechanistic point of view and the finalist point of view) in return for certain critical limitations that clearly need to be spelled out. This antinomy and its solution include three assertions that I shall analyze in all their rigor before extracting their significance.

(1) The thesis (asserting that all production of material objects is possible through mechanism) and the antithesis (asserting that certain productions are not possible through simple mechanical laws, but require the finalistic or purposive point of view) irremediably bear on the objects of the phenomenal world such that a solution like the one to the third antinomy (one principle for the in-itself, another for the phenomenon) is not only impossible but absurd. (We already know that outside of experience mechanism makes no sense, and finality even less, as we shall see in what follows.) Hence the fact that the antinomy takes the form of an *absolute* and, in a sense to be spelled out, irreducible contradiction, and escapes the usual structure of the Kantian antinomies.[13] Hence also the question leading to the second assertion: Isn't it both illegitimate (because of the "second analogy" demonstrating the validity of mechanism) and costly (because of the insurmountable contradiction thereby raised) to admit into the phenomenal world another point of view in addition to mechanism? And what are the philosophical bases for this "intrusion"?

(2) Despite the evident legitimacy of mechanism, finality is still an indispensable viewpoint for the comprehensive explanation of certain phenomena: organized beings, and more generally, living things.

For many reasons this statement can (and must) seem paradoxical. I shall confine myself to the most obvious ones.

First, as we already know, mechanism is solidly proven at the level of the first *Critique* so that the point of view positing finality as real (the "realism of ends" analyzed in §72 and §73 of the *Critique of Judgment*) must absolutely be rejected.[14]

Next, and the fact does not cease to surprise us, the antinomy of teleological judgment is the lone Kantian antinomy in which the thesis and antithesis are merely posited but not apagogically *demonstrated*.[15] The reason for this is very simple: we can easily imagine an apagogical proof of the mechanistic thesis,[16] that is, the proof of mechanism that is based on the absurdity of finality, but "on the other hand, it is impossible to formulate an apagogical proof of the judgment that is based on the second maxim, that is, on finality. How can we imagine a proof that is the demonstration of the absurdity . . . of mechanism? The proof of the antithesis would be the refutation of the 'Transcendental Analytic.'"[17] Under these circumstances we realize that Kant preferred to give us an antinomy without proofs, even if that means it consequently escapes the general definition of an antinomy. Finally, to complete giving the impression that this antinomy was not really grounded, the antithesis seeming to lack legitimacy, Kant himself had to stress, in §61 of the *Critique of Judgment,* the purely contingent nature of the finalistic principle, explicitly admitted as purely subjective, without necessity, simply as "one more principle for bringing nature's manifestations under rules, there where the laws of causality according to mere mechanism are not sufficient." Moreover, the subjective and contingent nature of this principle is constantly strengthened by the idea that, from the point of view of the in-itself, only mechanism (or at least a principle higher than finality) would rule the world.

Why then isn't finality, as in Spinozism, a simple "delirium" due in reality to an ignorance of true causes, the antinomy of the teleological judgment itself being no more necessary than the antithesis that destroys it?

We thus need to ask ourselves (since we are hypothesizing that Kant was not thinking superficially) three questions: (*a*) In what circumstances can finality be admitted? (*b*) For what reasons should we resort to it? (*c*) In what mode and with what status?

(*a*) We can answer the first question—the question of legitimacy—only if we assume that mechanism has some *limitation.* But what limitation of this principle is compatible with the proof of it in the first *Critique?* Paradoxically (though, as we shall see, the paradox is merely apparent), the only possible limitation on mechanism consists of positing the principle of causality as a *reflective judgment,* that is, a maxim or subjective principle for reflection. It may be objected that the *Critique of Pure Reason* establishes quite the opposite, that the principle of causality is the very prototype of the determinative judgment *constitutive* of experience. That would be correct, but would in no way constitute an objection: for we should not forget that the principle of causality, which is constitutive in relation to *possible* experience, is merely "regulative" in relation to intuition, that is, in relation to *real* existence (which is why it is precisely a "philosophical" and not a "mathematical" analogy that does not permit the construction of a "philosophy of nature" in the sense that this expression took in German idealism). In plain language, the principle of causality is an indispensable *method* in the *experiential* search for the determinants of a phenomenon, but it cannot be an a priori principle governing the totality of *being*. A proof that mechanism dominates the *totality* of *being* would require taking a nonhuman point of view: one would have to take in the totality of the real, which for us finite beings presupposes an infinite amount of time. In short, as always, dogmatism cannot ground the point of view from which it performs its proof: with realizing it, it oversteps the to-its-eyes-imperceptible limit separating the form and the content of experience: the fact that the causal method is absolutely necessary does not mean that the real is wholly and totally subject to it (which, once again, would require a completely different proof, a strictly metaphysical one). The principle of causality is thus *determinative* at the level of possible experience and *reflective* at the level of real experience.

(*b*) Consequently, and here we touch our second question, *if* it turns out that certain phenomena (in order: products made with skill, organized beings, living beings, human actions) reflect an infinite improbability of production by mechanism, we can admit a second *maxim* to attempt to *think* of them. This maxim will certainly not be constitutive either in relation to experience (to the possible) or in relation to intuition (to the real)—without which we would founder anew in the "realism of ends"—but it will be thoroughly "reflective," and yet (here is the difference from Spinozism) *a priori uneliminable,* for its elimination would require the ability to take the point of view of God and of the in-itself, that is, confusing the form and the content of experience (of the possible and the real). Two points need to be strongly emphasized here for this reasoning not to seem specious: What is a being that is "improbable" through mechanism? How is this criterion of "improbability" *sufficient* to lead us to admit a finalistic maxim? (By definition, improbability cannot yield the certainty that *seems* to be required to posit this second maxim.) I shall not insist on the "proof" of the first point which rests essentially on a careful refutation of Descartes's likening the organism to a machine. Kant does this in §64 and §65 of the *Critique of Judgment,* and it is masterfully discussed by Philonenko:[18] no point then in repeating here a detailed analysis aiming to show how, if the mechanical production of a fabricated product is infinitely improbable, one can say that in a sense the mechanical production of an organized being (of a plant) is "triply infinitely improbable," it being distinguished from the machine by an "indivisible trinity" of criteria (reproduction, growth and preservation):[19] indeed, the organized being seems to be the cause and effect of itself in reproduction, growth and preservation, properties that can never be more than juxtaposed in even the most perfect automaton.[20] But how (second point) can the improbability of an organized being's production by mechanism justify admitting an "additional" maxim? The answer is simple but conclusive: we shall apply the finalistic maxim when mechanism proves insufficient, not de jure (which would be once again to contradict the second analogy), but de facto, and we are justified in doing this precisely because, since mechanism is merely a method, this method will no longer be *totally* constraining when it is de facto perfectly empty. To make oneself better understood, one might go so far as to say that mechanism *as a method* would contradict itself if it claimed at any cost to lay down the law *by itself* in the face of the infinitely improbable, for it would then be equivalent to chance. (This argument would of course make no sense if mechanism were a principle a priori holding for the totality of being.) In short, to use another image, we can say that if the mathematician who works on artificial intelligence senses that he or she will never produce an organized intelligent machine, the biologist studying organized beings cannot help having the symmetrical feeling of the impossibility of an exhaustive mechanistic reduction of organization.

(*c*) Hence the mode in which the finalistic maxim is admitted, without *proof* and as *purely* reflective: the oddity of the teleological antinomy—no proof was given of either the thesis or the antithesis—thus is, we dare say, normal: mechanism (the thesis) has no need to be proven (it already has been), and since finality has legitimacy only in the space separating the form and the content of experience, finality cannot be proven: finality is a fact and nothing more, but a fact that, to be challenged, presupposes taking the viewpoint of God and the transforming of mechanism into an ontological principle that held *in itself and in its totality for the real*. Thus, the antithesis could be no more than a "refutation by example: in other words, the apagogical proof required of the antithesis *coincides with the antithesis* to the extent that the antithesis is the counterexample to the thesis." [21] Kant can thus avoid the two pitfalls characteristic of the *dogmatic* idea of finality and locate the finalistic maxim at a distance from both the "idealism of ends" that denies finality (either by mechanism, as in Spinoza, or by the doctrine of chance, as in Democritus) and the "realism of ends" that posits its real existence in nature (hylozoism) or in God (theism). Hence the third noteworthy aspect of this antinomy.

(3) The solution does not eliminate the contradiction between mechanism and finality but "deobjectifies" or "deontologizes" it. In their dogmatic formulation (concerning being), the thesis and the antithesis produce an absolute and irreducible contradiction. The thesis states: "All production of material things *is* possible through purely mechanical laws," while the antithesis maintains that "Some productions of these material things *are not* possible by simple mechanical laws" (my emphasis). In their critical formulation, however, we clearly go from *being* to *judgment* (to method): Kant writes, in *Critique of Judgment,* §70, that "All production of material things and of their forms *must be judged* [*muss . . . beurteilt werden*] possible according to purely mechanical laws," "Some products of material nature cannot be judged according to purely mechanical laws (their *judgement requires* [*ihre Beurteilung erfordert*] a completely different law of causality, that of final causes [*Endursachen*])" (emphasis added). In their dogmatic form, neither the thesis nor the antithesis can be proven: "Reason can prove neither one nor the other of these principles, because we can have no determining a priori principle of the possibility of things *according to purely empirical laws* of nature." In their critical form, both maxims are on the contrary "demonstrable," one a priori, the other by fact. We can thus judge that *in a sense* the contradiction disappears:

> As for the firstly exposed maxim of a reflecting judgment, it in fact contains no contradiction. For when I say: I must judge all events in material nature, including all forms as its products, in their possibility according to purely mechanical laws, I am not thereby saying: they are only thus possible (exclusive of any other kind of causality); that only announces that: I *should* on every occasion *reflect* on such events following the principle of the pure mechanism of nature, and conduct my research according to it as far as I can, because if it is not posited as the basis of research, there can be no real cognition of nature. This does not hinder the use of the second maxim on occasional instances, specifically with some forms in nature (and on their instance, even all of nature) which can be traced and reflected on following a principle very different from that of the explanation according to nature's mechanism—namely, the principle of final causes.

So, for Kant, once they are "deontologized," the two maxims are clearly not contradictory. Yet, clearly, *in another sense,* the *opposition* remains and cannot be evaluated if it is true that "to displace the contradiction in the maxims is to chase it from the real to settle it in the mind."[22]

Can the difficulty be overcome? This question is in fact unanswerable, for it is the very example of the false problem: what is the putative contradiction that would settle in the mind and from what viewpoint would it be noticed? Very precisely, the contradiction consists in this: even when "deontologized," the maxims continue to point to their dogmatic formulation, so that only by taking a metaphysical point of view, the point of view in which the totality of the real were visible, do the maxims contradict each other and hence would have to be unified to the advantage of the mechanistic principle, or of some undetermined principle that would be a synthesis of mechanism and finality. This is the point of view from which Schelling and Hegel resolve the "contradiction." Consequently, there is no nondogmatic point of view from which the opposition beween the two maxims could be declared a contradiction, for from the *philosophical* point of view I am not warranted in judging this opposition a contradiction (I cannot coincide with the point of view from which they become dogmatic principles, and *effectively* contradict each other and need to be reconciled in a third principle), and from the *scientific* point of view, the two maxims agree without difficulty, the reflective finalism, which is necessary for *comprehending* organized beings, not suppressing but rather integrating the indefinite search for efficient causes. In short, we must say that if from the viewpoint of metaphysical reason the principles are contradictory, from the viewpoint of science the maxims are complementary and from the viewpoint of reflection they are merely antithetical.[23] A contradiction that can be seen only from a dogmatic viewpoint is, strictly speaking, not a contradiction but an opposition that it would be disastrous to try to eliminate; for that would amount to eliminating the very possibility of reflective judgment (of reflection),[24] as can be seen in Schelling and Hegel: eliminating the opposition between the two maxims would mean assuming a viewpoint from which the form and the content of experience are but one, and reflective judgment (which absolutely presupposes this distinction, meaning the contingency of the real) would disappear. Schelling's and Hegel's philosophies can thus "resolve" the antinomy of teleological judgment only by simply eliminating the conditions of reflection, that is, of human finitude. In other words, the opposition between the two maxims can and must be legitimately maintained even if one can (with some difficulty, moreover) *negatively* imagine (through the *negation* of finitude) a monistic point of view in which they would be reconciled.[25] The important thing is that this "imaginary" not be "reified" by speculation, nor used to relativize this opposition in relation to the point of view of the in-itself or God.[26]

3. Of Finality as a Sign of Freedom: The Human Body as a Symbol of Individuality

When we combine the three aspects of the antinomy just examined—(1) the fact that both the mechanistic and the finalistic points of view focus on the same world, the world of phenomena, (2) the legitimacy and necessity of positing the finalistic point of view, and (3) the fact that the opposition between the two viewpoints does not form a contradiction and, as such, does not have to be overcome— the main difficulties created by the moral view of the world can largely be resolved: the idea of freedom can be sustained in the phenomenal world (along with mechanism), for the finalistic point of view, being reflective, is uneliminable and necessarily refers to the *supposition* of an intelligent creator: through reflection, the finalized (intentional) character of human actions should be referred to the *hypothesis* of a freedom (of an intelligent human creation), while the finalized character of certain natural objects, organized beings, should be referred, also by reflection, to the *hypothesis* of a divine power (a divine intelligent creation); because nature is merely physical, it would be absurd to attribute it any intelligence (an intention) whatever. From this vantage point, the postulates of practical reason will have the status of principles of reflection and as such they will be, at the very level of phenomena (hence history), compatible with, though infinitely opposed to, mechanism.

This "critical solution" opens the way to another "critical solution": that of the problem, posed in the introduction, of the articulation of the philosophies of history (of rationalism, the moral view of the world, and phenomenology). Nevertheless, using the teleological antinomy as a reinterpretation of the solution of the third antinomy runs into two difficulties that cannot in all rigor be evaded. One was formulated by Schelling and the other by Fichte, and we shall have to examine them before we can come back to the question of the articulation of the philosophies of history.

(1) It is fairly easy to explain Schelling's objection[27] to Kant's solution to the teleological antinomy, but it still remains fundamental

and requires special attention. Essentially, he objects that the Idea of an intelligent creative God, even when understood as a principle of reflection, is "unknowable," contradictory ("unthinkable"), and hence cannot serve to ground the sense of finality felt at the sight of an organized being. Indeed, as Spinoza realized, an infinite being (which God is by definition) cannot have consciousness and intention. For intention (project) presupposes that the representation of an end precedes its actualization, thus, that the possible and the real are distinct, which is precisely the sign of finitude. From the viewpoint of an infinite understanding (unlimited by external objects), thinking and being are necessarily identical, and there thus cannot be intentionality, intelligence in the human sense of the term. Let us suppose, writes Schelling, that one introduces into the divine creator "the concepts of endgoals, etc. . . . he thereby ceases to be a creator and becomes a simple artisan; he is at most the architect of nature," for in attributing him with the capacity to have conscious intentions, hence thoughts that precede existence, one finitizes him: "Thus, from the moment you *finitize the Idea* of the creator, he ceases to be creator, and if you raise this Idea to the *infinite,* all concepts of purposiveness and understanding disappear and nothing but the idea of absolute power subsists." One will seek, like Kant in §77 of the *Critique of Judgment,* "to explain everything by the particular nature of the finite mind. But if you do that you no longer need an infinite posited as being outside of you." The idea of an intelligent creative God is thus—and Schelling is essentially only following Spinoza here—as absurd as it is useless for explaining finality.

Let's go further: the same reasoning can also hold in the converse sense, as regards the "second intelligent creator" to whom finality refers when it applies to actions: man. For if it is clear that an infinite being cannot be endowed with representations and projects, it is no less obvious that a finite being, although on the contrary easily capable of these two properties, cannot, however, create anything—"a being in whom concept *precedes* action, and project realization, cannot produce"—so that the idea of an intelligent causality toward which the reflective use of finality points in thinking of human action is also strictly meaningless: man can certainly conceive of plans, that is, representations of certain ends that precede the actualization of these ends, but he can never have the power necessary for their actualization ex nihilo.

The inference from the sense of finality to the hypothesis, if only "reflective," of two "intelligent creators" would thus be absurd, for whether ascribed to man or God, the very idea of intelligent creation is not just unknowable (which Kant admits), but also unthinkable (contradictory).

Undeniably, Schelling's objection touches on a fundamental problem with criticist thought: easily surmountable from a metaphysical perspective (to be convinced of this it is enough to think of Hegel's definition of the "good infinity," of the infinity that integrates and goes beyond the finite point of view, the viewpoint of reflection), it poses (it must be honestly recognized) an insoluble problem within critical philosophy. This observation must nevertheless lead us to *more reflection:* What are we to think of a question whose solution is conceivable only from a viewpoint that transcends the limits of human finitude? Must we "resolve" this question or, on the contrary, does it not behoove us to set about deconstructing it?

We should first note that this problem did not escape Kant, who stressed many times over (not only in the third *Critique,* but also in the essay called "On a Distinguished Tone Newly Adopted in Philosophy") the inconsequentiality of attributing to the infinite understanding both the intelligence and will that presuppose the *separation* of thinking and existence, and hence finitude. In considering nature, says §77 of the *Critique of Judgment,* we as finite beings always go, depending on the effective causes, from the parts to the Whole. Only from the point of view of God—from the standpoint of an infinite understanding that we imagine through the negation of our own, through abstraction—can nature be considered a Totality whose parts are *deducible.* If man can go only from the parts to the Whole, God alone can go from the Whole to the parts. Let us apply this remark to the problem of finality: finality presupposes that the parts of a totality (the organized being or nature as a system) are considered, not the effect of this totality but of the *representation* of this totality (intention). Thus there cannot be—Schelling is correct—finality for God (or *in* him, it's hard to know how to put it): "The whole would be an effect (product) whose representation is seen as the cause of its possibility; we call end [*Zweck*] the product of a cause whose determining principle is simply the representation of its effect: it follows that it is merely the consequence of a special characteristic of our understanding when we represent the products of nature to ourselves as possible according to another kind of causality . . . that of purposes [*Zwecke*] and final causes."[28] And Kant is so keenly aware of the difficulty that Schelling was to present him with that he goes as far as proposing, in the same paragraph, the analogy

of space to "imagine" the viewpoint of God, space having "this similarity to the real foundation we are looking for, that in it no part can
be determined without a relation to the whole," although the *perfect*
representation of this totality, which is merely a "horizon," is impossible.[29]

But aren't we forced back to the second aspect of Schelling's objection: If the idea of finality is purely connected to the finite structures of our understanding—as §77 itself recognizes—what is the
difference between Kant and Spinoza? Isn't finality simply "delirium"
and aren't we forced back to the "idealism of ends"?

Here we reach the ultimate limit of the attempt by any finite
being to think the infinite, hence the limit in which the essence of
criticism is best expressed. I shall therefore try to be clear: the infinite can be thought of according to two quite different "logics," that
of the pure concept and that of the schema,[30] and these two logics
themselves correspond to quite distinct speculative interests: if I
think of the *concept* of an infinite being by totally abstracting from
my view of this concept and thus avoid finitizing it, Schelling and
Spinoza are clearly correct and it is absurd to attribute God with representations that would presuppose that, thought and existence
being unconnected in him, he is in fact a finite being—which contradicts his concept. But can I abstract myself out? What's more, should
I? For it will be granted that if the concept of God thus obtained is
coherent, for me it is completely unrepresentable (perfectly unschematizable). But I was the one who posited and defined this concept!
If I take my own point of view again, then I must (1) say that the
concept of God is only an *Idea* and not an existing *reality* and (2)
distort this Idea in such a way that it becomes representable for me.

What does this operation signify? Just this: a finite being who
tries to think the infinite can never escape contradiction, but can
merely choose to locate this contradiction in the fact of denying his
own point of view (then, following the logic of the concept, he will
obtain a noncontradictory but unrepresentable concept), or in the
fact of distorting, from his own point of view, the concept that he is
trying to think of (then, following the logic of the schema, the concept will become representable but contradictory).

This is the inevitable aporia reached in any finite being's attempt
to think the infinite; and the greatness of criticism is to lead us to it,
to analyze it, and not to claim to overcome it; for a conceptual overcoming of the aporia is wholly illusory. In truth, the very project is
infracritical for it consists in deepening a single aspect of the prob-

lem (the logic of the concept) at the expense of the second (the logic of the schema) without seeing that the aporia lies in the coexistence of the two.

We can state therefore that the thought of man and of God, as intelligent creators, refers to an insurmountable inverse symmetrical difficulty:

—In the case of God, reflection finitizes the idea of infinity such that, for man, God defines himself as a point of view of a point of view (the point of view that *reflection* has on one of reason's *Ideas*).

—In the case of man, however, it is the idea of infinity (the idea of freedom given through practical reason) that distorts the structures of finitude and to the idea of project adds that of intelligent creation without which the finality of human actions remains unthinkable.

It is no more possible to get beyond the aporias created by these two Ideas without overstepping the limits of finitude than it is to get beyond the antithesis of mechanism and finality. Every "solution" that gives conceptual "internal coherence" to the *Ideas* of man and God will inevitably be produced from a *fetishized* (unschematizable) point of view by abstracting from the conditions of reflection.[31] But as we shall see in examining the second objection—this time formulated by Fichte—to a certain use of the teleological antinomy as a solution to the third antinomy, if the finite thought of the infinite is always somehow doomed to contradiction, if the idea of man is itself "unthinkable," the reason may be that man—unlike the thing, the organized being, or even the animal—is, at bottom, *nothingness.*[32]

(2) Fichte, as has been mentioned, judged the solution to the third antinomy inadequate and asked the decisive question about the criteria for applying the categorical imperative to the phenomenal world, that is, the criteria for recognizing Otherness as humanity. Because the analysis of the teleological antinomy indicates the existence of two viewpoints (mechanism and finalism) in the very sphere of the phenomenal world, we find a *sign* (a symbol, one could say) of finality in human actions. But is this sign enough? This is Fichte's new question:

> That which has the character of purpose or finality can have a rational originator; that which does not permit the concept of finality to be applied to it has certainly no rational originator. But this distinguishing mark [*Merkma*] is ambiguous; concordance of the manifold into unity is the character of finality, but there are various types of such concordance explainable from strict natural laws—not mechanic but

> organic ones. We need another distinguishing mark to be able to con-
> clude with conviction from a certain experience to a rational origin
> for it. There also where she acts with purpose, nature acts according
> to *necessary* laws; reason acts always with freedom ... the question
> remains: how to distinguish an effect produced in experience by ne-
> cessity from a similar effect produced through freedom?[33]

It will be noted—as could be expected from Fichte—that the problem is well posed since it touches the distinction between freedom
and necessity at the very level of the phenomenal world, when the
effects in question are "similar ... [as] produced in experience."
Nevertheless, in the *Science of Rights* Fichte asks a sharper question
clearly aiming to discover not an "ontological" (in the current sense
of the term) but a *methodological* criterion for the faculty of judging:
"The question has rightly been asked: 'What effects can be explained
only as the effects of a rational cause?' The answer: 'the effects that
must necessarily be preceded by a conception of them' is true but not
sufficient, for the higher and more difficult question remains: 'What
effects must we then say were possible only after a prior conception of them?'" a question that Fichte says has not yet been resolved
by philosophy, not even by Kant's philosophy (*SR* 57–58; *SW* 3:37).

Fichte proposes his own solution in a passage so commendable
(*SR* 76–85)[34] that I must be forgiven for repeating long extracts from
it here. In fact, Fichte very largely confines himself to drawing from
the teachings of §64 and §65 of the *Critique of Judgment*. But he
clarifies them on one essential point: the distinction between organization and life.[35]

The opening chapter of the *Science of Rights* is devoted to per-
forming the difficult "deduction of intersubjectivity." As it is clearly
beyond the scope of this book to show all Fichte's argumentation,[36] I
shall merely recall that he describes how the existence of others is
an absolutely indispensable theoretical condition of possibility for
self-consciousness ("No you, no I—no I, no you," Fichte writes in his
own special style). Continuing to explore the conditions of possibility for self-consciousness, in an analysis that announces—and sur-
passes—the phenomenology of Husserl and Merleau-Ponty (see *LH*
54ff.), chapter 2 (§5) shows that this consciousness must be incar-
nated in a body thought of as the sphere of *individual* freedom: the
visible sign of freedom is *articulation* (*SW* 3:61), for it manifests the
capacity of the parts of the human body to move in an autonomous
way "according to concepts," that is, according to the human will.

This symbol of articulation enables us to distinguish, more

clearly than we can in Kant, three "orders of the real"—to adopt the vocabulary Philonenko has borrowed from Leibniz. It is very important to distinguish these three orders so as to follow Fichte's argument which Merleau-Ponty's *Phenomenology of Perception* echoes on two points: the human body is immediately meaningful, the reason being that man is nothingness (or, to echo Sartre, does not have a "nature").[37]

The first order is that of natural things including machines (like the watch, which Cartesians use to think of the organism).

The second order is that of organized beings, the model of which is the plant (the tree in §64 of the *Critique of Judgment*). For both Fichte and Kant, the organized being cannot be lumped together with the machine, as Cartesianism would have it, for with regard to mechanism it is infinitely improbable. Moreover, the likening of the organized being to a machine rests on a second error: it leads to making God an artisan, certainly very skilled but still qualitatively similar to man. In the order of organization, we have not yet reached the sphere of absolute individuality, but merely that of *relative* individuality, the criterion of this relativity being the graft: "That is why," writes Kant in §64, "we can consider each branch, each leaf from the same tree as simply grafted or transplanted on the tree, that is, as an existing tree in itself that simply attaches itself to another tree and is nourished by it like a parasite."[38]

The third order is that of life, and one cannot overemphasize the importance of distinguishing it from both natural things and plants. Philonenko writes:

> It is . . . on the subject of the idea of the *living* that Kant has been most poorly understood. One likened the living thing to the organism. While everything true of the organism is also true of the living, the reverse is not true. The tree does not have *articulation*. In sum, it is a republic defined by a very precise limit, the graft or scion. . . . On the other hand, the living thing that is subject to articulation resists a great number of grafts. For example, one cannot transplant my hand onto another individual and vice versa. This commonsensical notion has totally escaped the readers of Kant who at the same time have misunderstood the significance of the third *Critique,* so true is it that taste defines the cutting edge of individuality.[39]

Written from a Fichtean perspective, this somewhat enigmatic passage deserves some comment, for it leads us to the heart of our problem. First, let's be fair: if Kant was misunderstood, it was because he failed to indicate the *empirical criterion* of the living thing: articulation and the impossibility of its grafting, and Fichte deserves honor for discovering this criterion in chapter 2 of the *Science of Rights*. Kant, in *Critique of Practical Reason,* consistently defines life as the "faculty a being possesses of acting according to its representations." Kant does not, however—and we shall see the importance of this point for the solution of the problem posed by Fichte—indicate the criterion for identifying life or organization in the phenomenal world. The impossibility of a scion thus removes us from the sphere of relative individuality (organization) and ushers us into that of absolute individuality (life). Hence the political importance of the metaphor Philonenko takes from Kant: the tree is a "republic," and individuality has a very different place in relation to the totality depending on whether the body politic is thought of as a machine, an organized being, or a living thing. In the same article Philonenko stresses that we can also reverse the metaphor and say that in the republic the social contract (the general will by which individuals form a compact) is a graft: the individual then keeps his autonomy. If the body politic is alive, however, and the Whole is absolute individuality, the parts are no longer "transplantable": they lose their autonomy, and totalitarianism (or at least, what the Germans call "universalism") is not far off!

Thus, only at the level of the third order can the individual, as a living being with an articulated body enabling him or her to act according to representations, be considered a person, that is, a reasonable being. And only the living being is capable of direct communication with others, in esthetics for Kant,[40] in the legal system for Fichte.

We can thus begin to glimpse the solution to our problem: we find the empirical sign of freedom in the analysis of the human body itself: for with life as the ability to act according to representations we have the *analogue* of this freedom! And with articulation we have its criterion! (The reader may already be wondering what difference to make from this point of view between man and animal, for animals also clearly are more than simple organized beings and have articulated bodies. We shall shortly see how Fichte deals with this problem.)

Let's return to our text. We know what its purpose is: not, as is sometimes believed, to "deduce the human body" (always that legend of Fichte as a fantastical idealist!), but to construct a "phenomenology" of it,[41] to show how, in its simple perception and without intellectual construction, I must think of it as an alter ego, another self. It is indeed necessary that the phenomenon of my body, says Fichte, "be such that it is in no way comprehensible and conceivable, without the presupposition that I am a reasoning being; that accordingly the following can be presumed of the other: when you saw this figure [*Gestalt*] you had to take it necessarily as the representation of a reasoning being in the sensible world, if you yourself are a reasoning being. How is this possible?" This is indeed the question of the empirical sign of freedom that, by giving some content to the idea of free finality, will enable us to distinguish it not just from mechanism but also from the natural finality of the organized being. Fichte thus links up with Kant by going beyond him: he finally completes the solution of the teleological antinomy by finding the criterion of free finality at the level of phenomena.

But how can we resolve this question without forcing the comparison with phenomenology? Doesn't Fichte say that it is a matter of "understanding and conceiving" (*verstehen und begreifen*) the human body as the body of a free being? Isn't it thus a matter not of an immediate recognition, but an intellectual construction?

We should be wary of overhasty judgment: Fichte very carefully defines what he means by "understanding and conceiving": "I have conceived an appearance when I have obtained a completed whole of cognition of it so that in its every part it is grounded in itself. . . . I have not conceived it, when I am still driven away from one part to another of my cognition" (*SW* 3:77). He expresses the problem of the recognition of others at the level of perception: "that I cannot conceptualize the appearance of a human body, except through the presumption that it is that of a reasoning being, means therefore: I cannot, in collecting the parts of its manifestation, come to a standstill before I have arrived at the point at which I am forced to think of it as the body of a reasoning being" (*SW* 3:77). In this passage Fichte means to give a rigorous description of the elements of that "genetic proof" (*SW* 3:77), and the necessity for thinking of the human body as a *sign* of the reasoning being comes just from the fact the latter is not thinkable in *any* concept and that I can *immediately* see him as an alter ego only in relation to what is most intimate to me, the idea of freedom. Under these circumstances, the different stages of this process will involve showing how the articulated body progressively explodes any concept in which one would like to subsume it. In short, as Fichte will admirably put it, "the articulated human body is *sense"* (*SW* 3:65), and if it is immediately perceived as such, the reason is that man is the lone being who "is originally nothing at all" (*SW* 3:80): immediacy here is due to nonconceptuality.

We can now easily understand the stages of this recognition of others. I shall confine myself to identifying them, interesting myself more in the *movement* leading to the "definition" of man as a "nothingness" than in the detailed argumentation which the reader can easily reconstruct:

(1) The human body must first be thought of as an organized being—the organization that cannot be confounded, and here Fichte repeats Kant's arguments, with a simple product of skill (a machine) (*SW* 3:77–78).

(2) Nevertheless, the concept of organization does not succeed in fully "containing" the perception of the human body, for man is not only organized, but living: "He is a perfect plant, but he is also something more" (*SW* 3:77; *SR* 118). What is the sign of this life, of this faculty of moving according to representations? It is of course a matter of *"articulation,"* which must necessarily be visible, and which is in any case a product of organization. But articulation does not in return produce organization; it indicates [*sie deutet auf . . . hin*] another endgoal, i.e. another concept wholly resumes it and reduces it to unity" (*SR* 118). What is this concept? As one would expect, Fichte (without saying it, but for one who knows his Kant, it goes without saying) gives Kant's definition of life: "This . . . conception could be [that] of determined free movement, and to that extent man would be an animal" (*SW* 3:79; *SR* 118). This passage, however, poses two problems: Why a conditional (man "could")? What does "determined free movement" (*die "bestimmte freie Bewegung"*) mean? These two problems can be reduced to one: how to think the difference between man and animal when *both* are not just organized beings (plants) but also living beings (beings able to act according to representations and having articulated bodies)? Fichte tells us that articulation (the living) "indicates another end" (*SR* 118) than organization (the plant): it points to freedom (free movement). But is this freedom the same in man and animal? In short, isn't it necessary in these circumstances to get beyond the simple criterion of articulation? This is what Fichte tries to do by producing the surprising concept of "determined free movement": the animal has a free movement, it even acts according to representations (it is a living creature); but, as Kant realized,[42] the free movement characteristic of animal life is determined by instinct (enclosed again, consequently,

within certain limits): "Animals are by their instinct all that they can ever be; *some other reason* has provided everything for them at the outset ... but man, on the contrary, comes, so to speak ... as raw material to the world."[43] The concept of "determined free movement" amounts to Fichte's equivalent of Kant's "some other reason." Man is neither a machine, nor a plant, nor an animal. If "this presupposition of determined free movement also must be insufficient for the comprehension of the human body" (*SW* 3:79), under which concept should we think it? One last stage should be crossed. Let's listen to Fichte:

> (3) Its articulation ... must be incomprehensible in any *determined* conception. It must not refer to a definite, *determined sphere* of arbitrary motion [*der willkürlichen Bewegung*], as in the case of the animal, but to all infinitely thinkable motions. There must be, not a determinedness [*Bestimmheit*] of articulation, but an infinite determinability [*Bestimmbarkeit*] of articulation; not development, but developability. In short, all animals are perfect and complete; man, however, is merely suggested. A rational observer of the human body can unite its parts in no conception except in the conception of a rational being like himself, or in the conception of freedom as given to him in his self-consciousness. He must subsume the conception of his own self to his contemplation of that other human body, because that body expresses no conception of its own. ... Every animal is what it is; man alone is originally nothing at all. (*SW* 3:80; *SR* 118–19)

And because nothing rigorously allows us a priori to distinguish man from animal (insofar as they are living things in the Kantian sense and articulated in the Fichtean sense, they theoretically belong to the same "order"),[44] Fichte endeavors in the corollary to this "proof"[45] to point out the visible signs distinctive of "determined free movement" that is indicative of instinct, from the free movement that could be called *undetermined* and which in turn point to the supreme order, that of moral freedom. I leave to the reader the pleasures of analyzing them himself.

It is impossible here to spell out all the consequences of this "phenomenology of the body": notably, it suggests that no science of man is ever identical to a science of nature. (Expressions like "political science" or "educational science" are in this sense highly problematic: rather, we should speak of a political "art" of the "art of education" to preserve the dimension of "prudence" implied by the definition of man as nothingness, that is, "infinite perfectibility.")[46] I shall merely indicate what is of direct relevance to our aim and will enable us to resolve the difficulty raised by Fichte against Kant: we first note that Fichte, at least in the passage just discussed, keeps within the limits of criticism and is merely completing Kant's project in the *Critique of Judgment,* which was not to posit the freedom of man as an ontological truth, but to show that at the level of phenomena (of perception) one can think of man only as a free and reasonable being, at least theoretically, that is, as *capable* of being so. Consequently, the criterion of finality or purposiveness is not really superseded, but rather completed through the analysis of the symbols that justify—or better, compel—thinking of finality as the symbol of freedom: Fichte objects to the inadequacy of Kant's criterion of finality not in order to go *beyond* this criterion to an "ontology," but merely, I believe, because he finds it insufficiently elaborated in Kant, the confusion between organization and life, and then, within life itself, between determined free movement (instinct) and undetermined free movement (freedom) remaining possible in the absence of this phenomenology of empirical signs.

Thus, with the supplements produced by the Fichtean perspective, the solution to the teleological antinomy does not contradict but clarifies the solution to the third antinomy. For reflective judgment, finality—with all the signs that need to be added to it—can well remain the criterion of the phenomenal difference between thing and man, movement and action, and as §53 of the *Prolegomena* already shows, it is in this indeterminacy of man, his "nothingness," that lies the possibility (which Kant calls the "arbiter")[47] of his choosing between heteronomy (animality) and autonomy (morality). Only in autonomy is his action, henceforth fully sensible, thinkable under the noumenal idea of freedom in an order that is no longer that of fact, but, as Cassirer realized, value.[48]

The two fundamental philosophies of history—the one that, resting on the principle of reason or causality, refers to theoretical ontology, to the idea of a system, and manifests itself in nature through the law of mechanism, and the one that rests on the principle of an intelligent causality and refers to practical ontology, to the idea of freedom, and manifests itself in nature through finality, with its panoply of symbols—can now be reconciled without contradiction. It will thus be possible for us now to see in its totality the "system" of philosophies of history.

The System of Philosophies
of History

The diagram of the philosophies of history presented in the introduction indicates two central tasks (see p. 19): the first, to reconcile
rationalism and irrationalism by resolving the antinomy they create
in their common, although differently grounded, rejection of the
moral view of the world. Sketching a critical solution to this antinomy, part 1 of this book (chap. 3) opened up a space for the moral
view of the world. Still, it was necessary (second task) that the moral
view of the world be thought of as compatible with the conclusions
of part 1: in plain language, the moral view of the world had to be
given a status that would not make impossible the rationality and the
contingency of the real which the solution of the antinomy of rationalism and irrationalism had made room for.[1]

It is precisely this status that appears in the "reflective use" of the
idea of "intelligent creation" (the correlate of finality): thus, through
the solution to the antinomy of mechanism and finality (that is
merely the "visible version" of it), the antinomy of rationalism and
ethics receives a solution perfectly analogous to that of the antinomy
of rationalism and irrationalism, which also made reflective use of
the idea of system.

Rationality, contingency, and freedom (finality) can thus be reconciled, or better, they are strictly inconceivable without each other,
and that is what I have tried to designate by the term "system" which
must here be understood etymologically, as what is *posited together:*
it is because the real is contingent (which one can well, if one likes,
call the "ontological difference" or "miracle of Being"),[2] that at their
culminating points (in the idea of system and in that of freedom)
rationalism and ethics must take on the methodical status of principles of reflection. And vice versa: only if we make these two ultimate ideas of theoretical and practical ontology methodical principles for reflection and hence points of view that leave room for the
contingency of the real is it possible to undo the contradiction that
otherwise makes them opposed.

If criticism is a problematic of limits, dogmatism can be defined as the bias that ontologizes one of the points of view at the expense of the other two, takes the part for the whole, and makes inevitable the no-less-inevitably denied emergence of the highly antinomial contradiction of the two points of view that have been left out: hence the absurdity of trying to construct a *whole* philosophy from only one of these three points of view.

Critically conceived as the "defetishization" of the principles of ontology that a constantly reemerging metaphysics—even in the sciences—tries persistently to reify, philosophy is thus in essence an opening on the real. Thus like the "common consciousness" that it wants to rejoin, it must have "applications."

One such application seems to me particularly important today: it concerns the relation between political philosophy and the social sciences. Today, the opposition of these "disciplines" may have reached its height, everything happening as though the social sciences (predominantly, there of course being exceptions) tended to settle on a "rationalist model" inevitably oriented to historicism, with political philosophy divided between the two other "models," depending on whether it sets out to be normative (the heir of a certain jus naturalism) or "phenomenological" (forever doomed, it appears, to "deconstructing" its chief object: totalitarian ideologies).

This opposition—which a deeper analysis could show reproduces that of the three philosophies of history just mentioned—seems to me (I say this not out of any spirit of ecumenicism) profoundly sterile and harmful: positivism, in the sense in which Leo Strauss and Jürgen Habermas use the term to mean the Weberian or Popperian separation of facts and values, seeming to me to be, all things considered, only a lesser evil. The critical examination of what I have called the "system of philosophies of history" should empower a fresh approach, at least from the vantage point from which this book was conceived, to two classic questions that I consider indissolubly linked: can we conceive of a political philosophy that, leaving room for a reflection on values and even on the irreducibility of political phenomena (the "new" as they say), does not, for all that, deny legitimacy to the necessarily causal analyses produced by science? Reciprocally: can, without losing its very existence, a *human* science keep open the space of values and the contingency of the real, that is, if we reflect on it further, can it cease taking the natural sciences as a model?[3]

NOTES

INTRODUCTION

1. I am thinking here of the work done in collaboration with Alain Renaut in the Collège de Philosophie since its formation in 1974, then at the Center for Study and Research on Kant and Fichte at the Ecole Normale Supérieure in Paris. A presentation of these works appeared in the journal *Esprit* in April 1982.

2. André Glucksmann's book *The Master Thinkers,* trans. Brian Pearce (New York: Harper and Row, 1980), remains the foremost example in this vein.

3. It largely repeats, along with my earlier study, *Political Philosophy 1: Rights: The New Quarrel between the Ancients and the Moderns,* trans. Franklin Philip (Chicago: University of Chicago Press, 1990), material contained in my dissertation for the *doctorat d'état* on Fichte defended in June 1980 under the directorship of Miguel Abensour.

4. Cornélius Castoriadis, *The Imaginary Institution of Society,* trans. Kathleen Ramey (Cambridge: Polity Press, 1987). This text was written in 1964, and, since then, the analyses of the USSR made by Castoriadis have changed significantly.

5. See on this point Luc Ferry, "Stalinisme et historicisme," in Evelyne Pisier-Kouchner, ed., *Les Interprétations du stalinisme* (Paris: Presses Universitaires de France, 1983).

6. See on this point, the articles of Alain Renaut and of T. Maclet, in Pisier-Kouchner, *Interprétations du stalinisme,* on the interpretation of Louis Althusser and Leon Trotsky.

7. With the obvious exception of works produced or inspired by Raymond Aron, that were written from a Weberian or neo-Kantian point of view.

8. Simone de Beauvoir, "La Pensée de droite aujourd'hui," *Temps Modernes* (1955):1539.

9. Nothing will be said here about the different attempts within Marxism to devise a theory of the "relative autonomy" of superstructures, and particularly about Althusser's "practical texts," the very absurdity of the project being disconcerting. See article by Alain Renaut in Pisier-Kouchner, *Interprétations du stalinisme.*

10. See, for example, Hannah Arendt's homage to Heidegger: "Martin Heidegger at Eighty," *New York Review of Books* 17 (3 October 1971).

11. See Hannah Arendt, *The Human Condition* (Chicago: University of Chicago Press, 1958).

12. Hannah Arendt, "Understanding and Politics," *Partisan Review* 20 (July–August 1953):388.

13. Hannah Arendt, *The Origins of Totalitarianism* (London: André Deutsch, 1986), 469.

14. Arendt, "Understanding and Politics," 389.

15. Arendt, "What Is Freedom?" in *Between Past and Future: Six Exercises in Political Thought* (New York: Viking, 1961), 168.

16. Ibid., 169.

17. Ibid., 169–70.

18. Martin Heidegger, *Der Satz vom Grund* (Pfullingen: Gunther Neske, 1957), 154.

19. On this argument see Luc Ferry and Alain Renaut, "D'un retour à Kant," *Ornicar* 2 (1980); also Luc Ferry, "Sur le dilemme: La raison ou ses marges," *Débat* 4 (1980).

20. On this notion of model, particularly in its relation to the social sciences, see the interview in the journal *Esprit* (April 1982), as well as Ferry and Alain Renaut, "Heidegger en question," *Archives de Philosophie* 4 (1978), and Ferry, "Horkheimer et l'idéalisme allemand," *Archives de Philosophie,* April 1982.

21. See Luc Ferry, in collaboration with J. -P. Pesron and Alain Renaut, *Philosophies de l'université, présentation* (Paris: Payot, 1979).

22. See Ferry, "L'Idéalisme allemand et la Terreur," *Passé-Présent,* Fall 1983.

23. See the preface to part 3 of Arendt's *Origins of Totalitarianism.*

24. See Heidegger, *Discourse on Thinking,* trans. John M. Anderson and E. Hans Freund (New York: Harper and Row, 1966).

25. Arendt, "Martin Heidegger at Eighty," 54.

26. See Leo Strauss, "The Three Waves of Modernity," in *Political Philosophy: Six Essays by Leo Strauss,* ed. Hilail Gildin (Indianapolis: Pegasus/Bobbs-Merrill, 1975).

27. Pierre Manent, *Naissance de la politique moderne* (Paris: Payot, 1977), 12.

28. See Ferry, *Political Philosophy 1,* as well as idem, "De l'historicisme à la question du droit," in *Rejouer le politique* (Paris: Galilée, 1980).

29. The model is clearly evidently sketched out by Leibniz, and we find many less philosophical versions in the course of the seventeenth and eighteenth centuries, in authors such as Bernard Mandeville, who had a considerable influence on Kant.

30. In the following pages I repeat without significant modification some passages from an article that appeared on this theme in the journal *Passé/Présent,* Fall 1983.

31. See, for example, Xavier Léon, *Fichte et son temps,* 1:167ff. It goes without saying that I am here disregarding the historical relevance of this interpretation.

32. Maurice Boucher, *La Révolution de 1789 vue par les écrivains allemands, ses contemporains* (Paris: Didier, 1954), 8.

33. Jacques Droz, *L'Allemagne et la Révolution française* (Paris:Presses Universitaires de France, 1949), 49, explains how the situation in Germany before the Revolution made it possible to at least partially understand this enthusiasm.

34. Edmund Burke's *Reflections on the Revolution in France* was first published in 1790.

35. Alexis Philonenko, *Théorie et praxis dans la pensée morale et politique de Kant et de Fichte en 1793* (Paris: Vrin, 1968).

36. August W. Rehberg, *Untersuchungen über die französische Revolution* (Hannover, 1793). On Burke's other German "disciples," particularly Brandes, see Frieda Braune, *Edmund Burke in Deutschland* (Heidelberg, 1917).

37. Philonenko, *Théorie et praxis,* 14. See also Droz, *L'Allemagne et la Révolution française,* 360ff.; Léon, *Fichte et son temps,* 1:176ff.

38. Quoted by Léon, *Fichte et son temps,* 1:170.

39. Rehberg, *Untersuchungen,* 18–19.

40. Ibid., 18.

41. Ibid., 23.

42. See Philonenko's introduction to his translation of Kant's *What Is Orientation in Thinking, Qu'est-ce que s'orienter dans la pensée?* (Paris: Vrin, 1959).

43. On the texts of the conflict, see Heinrich Scholz, *Die Hauptschriften zum Pantheismusstreit,* Neudrück selt. ph. Werke de Kant-Gesellschaft., Bd 6 (Berlin, 1916); see also H. Schmoldt, *Der Spinozastreit* (Wurzburg, 1938). See also Martial Gueroult, *L'Evolution et la structure de la "Doctrine de la Science" chez Fichte, I* (New York: Olms, 1982).

44. Edmund Burke, *Reflections on the Revolution in France* (London: S. M. Dent, 1960), 58. Burke clearly drew from it a criticism of the very idea of revolution: because politics presuppose broad experience, "more experience even than any person can gain in his whole life," it should definitely be imprudent to "pull down an edifice which has answered in any tolerable degree for ages the common purposes of society" (p. 59). On the Aristotelian version of this criticism of a politics deduced from theory, see Pierre Aubenque, *La Prudence chez Aristote* (Paris: Presses Universitaires de France, 1963), 51ff.

45. Jacobi's letter, dated 5 May 1790, appears in volume 2 of Jacobi's *Werke* (Leipzig, 1815), 513ff. A more recent edition was published in 1980 by Wissenschafliche Buchgesellschaft. The quotation, which Jacobi attributed to Mirabeau, is in fact from Rabaud Saint-Etienne: see A. Ayrault, *La Genèse du romantisme allemand* (Paris: Aubier, 1961), 120.

46. Jacobi, *Werke,* 2:516.

47. Jacobi's frequent reference to English empiricism in contrast to German idealism is significant in other respects.

48. Philonenko, *Théorie et praxis.*

49. Ibid., 25–27.

50. Immanuel Kant, "First Supplement," in "Perpetual Peace: A Philosophical Sketch," in *Kant's Political Writings,* trans. H. B. Nisbet (Cambridge: Cambridge University Press, 1970), 108.

51. I shall come back to this further on, but it is already clear that one cannot omit what separates the "design of nature" and the "cunning of reason."

52. This is the basis of the fact that Hegel and Kant have a nearly identical attitude toward the French Revolution. See Ferry, "L'Idéalisme allemand et la Terreur."

53. See part 2, the Fichtean criticism of Kant.

PART 1, PREAMBLE

1. Theodor L. Häring, *Hegel, Sein Wollen und Seine Werke* (Leipzig, 1929–38), 2:319. See also Bernard Bourgeois's introduction to his translation into French of Hegel's *Encyclopedia* (Paris: Vrin, 1970), 109.

2. Dieter Henrich attempted to assess the possible readings of this question. See his article on the Hegelian theory of the contingent in his *Hegel im Kontext* (Frankfurt: Suhrkamp, 1967).

CHAPTER 1

1. Bernard Bourgeois, *Hegel à Francfort: Ou Judaïsme, christianisme, Hegelianisme* (Paris: Vrin, 1970), 89. On Hegel's development as a general critic of Fichte's philosophy, see also Bourgeois's *La Pensée politique de Hegel* (Paris: Presses Universitaires de France, 1969), 27–81. I was often inspired for the writing of this chapter by discussions with Jacques Rivelaygue in his brilliant seminars on German idealism as well as lectures he has given since 1974 at the Collège de Philosophie and at the Center for Study and Research on Kant and Fichte at the Ecole Normale Supérieure in Paris. I warmly thank him.

2. From Tübingen to Jena where Hegel's final philosophy was formed, we can identify four elements in his development, each marking a certain progress in the criticism of the "moral view of the world." In Tübingen and in Berne, Hegel's thinking was dominated by a double reference: on the one hand, a romantic vision of Greece as the realization of an ideal of freedom defined as the reconciliation of the particular individual with the universal which the city represents; on the other hand, the allegiance to the French Revolution as a means of restoring this ideal, which was lost with the emergence of the Roman world and the Christian religion. For Hegel, the revolutionary project consists—as clearly announced in the "Tübingen Essay," see *Three Essays, 1793–1795: The Tübingen Essay, Berne Fragments, the Life of Jesus,* trans. Peter Fuss and John Dobbins (Notre Dame, Ind.: University of Notre Dame Press, 1983)—in transforming the Christian religion into the religion of a free people by eliminating its "positivity" through a return to Kant and Fichte (see the letter of Schelling of 16 April 1795) (see Nohl, *Theologische Jugendschriften* [Tübingen, 1907], 89) and also in changing political reality (hence Hegel's allegiance to the Revolution) to accord with the principles of Rousseau. Consequently, during this period, Hegel has the "modern freedom" (whose most ardent defender was Fichte) function in the framework of a philosophy of history already marked by the compound structure (in this case, the Golden Age is Greece, the decline of Rome and the restoration brought about by a twofold process: through Kant's and Fichte's criticism of religion, and through the transformation of politics according to the model of France). It was during the Frankfurt period that the second philosophy of history was formed (through reference to the concept of Life), which may rightly be considered as the first original version of the properly Hegelian thought, for (as shown by Bourgeois, *Hegel à Francfort,* 105) it marks the will to reconcile thought and the real by getting beyond the separations inherent in the ethical point of view. The aporetic plan at Frankfurt received its first solution in the start of the Jena period, in the writing on *The Difference between the Fichtean and Schellingian Systems of Philosophy,* trans. Jere Paul Surber (Reseda, Calif.: Ridgeview, 1978), and above all in the short article on the "Essence of Critical Philosophy." Hegel echoes Schelling's theory of the "need for philosophy," trying to reconcile thought with the real by showing that the real (essentially characterized by this division) points toward the philosophy of Identity (whose model for Hegel is still Schelling's System of Identity). This position, very close to his final philosophy—which will appear with the *Phenomenology of Spirit,* trans. A. V. Miller (Oxford: Oxford University Press, 1977)—still should be carefully distinguished from it, as Jürgen Habermas showed (see his "Hegel's Critique of the French Revolution," in *Theory and Practice,* trans. John Viertel [Boston: Beacon Press, 1973]). It is, moreover, criticized as dogmatism in the beginning of the introduction to the *Phenomenology.* As we see, each of these stages of

Hegel's thinking represents a distancing from the initial positions, at the same time as a constant progress toward a philosophy of the identity of the will and the understanding.

3. Translation is modified.

4. It is precisely in this that Hegel's philosophy of history *explicitly* echoes Leibniz's project in his *Theodicy.*

5. Consequently, this seems equivalent to denying chance or contingency; see *VG* 29. Later I shall return to the problem of this negation of the contingent.

6. To a great extent, starting with such questions would make it possible to understand the return in human sciences (Marxism or psychoanalysis, for example) of a metaphysics of history that has long been thought refuted.

7. Karl Marx, *Capital: A Critique of Political Economy,* trans. Ben Fowkes (New York: Random House/Vintage, 1977), 1:929.

8. Hegel, *The Philosophy of Right,* trans. T. M. Knox (Oxford: Oxford University Press, 1952), 34–35.

9. In Leibniz's terms, the universal will is to the particular will what the consequent will is to the antecedent will.

10. It is at bottom this hiatus that makes of Fichte's philosophy a philosophy of the Terror, as is shown by the close connection between the criticism of the French Revolution in the *Phenomenology* with that of the moral view of the world. In other respects it is the same criticism that underlies the analyses of the *Science of Rights* in Hegel's *Natural Law: The Scientific Ways of Treating Natural Law, Its Place in Moral Philosophy, and Its Relation to the Positive Sciences of Law,* trans. T. M. Knox (Philadelphia: University of Pennsylvania Press, 1975), as in his *Difference between Fichtean and Schellingian Systems.* It is very clear that for Hegel, formalism must lead to a philosophy of constraint: indeed, if the universal will and the particular will cannot *be* reconciled, but merely *should* be, they can have only the negative relations of domination and submission. Thus, the will is merely "moral *consciousness* as negative essence, for whose pure duty sensuousness has only a *negative* significance, [and] is only *not* in conformity with duty "(*PS* §603, p. 368).

11. In *Hegel's Lectures on the History of Philosophy,* in an analysis of Kant's *Critique of Practical Reason,* Hegel examines in great detail the contradiction of the moral view of the world; see notably the study of the Kantian *postulates* in which Hegel "discovers" a veritable "nest of contradictions": "For example, the immortality of the soul is postulated because the latter is affected by sensibility. But the sensible conditions moral self-consciousness; it is the goal—perfection—which suppresses [*aufhebt*] morality as such. In the same way does the other goal, that of the harmony of the sensible and the rational, also suppress morality, since this latter consists precisely in this opposition toward the sensible." Hegel, "Theorie Werkausgabe," in *Werke in zwanzig Bänden,* (Frankfurt: Suhrkamp, 1971), 20:371.

12. Translation is modified.

13. This is true from a diachronic as well as a synchronic point of view.

14. In studies of Hegel, the lack of interest in and even utter contempt for Fichte's thinking is frequent, as is testified, for example, by the way Ritter judges the philosopher who, according to him, "embarrassed by the narrowness of what goes on in Germany . . . pulls from his head as if from an 'absolute self' by force of a priori deduction and of postulate, political and legal systems. Joachim Ritter, *Hegel and the French Revolution: Essays on "The Philosophy of Right,"* trans. Richard Dien Winfield (Cambridge:

MIT Press, 1982). It is hard to see how such superficial judgments can be made in this otherwise well-documented study.

15. An illustration of this would be Horkheimer's "Materialism and Morality," in *Critical Theory: Selected Essays*, trans. Matthew J. O'Connell and others (New York: Continuum, 1982).

16. See also *VG* 75, 78. Secularized, this idea is again manifest in a Marxist context. See Engels's letter to Bloch of 21 September 1890: the historical event must be considered "the product of a force acting as a whole, in an unconscious and blind way."

17. We need to recall that here the essential difference is that nature never reaches the "for itself."

18. See, for example, *E*, addendum to §209. This "naturalism" conveyed by the mechanistic schema of the composition of forces will also be repeated in Marxism: see, for example, beyond the first preface to *Capital*, the letter of Engels to Bloch (September 1980) and chapter 4 of Engels, *Feuerbach: The Roots of the Socialist Philosophy*, trans. Austin Lewis (Chicago: Charles H. Kerr & Co., 1903).

19. On the echo of these two last points by the Marxist idea of history, see, for example, Engels, *The Origin of the Family, Private Property and the State* (London: Lawrence and Wishart, 1972).

20. Hegel, *Lectures on the History of Philosophy* (Oxford: Clarendon Press, 1985), 71–72. Translation is modified.

21. Bourgeois, *La Pensée politique de Hegel*, 47.

22. Hegel, *Briefe von und an Hegel* (Hamburg: Felix Meiner, 1952), 23.

23. Hegel tells Schelling that he is reading Fichte's *Science of Rights*.

24. It should be noticed, however, that despite the evident rapprochements with Fichte's thinking, Hegel was at the time already preoccupied by the necessity, for transforming the world, of finding something in the real itself which calls for this transformation. This is why he did not think of brutally imposing some religion other than Christianity (although, as we learn from the "Tübingen Essay," he was not at the time kindly disposed toward it), but simply to transform it such that, freed of all positivity— see his "Life of Jesus"—it can become the religion of a free people. It is basically, already in embryo, the announcement of what was to be Hegel's third philosophy of history (at the end of the Frankfurt period and at the start of the Jena period) in which it is the self-differentiation proper to the spirit of the time that is, in itself, a "need for philosophy," calling negatively, through its own lacunas, for the actualization of identity.

25. I think one can see in Hegel scholarship three types of interpretation of his development with regard to the French Revolution. That of Rudolf Haym (*Hegel und seine Zeit: Vorlesungen über Enstehung und Entwicklung, Wesen und Werth der Hegel'schen philosophie* [Berlin: Rudolph Gärtner, 1857]) which basically considers the young Hegel's allegiance to the French Revolution as merely a "youthful sin" soon disavowed by the philosopher who was to become "so totally antirevolutionary" (p. 33). Haym's theses are in other respects well known: they make Hegel "a philosophical dictator of Germany" (p. 347), a universalistic theoretician of the state, and Haym sees in the preface to Hegel's *Principles of the Philosophy of Right* "nothing other than a scientifically formulated justification of the police system of Karlsbader and the persecution of demagogues." We find, in French, an echo of these themes in the article, also more than debatable, of Alfred Stern, "Hegel et les idées de 1789," *Revue Philosophique de la France et de l'Etranger* 128 (1939): 353–63. Casting doubt on Hegel's "sincerity," Stern judges that "the liberal ideas born of the Revolution and propagated by Napoleon

find little approval from his enthusiastic admirer. In the chapter on the Revolution . . . in his *Philosophy of World History,* Hegel rejects liberalism. . . . To the 'aggregate of volitional atoms' which the liberal state is for him, he contrasts the 'individuality nation' . . . as a precursor of the authoritarian state as later conceived by the phenomenologist Scherer . . . then realized by fascism and National Socialism" (p. 361). Karl Popper's criticism also falls into this line of thought. Repeating Eric Weil's project in *Hegel et l'état* (Paris: Vrin, 1950), Ritter tries to refute the aberrant criticisms of Hegelianism by taking as his precise themes the study of Hegel's position regarding the French Revolution. Judging that "the event round which—for Hegel—all determinations of philosophy in relation to time . . . gather, is the French Revolution" (*Hegel and the French Revolution*), Ritter argues that "there is no other philosophy which is so much and so deeply in its innermost impulses the philosophy of revolution as that of Hegel" and that, far from being reactionary, Hegel's criticism, since it constantly, at times passionately, opposes itself to political restoration," is much more a progressivist attempt to get beyond the indissolubly interconnected aporias of this inseparable couple formed by the Restoration-Revolution antinomy. Finally, Habermas's "Hegel's Critique of the French Revolution," while claiming simply to "amplify" Ritter's thesis (see p. 121), seems to me in reality to have opened a new vista by showing how "Hegel's philosophy of revolution is his philosophy *as* the critique of revolution" (p. 121). I shall return to this point.

26. Hegel, *Werke,* 12:539.

27. Ibid., 526.

28. This passage is discussed by Weil, *Hegel et l'etat,* 49–50.

29. Habermas, "Hegel's Critique of the French Revolution," 121.

30. Hegel, *Werke,* 12:529.

31. "We now have to consider the French Revolution as world-historical, because this occurrence is world-historical as to its *content,* and formalism's struggle must be differentiated from it" (ibid., 535).

32. Again, let us note, he was not a Robespierrist, as seen in a letter to Schelling dated December 1794: "You have heard no doubt that Carrier has been beheaded . . . . This trial is very important; it has shown up the ignominy of the robespierrists. " Hegel, *Briefe.*

33. See on this point Jean Hyppolite, "La Signification de la Révolution française dans la *Phénoménologie de Hegel," Revue Philosophique de la France et de l'Etranger* 28 (1939):321ff. This also is a point that, despite his perspective, Ritter could not but stress, while trying to minimize the importance for Hegel of the criticism of the revolutionary form: "One could even say that the essence of the modern political revolution, what distinguishes it from all other forms of overthrow, revolt, insurrection, and coup d'etat, lies for Hegel not so much in the particularly political form that violence takes, as in the social emancipation that serves as its base" (Ritter, *Hegel and the French Revolution,* 63). Thus, Ritter must continually recall that the positive interest Hegel felt for the Revolution always presupposes that an abstraction be made from its form, that is—it must be pointed out—from everything that makes it revolutionary for subjective consciousness and political action: it is thus necessary to "break through the 'formalism' of political oppositions and inquire after the revolution's 'content'," (p. 26). It is precisely the necessity of this distinction that in my eyes justifies Habermas's point of view.

34. Habermas, "Hegel's Critique of the French Revolution," 126.

35. Ibid., 128. We must, moreover, stress the similarities between Kant's and Hegel's

positions regarding the French Revolution. Both were "filled with enthusiasm" by its *result,* and therefore enemies of any restoration of the ancien régime, but attached as they were to Luther's spirit of reformation, they remained no less deeply antirevolutionary. Here again, it is clear that this can be largely understood on the basis of the philosophy of history when we cease interpreting Kant's philosophy of history as a moral idealism and see it as a theory of the cunning of reason, one that essentially differs from Hegel's in its ("reflective") status and not in its content.

36. Habermas writes that Hegel "reintroduces on the level of objective spirit what he rejects on the level of subjective spirit: for, after all, he designates Robespierre, whom he has rejected, as world spirit" (ibid., 137). One point of Habermas's, however, seems to me debatable: he seems to think that Hegel abandoned his third philosophy of history (the one, at the beginning of the Jena period, characterized by the notion of the "need for philosophy") because of its "dangerous" revolutionary potentials (which Habermas likens to "Critical Theory"). It seems to me, more simply, that Hegel got beyond this position because it didn't yet allow for the reconciliation with the real world. (See the criticism of the "need for philosophy" in the introduction to the *Phenomenology.*)

37. Hegel, *Lectures on the Philosophy of History,* trans. Walter Kaufmann (New York: Vintage, 1967), 60.

38. Habermas, "Hegel's Critique of the French Revolution," 138–39.

39. Ibid

40. Ibid., 141.

41. See Theodore F. Geraets, "Les Trois Lectures philosophiques de *L'Encyclopédie* ou la réalisation du concept de la philosophie chez Hegel," *Hegelstudien* 10:231–54.

42. Geraets, "Trois Lectures philosophiques," 243.

43. Geraets, "Trois Lectures philosophiques," 247.

44. The differences between the first and third edition of the *Encyclopedia* are significant. See Geraets, "Trois Lectures philosophiques," 250–51.

45. Ibid., 252.

46. Ibid.

47. See in *The Logic of Essence,* the chapters corresponding to these criticisms of Kantianism.

48. Not being dialectical, it cannot be part of the truth either. In others words, it must be considered a thesis on the system and thus have, if you will, the status of an afterword.

49. On the meaning of "archetypical understanding," see chapter 3 of this book.

50. The term "concept" is used here in the Hegelian sense, i.e., the movement of the production of otherness from oneself, then of return in itself from otherness.

51. If the absolute syllogism is not posited dialectically, logic demands that it have the status of what Kant calls an Idea or "principle of reflection." I do not see what other meaning could have, in the Hegelian system, a point of view that the finite consciousness posits as external to itself.

52. That is nevertheless the position of many exegetes, and not the lesser among them. See, for example, Häring, *Hegel, sein Wollen und sein Werk,* 2:319.

53. On this interesting point see Dieter Henrich, "Hegels Theorie über den Zufall," in *Hegel im Kontext,* 157–86.

54. Still, to my mind, rather incoherently: it seems to me barely comprehensible that one can first criticize the "moral view of the world" with ready-made formulas and

then find, with relief, as proof of the "non-immoral" character of Hegelianism, the ethical point of view that enters into it at the level of the state: if in Hegel the return to an ethical point of view is possible, the reason is that it was never gotten beyond, and conversely, if it had been, there wouldn't be any reason to rejoice at seeing it come back at such a central point in the system: that would be quite simply the surest indication of its triviality. In this regard, Eric Weil's book is one of the most striking examples of an inability to admit the consequences of a real refutation of the ethical point of view.

55. Weil, *Hegel et l'état,* 100.

56. Small indeed, since the contingent, if Hegel does not deny it, is of no philosophical interest.

57. Heidegger, *Der Satz vom Grund,* 72:"aus dem Machtbereich des grossmächtigen Prinzips."

58. Heidegger, "Hegel und die Griechen," in *Wegmarken* (Frankfurt: Klostermann, 1967).

CHAPTER 2

1. What follows repeats and elaborates the first part of a study written in collaboration with Alain Renaut, "La Dimension éthique en la pensée de Heidegger," in *Nachdenken über Martin Heidegger* (Hildesheim: Gerstenberg, 1980). See also our contribution to the *Colloque de Cérisy* on the "ends of man" (Paris: Galilée, 1981). The reader unfamiliar with Heideggerian "jargon" can refer to the interview with the Collège de Philosophie published in the journal *Esprit* (April 1982) as well as the introduction to my *Political Philosophy 1: Rights, the New Quarrel between the Ancients and the Moderns.*

2. "[O]ntology always thinks solely the being (*on*) in its Being. But as long as the truth of Being is not thought, all ontology remains without its foundation. Therefore the thinking which in *Being and Time* tries to advance thought in a preliminary way into the truth of Being characterizes itself as 'fundamental ontology.' As such, "by initiating another inquiry" [that of Being, and not of the being of beings (*l'être de l'étant*), i.e., the question of the meaning of "the fact that there is being"—and not the question of the meaning of "the objectivity of the object"—or of the "beingness of beings" (*étantité de l'étant*)], "this thinking is already removed from the 'ontology' of metaphysics (even that of Kant)" (BH 184; LH 235). We know from other sources that Heidegger was later to abandon the expression "fundamental ontology" as its implied reference to a logic of foundation runs too great a risk of representing an attempt within the framework of founding rationality.

3. Heidegger, *Einführung in die Metaphysik* (Halle: Niemeyer, 1952), 105; *Introduction to Metaphysics,* trans. Ralph Manheim (New Haven: Yale University Press, 1959), 140.

4. See, for example, Heidegger,"Hegel's Begriff der Erfahrung," in *Holzwege* (Frankfurt: Klostermann, 1952), 162; *Hegel's Concept of Experience,* trans. J. Glenn Gray and Fred D. Wieck (New York: Harper and Row, 1970).

5. On this relating the notion of value to the metaphysics of subjectivity, see Jean Beaufret, *Dialogue avec Heidegger* (Paris: Minuit, 1973), 2:182ff.; Eryck de Rubercy and Dominique Le Buhan, *Douze Questions à Jean Beaufret à propos de Heidegger* (Paris:

Aubier Montaigne, 1983), 25ff. (P. 28: here it is a question of "ceding back the viewpoint of value finally to put us in the presence, in evaluated things, of a more essential dignity.")

6. This deepening of ethics—from *éthos* to *ethos*—toward an idea of "abode" within which man thinks and acts, is to be connected with the grasp of Being as Place (*Ort*), Country (*Gegend*), Homeland (*Heimat*).

7. Further on, I shall return to the significance of these denials.

8. To the lecture itself (1929) were added an afterword that appears in the fourth edition (1943) and an introduction (1949); one can also mention the prologue written in 1937 for the translation of the lecture and of extracts from *Sein und Zeit* into French (trans. Henry Corbin [Paris: Gallimard, 1951]).

9. Heidegger, "Was Ist Metaphysik?" in *Wegmarken*, 12; "What Is Metaphysics?" in *Basic Writings*, ed. David Farrell Krell (New York: Harper and Row, 1977), 106: "Without the original revelation of the nothing, no selfhood and no freedom."

10. Heidegger, "Metaphysik," 13; "Metaphysics," 106.

11. Heidegger, "Metaphysik," 14; "Metaphysics," 108.

12. Heidegger, "Metaphysik," 14; "Metaphysics," 108.

13. Heidegger, "Metaphysik," 19; "Metaphysics," 112. See also the 1937 prologue to the French edition of *Wegmarken* (*Questions 1,* 10): "Every time it will be within the respective capacity of this will and of this force that the first and ultimate question of philosophy will assure its watchfulness, spreading the glow of fire and making the shape of all things appear."

14. See Husserl, *Nachwort zu meinen Ideen* (Halle: Niemeyer, 1930), 371 (*Being and Time* as "new anthropology").

15. See Alain Renaut, "Qu'est-ce que l'homme?" *Man and World* 9, no. 1 (February 1976): 9ff.

16. Heidegger, *Nietzsche 2* (Pfullingen: Neske, 1961), 194; English ed. trans. David Farrell Krell (San Francisco: Harper and Row, 1979). It is consequently unsurprising that, of Heidegger's French disciples, E. Martineau is both the one who attempts a return to *Being and Time* and also the one in whom the ethical view is the most pronounced: see "La Provenance des espèces," *Critique* (February 1978), in which thinking is said to ought to be "decided for it ownmost destination"—which assumes that it takes itself far from the "twaddle that is offered to us these days" and that it "indefatigably fixes its attention" on the multiple deployment of Being: thereby a thought can finally escape what is "sordid" in the cultural world today—and that, concludes the author, "I say in all simplicity."

17. How indeed can we not speak of "values," for attention, watchfulness, insistence, and the like are ways of being for Dasein without which it cannot fulfill its essence (the relation to Being)?

18. Heidegger, *Gelassenheit* (Pfullingen: Neske, 1959), 37: "Wir *sollen* nichts tun, sondern warten" (emphasis added); *Discourse on Thinking,* trans. John M. Anderson and E. Hans Freund (New York: Harper and Row, 1966).

19. Heidegger, *Sein und Zeit* (Halle: Niemeyer, 1927), 167; *Being and Time,* trans. John Macquarrie and Edward Robinson (New York: Harper and Row, 1962), 211.

20. Heidegger, *Holzwege,* 325; "Anaximander Fragment," in *Early Greek Thinking,* trans. David Farrell Krell and Frank A. Capuzzi (New York: Harper and Row, 1975).

21. For example, see the opening pages of the introduction to "What Is Metaphysics?" or again in *Der Satz vom Grund,* 96; "Being and Ground [= reason]: The Same."

22. Heidegger, *Schelling's Treatise on the Essence of Human Freedom,* trans. Joan Stambaugh (Athens: Ohio University Press, 1985).

23. See "Letter to R. P.," in William J. Richardson, *Heidegger: Through Phenomenology to Thought* (The Hague: Nijhoff, 1963). The thought of Being "does not require so much a new language as a mutation in our relation to the old one."

24. "Séminaire du Thor," 7 September 1969, in Heidegger, *Questions IV* (Paris: Gallimard, 1976), 284. On the question of language in Heidegger, see Ferry and Renaut, "Heidegger en question."

25. Summary of a seminar on the lecture "Time and Being," in Heidegger, *On Time and Being,* trans. Joan Stambaugh (New York: Harper and Row, 1972), 50.

26. Hence the resort to quotation marks, italics, all ways of setting apart.

27. Heidegger, *Gelassenheit,* 64; *Discourse on Thinking.*

28. Heidegger, *Holzwege,* 311; "Anaximander Fragment," 27.

29. Heidegger, *Der Satz vom Grund,* 109.

30. Heidegger, *Holzwege,* 310; "Anaximander Fragment," 26.

31. Here I can only refer to the way in which Alain Renaut has shown how the interpretation of the History of Being by Jean Beaufret (in *Dialogue avec Heidegger*) consisted in thinking an inauguration of the forgetfulness, and thus tended to represent the forgetfulness as external to Being (the ethical accentuation, particularly clear in the writings of Jean Beaufret, then fitting perfectly into the logic of this interpretation): on these various points, see Alain Renaut, "Vers la pensée de déclin," *Etudes Philosophiques,* no. 2 (1975), and idem, "La Fin de Heidegger et la tâche de la pensée," *Etudes Philosophiques,* no. 4 (1977).

CHAPTER 3

1. As Heidegger very well realized (see *Kant and the Problem of Metaphysics,* trans. James S. Churchill [Bloomington: Indiana University Press, 1962]) the assertion of man's radical finitude does not represent an observation, as in empiricism, but it is thought of as an a priori condition of objective knowledge.

2. To do full justice to the Kantian "architectonics"—which, contrary to what the absurd accusations of formalism suggest, can provide a truly "philosophical" and not merely "historical" knowledge of the system—it would obviously be necessary to show how and above all *why* these three ideas are produced through the application of the principle of reason (of the hypothetical syllogism) to the three categories of relation. This would permit one to demonstrate that Kant's critique of metaphysics does not yield anything in rigor to Heidegger's deconstruction. Here I shall limit myself to recalling that only the categories of substance, causality, and reciprocal action are capable of a metaphysical significance, that is, of producing Ideas: the categories of the modality are not part of the constitution of the object, but merely describe the relation between the constituted object and the subject, and are thereby improper for grounding an ontotheology; on the other hand, the categories of quantity and quality have no possible *meaning* outside of scientific use (in other words, their meaning is exhausted by their presentation—*Darstellung*—in space and time). Only the categories of relation have a possible metaphysical meaning, that is, a meaning distinct from the one produced by their scientific use in space and time: thus the category of substance can mean both the subject that is not [a] predicate (metaphysical sense) and

permanence (the scientific sense; constancy of the quantity of force in the universe), the category of causality can designate production/creation (metaphysical sense) and the irreversible succession (scientific sense), just as reciprocal action can characterize both the system of all [possibilities?] (the divine understanding) and a system of physical forces like Newton's solar system. Although I will not dwell on this architectonic—the study of which would be beyond the scope of this book—I will nonetheless return farther on to the theoretical stakes of this duality of meaning.

3. See Alexis Philonenko, *L'Oeuvre de Kant* (Paris: Vrin, 1975), 1:170ff.

4. Kant, "What Is Orientation in Thinking?" in *"Critique of Practical Reason," and Other Writings in Moral Philosophy,* trans. Lewis White Beck (New York: Garland, 1976).

5. On these characteristics, see the appendix to the"Transcendental Dialectic," in Kant, *Critique of Pure Reason,* trans. Wolfgang Schwarz (Aalen: Scientia, 1982).

6. Gaston Bachelard, *Le Rationalisme appliqué* (Paris, 1949), 58–59.

7. Kant, *Critique of Pure Reason,* 206.

8. On the connection between theory of meaning and esthetic theory, see Ferry and Renaut, "La Question de l'éthique après Heidegger," in *Système et critique, essai sur la critique de la raison dans la pensée contemporaine* (Brussels: Ousia, 1985), p. 37ff. See also Ferry, "Sublime et système chez Kant," *Etudes Philosophiques* (1975).

9. Kant, *Critique of Pure Reason,* 212–14.

10. See Ferry, "Stalinisme et historicisme."

11. It could easily be shown that "reflective judgment" is always at the heart of "determinative judgment," as is clearly confirmed by the fact that the analogies of experience, if they are *constitutive* of objectivity, are only *regulative* in relation to intuition.

PART 2, PREAMBLE

1. By the expression "Copernican revolution," Kant means, as we know, the reversal of objectivity he established in relation to previous theories (notably the Cartesian ones): this reversal brought out the idea that it is the subject that, in possession of a general definition of objectivity, constructs objects through its *activity.* We shall see how Fichte extends to history and politics the idea of an activity of the subject through which it ceases to be subject to and determined by the world of objects. Thus, the notion of Copernican revolution already contains the critical idea of freedom.

2. Fichte, *Briefe* (Stuttgart-Bad Cannstatt: Frommann, 1968), quoted by Philonenko in *Théorie et praxis,* 78.

3. This of course is the Copernican revolution brought about by Kant's philosophy.

4. See Philonenko, *Théorie et praxis,* 78: "The French Revolution belongs to the order of the founded and the Copernican revolution to the order of the foundation."

5. Fichte, *Nachgelassene Schriften* (Stuttgart: Fromann, 1962), 2: 25.

6. Kant, "Preface," in *Critique of Pure Reason,* 3.

7. We shall see further on how this "legitimation" leads to the modification of certain theses supported in 1793. This is in no way paradoxical, however, for these modifications (notably regarding the question of the situation of the state of nature) merely *carry out* the plan of 1793: thinking of history exclusively in terms of the future and not the past.

8. In more "modern" language we would say that man is "in situation."

9. For example, see Martial Gueroult, *Nature humaine et état de nature chez Rousseau, Kant et Fichte,* passim; Pierre-Philippe Druet, *La Conversion de Fichte,* 66ff.

CHAPTER 4

1. See K. Schuman, *Die Grundlage de Wissenschafstlehre in ihrem Umrisse* (The Hague: Nijhoff, 1968), 6.

2. See Fichte's writings on Machiavelli.

3. See G. W. F. von Leibniz, *Theodicy: Essays on the Goodness of God, the Freedom of Man, and the Origin and Evil,* trans. E. M. Huggard (New Haven: Yale University Press, 1952), §22. Leibniz uses this model to distinguish between the "antecedent will" and the "consequent will," which is the decisive one:

> Full and infallible success belong only to *consequent will,* as it is called. It is all-encompassing, and it is to it that the rule refers, according to which one never fails to do what one wills when one can. Now, this consequent will, final and decisive, results from the conflict of all antecedent wills, those with a tendency towards the good as well as those which reject the bad; it is from the combination of all these particular wills that arises the total will; as, in mechanics, composite movement is a result of all the tendencies which combine in the same motive and satisfies each one equally, as far as it is possible to do all at once. It is as if the motive were shared among these tendencies, following what once I demonstrated in one of the newspapers of Paris (September 7, 1693), in giving the general law of the composition of movement.

This physical model constantly underlying the theodicy is present in *all* theories of the cunning of reason, even Engels's, so that it can be considered an indisputable sign of it. See, for example, Friedrich Engels's letter to J. Bloch, 21 September 1890, and his *Ludwig Feuerbach and the Outcome of Classical German Philosophy* (New York: AMS Press, 1981).

4. In reading these texts, moreover, it is hard to see how, since Hegel's "Natural Right," most of the exegetes, who were surely too much influenced by Kant's *Critique of Practical Reason,* could see in Kant's philosophy of history a "moral idealism" assimilable to that of Fichte (Hegel never made a clear distinction in this regard between Kant and Fichte). We find an example of this confusion in the book of V. Delbos, *La Philosophie pratique de Kant* (Paris: Alcan, 1926), 264ff. The author argues that Kant's philosophy of history is throughout "a refutation of Leibniz" in the sense that "the concept constitutive of the philosophy of history is for Kant the concept of freedom" (p. 269) which "can be saved only through an irreducible opposition to mechanical causality." (p. 266) Delbos even goes so far as to define the opposition between Kant and Herder in these terms: "In Kant reason goes through history as a militant faculty that must conquer the hold over sensory nature" (p. 290). This last assertion is simply incompatible with the assertion of a "design of nature" that is realized through the "madness" of particular acts. The difference between Leibniz and Kant on the subject of history is not so much at the level of the *content* of the theses expressed as in their *status* ("reflective" in Kant, "determinative" in Leibniz). In this sense, Kant's philosophy of history is based on the *Critique of Judgment* and not on the *Critique of Practical Reason,* as is otherwise clearly attested in the introduction and §83 of the third *Critique.*

5. A theme largely repeated in Kant, "Perpetual Peace"; see, for example, p. 112.

6. The reference to Newton at the beginning of the 1784 text is, clearly, not inno-cent, the "precinct" constituting the place in which the centrifugal force and the centri-petal force (i.e., the "unsociable sociability") end up forming a system (the laws). This is how we should understand Kant's famous remark in the margin of the *Observations on the Beautiful and the Sublime,* trans. John T. Goldthwait (Berkeley and Los Angeles: University of California Press, 1981), according to which Rousseau is "the Newton of the moral world." It is enough to liken the centrifugal force to pity and the centripetal force to self-love (unsociable sociability). Clearly, this "interpretation" of Rousseau is textually inaccurate.

7. For an excellent discussion of "twistedness" as Luther's metaphor for selfishness, see Philonenko, *Théorie et praxis,* 28.

8. It will be noticed, however, that the problem is raised in connection with the leader who in Kant's political theory is "outside the precinct" and hence outside the system of the cunning of nature.

9. Philonenko, *Théorie et praxis,* 29.

10. It is noteworthy, moreover, that "Perpetual Peace," written in the context of inter-European wars, works out a primarily deterministic philosophy of history to the exclusion of nearly any ethical point of view. Thus it is the only writing of Kant's not to declare the political problem somehow insoluble.

11. "[T]he morally practical reason utters within us its irrevocable veto: There shall be no war." Kant, "The Science of Right," trans. W. Hastie, in *Critique of Pure Reason and Other Writings* (Chicago: Encyclopaedia Britannica, 1952), 457.

12. We shall compare, for example, what Kant says about the beneficial function of war in "Perpetual Peace": "Even if people were not compelled by internal discord to submit to the coercion of public laws, war would produce the same effect from out-side. For in accordance with the natural arrangement described above, each people would find itself confronted by another neighboring people pressing in upon it, thus forcing it to form itself internally into a *state* in order to encounter the other as an armed *power*" (*Kant's Political Writings,* 112) with what Hegel wrote in the addition to §314 of his *Philosophy of Right:* "the nations which are hostile to one another find internal peace thanks to war" (trans. T. M. Knox [New York: Oxford University Press]). If it is correct to stress that Hegel's and Kant's ethics are opposed on the question of war (see Philonenko, "Ethique et guerre dans la pensée de Hegel," in *Essais sur la philosophie de la guerre,* 55ff.), it would be unwise to lay too much stress on their divergences on this matter in their philosophies of history.

13. We could still speak of an esthetic side to war: see Kant, *Critique of Judgment,* §28.

14. On the foundation of war in Kant's idea of nature, see Paul Natorp, *Kant über Krieg und Frieden: Ein Geschichtsphilosophischer Essay* (Erlangen, 1924).

15. The essential text in this regard of course remains §83 of the *Critique of Judgment.*

16. See Kant, "Perpetual Peace," 112.

17. Ibid., 113.

18. "The republican constitution is not only pure in its origin (since it springs from the pure concept of right); it also offers a prospect of attaining the desired result, i.e., a perpetual peace and the reason for this is as follows.—If, as is inevitably the case under this constitution, the consent of the citizens is required to decide whether or not war is to be declared, it is very natural that they will have great hesitation in embarking on so dangerous an enterprise" (ibid., 100).

19. It is surprising in this regard that "Perpetual Peace" was judged "utopian" because of its lack of specificity about the institutional means for achieving peace (see, for example, Georges Vlachos, *La Pensée politique de Kant* [Paris: Presses Universitaires de France, 1962], 573), the commentator frequently seeing a mere act of ethical faith in which the "great philosopher" joins "the camp of the common consciousness" (see P. Hassner, "Les concepts de guerre et de paix chez Kant," *Revue Française de Science Politique* 11 (1961). As Philonenko has shown, this *intentional* imprecision is due on the contrary to Kant's "realism," "naturalistic pessimism" dictating "its way to practical optimism" in a vision of history in which morality and politics have becomes relatively autonomous from each other. See Philonenko, "Kant et le problème de la paix," *Revue Guerre et Paix* (1968):26ff.

20. This is probably the point on which Kant's thinking clearly comes closest to Hegel's.

21. Kant, *Critique of Judgment*, §83.

22. Moreover, the location of this idea in the third *Critique* is not in any way surprising when we consider that it is essentially a question of completing the system.

23. We can judge that Kant prefigures Hegel here because he meets Leibniz's idea of the "system" of harmony. On this point, see the valuable remarks of Ernst Cassirer, "Introduction," in *Das Erkenntnisproblem in der Philosophie*, 3:16; *The Problem of Knowledge: Philosophy, Science, and History since Hegel*, trans. William H. Woglon and Charles W. Hendel (New Haven: Yale University Press, 1950).

24. "Perhaps it is because we have chosen the wrong point of view from which to contemplate the course of human affairs that the latter seems so absurd to us. The planets, as seen from the earth, sometimes move backward, sometimes forward, and at other times remain motionless. But seen from the sun—the point of view of reason—they continually follow their regular paths as in the Copernican hypothesis . . . It is our misfortune, however, that we are unable to adopt an absolute point of view when trying to predict free actions. For this . . . would be the point of view of *providence,* which extends even to *free* human actions. And although man may *see* the latter, he cannot *foresee* them with certainty (a distinction which does not exist in the eyes of the divinity)" (Kant, "The Contest of Faculties," in *Kant's Political Writings*, 180–81). Kant takes this point of view in the third *Critique,* but, it is true, in a simple "reflecting" way. It is clearly the same with "Perpetual Peace." Precisely because this viewpoint (the basis for optimism) is not objective, we can understand Kant's wavering on the question of the actualization of right.

25. It is basically a matter of applying Kant's distinction in the *Grounding for the Metaphysics of Morals,* trans. James W. Ellington (Indianapolis: Hackett, 1981), between actions simply conformable to duty and actions done out of duty.

26. It should be noted, moreover, that if war has a finality, it is as a *test of adaptiveness,* as a means of delivering man from the "lazy" pursuit of happiness.

27. See the second introduction to the third *Critique*. In his *System of Transcendental Idealism,* trans. Peter Heath (Charlottesville: University of Virginia Press, 1978), Schelling attributes this mediating function to history.

28. Here is Philonenko's opinion: "How can we not see that this solution (Kant's solution of the problem of peace) is based on a philosophy of history affirming the necessity of the progress of freedom, maintained by both nature and reason? The great philosopher coming after Kant, Fichte, doubted Kant's thesis of history; by the same token, he posed anew the problem of war and peace. Wasn't Kant a metaphysician in his judgment of history? Didn't he go beyond the logic of facts in asserting the reality

of an order tending toward the good, despite all events? Perhaps history is only a pure diversity, in itself neither good nor bad, similar to printing characters mixed in a chest and from which one can draw a mediocre and buffoonish comedy as well as a *Divine Comedy*. If that were so, the problem of peace would rest, and that for the first time, uniquely on human will and freedom" ("Kant et le problème de la paix," 20)

29. See Philonenko, *Théorie et praxis,* 75ff. I deliberately leave aside Fichte's "Reclamation of Freedom of Thought from Europe's Princes," in which he is still Kant's disciple in the matter of history.

30. I am of course thinking here only of the sole question of history; it is evident that Fichte remains in many ways, on other matters, Kant's disciple.

31. That, if you will, of a "reflective theology."

32. And this is true enough that, despite his manifest distaste for the revolutionary *process,* Kant was an ardent defender of the French Revolution's *results.*

33. The reference to the tree—which we know served as a model for the definition of the "natural ends" in the third *Critique*—may not be innocent. See Fichte, "Vocation of the Scholar," in *Fichte: Early Philosophical Writings,* trans. Daniel Breazeale (Ithaca, N.Y.: Cornell University Press, 1988).

34. To tell the truth, during this period Fichte did not yet thematically doubt the distinction between phenomena and things in themselves (hence, the solution to the third antinomy). In the *Beiträge* he was only aiming at the consequences of this distinction for the idea of history. He could thus believe he was a true Kantian at least in spirit when he refers to the *Critique of Practical Reason,* i.e., essentially to the part of Kant's philosophy anchored in the *thesis* of the third antinomy (the Kantian philosophy of history being seen more from the viewpoint of the antithesis or, at least, from a viewpoint of God as the "aesthetic" synthesis of the theoretical and the practical). This is what appears in Fichte's implicit reference to the second *Critique:* "Have you ever commanded to your soul an energetic 'I' and, after years of struggle, despite all sensual enticements, despite all obstacles, stood before the result and said *here it is?* Do you feel capable of telling the despot to his face you can kill me, but you cannot change my decision If you haven't—if you couldn't, then away from this place: it's too sacred for you. Man *can* what he *must;* when he says I *can* not, it means he *will* not." Here Fichte is clearly parodying one of Kant's most famous examples in which he conceives of his philosophy of history on the basis of ethics and not starting with the idea of a system.

35. See the second introduction to the *Science of Knowledge:* "Spinoza could not have been convinced; he could only *think* his philosophy, not *believe* it" (*SK* 81). Dogmatic metaphysics thus is, as in Kant, a perfectly coherent (thinkable) discourse, but because it denies the reality of the finite subject, it cannot think of it (conviction) without contradiction.

36. See also the first introduction to the *Science of Knowledge:* "We can show the dogmatist the inadequacy and incoherence of his system . . . we can bewilder and harass him from all sides; but we cannot convince him" (*SK* 16).

37. "If after everything I have said up to this point I assured my readers that *I* took everything I wrote to be true, I would not deserve to be believed. I wrote in a tone of certitude . . . it thereby follows that I am not speaking unreflectively and am not lying, but it does not follow that I am completely free from error" (*B*).

38. See the second introduction to the *Science of Knowledge:* "You will then claim to know no more in life than that you are finite, and finite in *this particular* way . . . and you will no more be minded to overstep these bounds than you are to cease being yourself" (*SK* 82). Dogmatism is thus the idea that oversteps the limits of humanity and

leads man to no longer be himself. The project of the *Phenomenology of Spirit* can in this sense be interpreted as an homage paid by dogmatism to criticism by taking into account—in the speculative proposition—the idea that the finite subject must not be excluded from discourse on the absolute.

39. We find examples of this kind of criticisms in *B* 94, 106. It seems to me that it is by taking these themes up again that the Frankfurt school's "critical theory" is still connected with the tradition of critical philosophy.

40. See the first patriotic dialogue in Fichte, "Machiavelli."

41. "Should we then let go of history? No, only take it out of your hands, for you remain eternal children never capable of anything other than *learning;* for you always allow yourselves to the *given* and can never yourselves *produce,* your highest creative power never going beyond *imitation*" (*B*).

42. Here we see how far the philosophy of history in Fichte's 1806 text *Die Grundzüge des gegenwärtigen Zeitalter* (The characteristics of the present age) has come from his earliest philosophy.

43. Quoted by Philonenko, *Théorie et praxis,* 79.

44. See *B* 103: "And if you came across a case that has not yet occurred in your history: what do you do then?"

45. The fact that the theodicy is "critical" and not "dogmatic" changes nothing in this particular matter. See Philonenko, *Théorie et praxis,* 98: "In Kant's thinking, though the activity of freedom does not have a determinate result—man has to solve his problems himself—it is determinate in its orientation. With this, man is still included in the perspective of creation (in the dogmatic sense). While the success of his destination in some sense belongs to him, the original plan of his destination is still taken away from him. Surely man is entrusted to himself and this is this sense in which he is responsible for himself, but just because he is entrusted to himself, he is still *ens creatum* and doesn't achieve absolute freedom."

46. "These are the principles according to which all investigations on the legitimacy or illegitimacy of a free action must be led" (*B* 99).

47. See on this point Peter Burg, *Kant und die Französische Revolution* (Berlin, 1974), 38 (paragraph entitled "Die französische Revolution als Wirkung der Natur") and 62 ("Die französische Revolution als Wirkung von Freiheit").

48. I refer to the note on p. 105 of the *Beiträge* which asserts the neutrality of the historical given.

49. Further on, we shall see how this conception of the historical given again implies a change of position in relation to Kant, particularly Kant's doctrine of radical evil.

50. This idea of history is, moreover, the only one compatible with Fichte's idealism as defined in the *Science of Knowledge,* provided one at least has a correct grasp of its meaning. As Philonenko has noted, "idealism is not the assertion that the world is 'in' consciousness, but in maintaining—as Descartes already did—that any experience is a 'deciphering,' presupposing a theory that fixes the perspective in which the cipher, i.e., the given real, is decoded according to precise rules. Idealism rests on a simple proposition: experience gets it meaning only through and in the operation of the mind" (*Théorie et praxis,* 88).

51. The passage quoted is undoubtedly directed against Kant; see the *Critique of Judgment,* §28: "War itself, provided it is conducted with order and a sacred respect for the rights of civilians, has something sublime about it, and gives nations that carry it on in such a manner a stamp of mind only the more sublime the more numerous the dangers to which they are exposed, and which they are able to meet with fortitude. On

the other hand, a prolonged peace favours the predominance of a mere commercial spirit, and with it a debasing self-interest, cowardice and effeminacy, and tends to degrade the character of the nation." Here again, Kant seems to prefigure Hegel more than Fichte.

52. It is certainly on this point that Fichte's philosophy most spectacularly changed; see his writing on Machiavelli.

53. It seems to me that in addition to Rehberg, this is at least obliquely directed at Kant, particularly the idea that the revolution is illegitimate because it establishes a state of anarchy to which one must always prefer order, even that of the harshest despotism.

54. *B* 158: "die erstere Bedeutung des Worts Gesellschaft."

55. The political system described in Kant's *On the Old Saw: "That May Be Right in Theory but It Won't Work in Practice,"* trans. E. B. Ashton (Philadelphia: University of Pennsylvania Press, 1974), is not, even if it contains certain difficulties, the description of an authoritarian state. In other respects, even if it is "constraining," its realization is due only to the historical process itself.

56. On the same page Fichte specifies that it is not "merely a sweet dream . . . its secure ground is the necessary advancement of mankind." (The necessity here is of course that of practical reason.)

57. This, of course, is a reference to Kant. See Fichte, "Vocation of the Scholar."

58. One can also say that they agree in the person of the enlightened sovereign, but not in any hypothesis, within the people.

59. See Ferry, "La distinction du droit et de l'éthique chez Fichte," *Archives de Philosophie du Droit* (1981).

60. See Jean-Jacques Rousseau, *The Social Contract,* bk. 3, chap. 18. Fichte explicitly repeats Rousseau: "The clause in the social contract declaring it inalterable would therefore be in the most complete contradiction possible with humanity's spirit" (*B* 136). See also the apology for Rousseau, in *B* 108.

61. The expression is Philonenko's; see *Théorie et praxis,* 164.

62. See Charles E. Vaughan, *Studies in the History of Political Philosophy:* BEFORE AND AFTER ROUSSEAU (New York, 1960), 2:196:"The political principle of the *Beiträge* . . . is individualism pure and simple"; see also 102. Nico Wallner establishes an interesting parallel between Fichte and Humboldt; see his *Fichte als politischer Denker* (Halle, 1926), 50ff.

63. See Ferry, "La distinction du droit et de l'éthique chez Fichte."

64. It is necessary always to keep firmly in mind the idea that, unlike Rousseau, Fichte thinks of the state of nature, right from the start of his political thinking, as a *neutral* state.

65. It is also clear that in this sense the *Science of Rights* will be conceived of as the realization of the aporetic project of the *Beiträge;* however the two texts diverge in other respects.

66. "Rousseau, whom you are one after another once again calling a dreamer, even as his dreams fulfill themselves under your eyes, was much too considerate with you, oh empiricists: this was his mistake" (*B*).

67. "Under your very eyes—and I may add, to your shame if you still don't know it, awakened by Rousseau—the human spirit has completed a work you would have declared the most impossible of all impossibilities, had you been capable of grasping its very idea: it has measured itself" (ibid.).

68. "Vigorous young men are perhaps quietly approaching the spirit of this work,

suspecting its influence on the system of human knowledge in its every part, the entirely new creation of the human way of thinking such a work must bring about, until they shall demonstrate it themselves" (ibid.).

69. These lines are taken from M. Vieillard-Baron's commentary in his French translation of the *Lectures on the Vocation of the Scholar,* 144.

70. "I have placed mankind's destination in the steady advancement of culture and in the uniformly continuous development of its dispositions and needs. To the social group that is to watch over the progress and the uniformity of this development I have assigned a most respectable place in human society.

"No one has contradicted this truth more resolutely and with more manifest reasons and more powerful eloquence than Rousseau. For him, the onwards movement of culture is the only cause of human corruption" (Fichte, "Fifth Lecture," 336).

71. M. Vieillard-Baron shares this opinion: "The essential difference between Rousseau and Fichte concerns the philosophy of history. For Rousseau, the future can only hold progressive deterioration; thus the only hope is to stop history to limit as much as possible the separation between the ideal and reality." On the contrary, "it is the theme of effort that orients all of Fichte's philosophy and gives him his confident optimism in the future."

72. Less, however, than it seems. Despite appearances, Fichte definitely does not commit the Voltairean counter-error. He simply wants to point out that Rousseau's critique of the present is essentially nostalgic.

73. We should again stress that the assertion of man's natural wickedness, i.e., his inertia, should not be confused with some Fichtean return to a Hobbesian state of nature, the two assertions being located on quite different levels. On the one hand, the state of nature will be defined, starting in 1794, as the future of man and hence as a state of perfection; on the other hand, the "wickedness" in question here is in reality wholly negative; it is defined as mere "inertia" and "laziness"; it is to say that, on this point, Fichte remains perfectly faithful to his conception of historical activity defined in 1793 as transformation of a historical manifold that is in itself *neutral.*

74. This theme was repeated by Fichte, against Schelling, in the "Lectures on the Vocation of the Scholar": nature "is not alive as reason is, and capable of an infinite development; she is dead, an existence frozen and closed in on itself. She alone, by this very obstacle, puts off for a while that which otherwise would erupt all at once as full and plentiful life" (*SW* 3:363, and in my translation, in *Philosophies de l'université,* 375).

75. This thesis was repeated in the "Lectures on the Vocation of the Scholar": "The human race . . . is surrounded by a nature without will which ceaselessly limits, threatens, and curtails its life. It had to be this way so that all life could win its unity through its own freedom" (*SW* 3:369–70).

76. Philonenko, *Théorie et praxis,* 148. Furthermore, Philonenko adds—an extremely valuable piece of information that unfortunately he does not elaborate on—that the reason for this reversal is to be found in the new way in which Fichte in 1794 conceived of the notion of synthesis. I shall return to this point.

77. Even though in a different mode, for Fichte, even in 1793, the state of nature already had the status of a practical "Idea" in the Kantian sense.

78. Fichte is in no way a "romantic" thinker, contrary to what one persistent legend suggests, as is attested to by certain interpretations even today. See, for example, Blandine Barret-Kriegel, *L'Etat et les esclaves: Réflexions pour l'histoire des états* (Paris: Calmann-Levy, 1979).

79. Pierre-Philippe Druet, "Introduction," in *Fichte* (Paris: Seghers, 1977).

80. See the letters to Kant of 2 April 1793 and 20 September 1793, as well as the *Science of Rights,* in *SW* 3:286, and Fichte's dedication to *Der Geschlossene Handelsstaat* (Hamburg: Meiner, 1979).

81. See Manfred Buhr, *Revolution und Philosophie: Die ursprüngliche Philosophie Fichtes und die französische Revolution* (Berlin, 1965).

CHAPTER 5

1. Here I follow the perspective opened by Alexis Philonenko whose radically new interpretation of Fichte I believe to be indubitable. See Pierre-Philippe Druet, "Fichte et l'intersubjectivité: Les thèses de M. A. Philonenko," *Revue Philosophique de Louvain* (1973):134–43.

2. This well-known theme is developed, for example, in the letter to Niethammer of 1793 in which we read that "Kant confined himself to indicating the truth, but neither exposed it nor proved it." See *SW* 1:420.

3. The "deduction" of time and matter from intuition thus does not have the "idealist" meaning commentators attributed to it before Philonenko's interpretation.

4. Kant, *Critique of Pure Reason,* trans. Norman Kemp Smith (London: Macmillan, 1933), 100 (Ak A = 63; B = 87–88). On the meaning of the concept of dialectics in Kant and Fichte, and on its evolution in Schelling and Hegel, see the masterful article by Jacques Rivelaygue, "La Dialectique de Kant à Hegel," *Etudes Philosophiques,* July–September 1978.

5. See *SW* 1:77. This goes against Hegel's interpretation.

6. See the article on Fichte in Hegel, *Lectures on the History of Philosophy,* in which Hegel regrets that "as early as the second principle, the deduction is over."

7. Thus it is effectively valid for Schelling's first two texts. It is in other respects interesting to note that this criticism is exactly the one Fichte made of Schelling and Spinoza, showing, in a text that Hegel would surely have concurred with, how methodologically absurd it seems to him to take the absolute as the starting point of philosophy. See Fichte, *Zur Darstellung von Schellings Identitätsystem,* in *Nachgelassene Werke* (Bonn, 1962), 2:371ff. Here again is an obviously weighty argument in favor of Philonenko's thesis.

8. It is this dialectics that Hegel repeats in the introduction to the *Phenomenology.*

9. That is why Fichte finds Spinoza's philosophy absurd, for in it everything happens as though it were "between two others": between a "subject" not-self and an "object" not-self (*SK* 101–2).

10. We have already seen how the positing of the first principle as an illusion implies the positing of the not-self, since it leaves free the reflection that "deduces" it from the same logical construction as the one that allowed for the positing of the absolute self. It is also clear, however, that the not-self presupposes the self or that, as Fichte says, "the possibility of counterpositing itself presupposes the identity of consciousness" (*SK* 103). The reasoning here can be quite simple: not-A presupposes A; not-A is identical to the proposition A = A. This last proposition (consistent with the first principle) is itself based on the proposition "self = self" from which we get the absolute self, "hence even the transition from positing to counterpositing is possible only through the identity of the self" (*SK* 103).

11. Fichte formulates this contradiction as follows (I add a commentary in paren-

theses): "[I]f I = I, everything is posited that is posited in the self. But now the second principle is supposed to be posited (because it has the same logical presuppositions as those we admitted to posit the first principle) in the self (because the absolute self contains everything), and also not to be posited therein (because it is precisely a not-self)" (*SK* 107).

12. It is clear that at the level of the first formulation of the third principle, the solution is still far from complete.

13. This idea of the self as substrate is still "dialectical" (illusory). See *LH* 256, n. 39.

14. The meaning of these three terms becomes clear only toward the end of Fichte's book. See *LH* 255–56.

15. This is an inevitable consequence of the attempt to reconstruct the *Critique of Pure Reason* by starting with the Ideas and then proceeding to the categories.

16. The categories are deduced this way: to the first principle corresponds reality, to the second, negation, to the third, limitation. The limitation is explained through reciprocal action (of the self and not-self in the absolute self) which, seen from the self's viewpoint, yields the category of substances, from the viewpoint of the not-self, that of causality, and so forth.

17. It is clearly quite impossible to get the sense of this unless we accept Philonenko's interpretation of the first three principles as forming a dialectics of illusion.

18. Gueroult, *L'Evolution et la structure de la "Doctrine de la Science" chez Fichte,* 1:342.

19. See Xavier Tilliette, *Schelling: Une philosophie en devenir* (Paris: Vrin, 1970), 487, 489 n. 28.

20. F. W. J. Schelling, *On University Studies,* trans. E. S. Morgan (Athens: Ohio University Press, 1966). It is also in this sense that in the *System of Transcendental Idealism* of 1800, the three elements of history are also fixed a priori: "The first period is one in which the dominant principle, still appearing as destiny, that is, as completely blind power, coldly and unconsciously destroys all that is greatest and most magnificent; to this period of history, which we can call the tragic, belongs the downfall of the splendor and miracle of the ancient world, the collapse of those great empires, of which hardly any memories remain, and about whose greatness we can conclude only from their ruins; the downfall of the noblest humanity that ever flourished, and whose return to earth is now but an eternal wish" (pp. 272–73). We see in the description of the first period, the three elements of history (paradise, fall, restoration) are determined. The second epoch will thus be that of the return being carried out, and the third, that of the return completed (p. 273).

21. Fichte, *Zur Darstellung von Schellings Identätsystem* (Remarks on the exposition of Schelling's *System of Identity*), in *SW* 11:372ff.

22. This appears even more clearly when we recall that in Plato this structure of the fall is that of the truth as anamnesis. It thus seems to me impossible to naïvely resituate oneself in this schema without suffering the consequences. We can observe, however, that a large part of the post-Engels discussion in anthropology about the status of the state in primitive societies seems circumscribed by critical inadequacy regarding this heavy philosophical inheritance. In his *Origin of the Family, Private Property, and the State* (London: Lawrence and Wishart, 1972), Engels's thinking subscribes to a tripartite representation of history—comparable on many if not all points to that of Schelling—which has never seemed to me to have been criticized *as such:* "The state, therefore, has not existed from all eternity. There have been societies which have managed without it, which had no notion of the state or state power. At a definite stage of economic

development, which necessarily involved the cleavage of society into classes, the state became a necessity because of this cleavage. We are not rapidly approaching a stage in the development of production at which the existence of these classes has not only ceased to be a necessity but becomes a positive hindrance of production. They will fall as inevitably as they once arose. The state inevitably falls with them" (p. 232). A critique that attempted to refute only the mechanistic view of history, or that confined itself to condemning the relation that Engels established between the economy, classes, and the state, would leave what may be the essential thing still intact: the metaphysical representation of truth and history implied by the *tripartite* character of the three epochs. Thus in arguing against Hegelian or Marxist dialectics, it is not enough to cite, as for example Heidegger does (see his *Der Satz vom Grund*, p. 154), the "fact" that the epochs are not necessarily linked to each other to get out of the Platonic scheme of the Fall or decline and so to avoid the nostalgic romanticism inherent in any idea of the restoration of a lost "authenticity"—as is shown in many respects by the role played by the pre-Socratics in Heidegger's thinking.

23. Schelling, *System of Transcendental Idealism.*

24. Ibid.

25. See ibid., where Schelling shows how at the transcendental level this philosophy of history is based on the initial assertion of absolute identity.

26. Ibid., 274.

27. Schelling, *On University Studies,* 12.

28. We have seen how, even in Kant, the hypothesis of the cunning of reason presupposes the identity of the rational and the real, if only in the mode of an Idea.

29. Fichte, *Nachgelassene Werke,* 2:213.

CHAPTER 6

1. It is the philosophy of law that will truly complete this deconstruction of metaphysics by solving the problem of representation; see my *Political Philosophy 1: Rights, The New Quarrel between the Ancients and the Moderns* (Chicago: University of Chicago Press, 1990) which attempts, by following the path opened by Alexis Philonenko, an interpretation of the first chapter of the *Science of Rights.*

2. Raymond Aron, *Les Etapes de la pensée sociologique* (Paris: Gallimard, 1967), 515.

3. Farther on we shall see why the antinomy of teleological judgment is the lone exception to this rule.

4. For an analysis of these difficulties I refer the reader to Rivelaygue's masterful article "De quelques difficultés concernant la troisième antinomie," in his *Passion de la raison: Hommage à Ferdinand Alquié* (Paris: Presses Universitaires de France, 1983).

5. Cassirer's interpretation (see his *Erkenntnisproblem,* vol. 2, final page) is surely the one that coincides best with the spirit of Kantianism, even if, as Rivelaygue suggests in the article cited, it does not resolve all the questions raised by the third antinomy.

6. They are indeed unequaled, and I have frequently been inspired by them in what follows. See notably Philonenko's remarkable *Etudes kantiennes* (Paris: Vrin, 1982).

7. Kant, *Critique of Practical Reason,* trans. Lewis White Beck (New York: Macmillan, 1956), 102–3.

8. Philonenko, *L'Oeuvre de Kant,* 2:144.

9. Letter to Reinhold of 29 August 1795, quoted in *LH* 52–53.

10. Ibid.

11. Philonenko, "Kant und die Ordnungen des Reellen," in *Etudes kantiennes;* see also *LH* §13.

12. Philonenko's analysis of this antinomy in his *Etudes kantiennes* seems to me altogether correct; see *Revue de Métaphysique et de Morale* 1 (January–March 1977):13ff. I can but repeat the main features.

13. See Philonenko, "Kant und die Ordnungen des Reellen," 23–36. In the usual antinomies, both theses are false (when they are contraries) or true (when they are subcontraries). Well, here both viewpoints will be true, although absolutely opposed! The legitimacy of this opposition remains, of course, to be established.

14. It will be recalled that the "realism of ends" can take two different forms depending on whether it attributes finality, in an animistic way, to nature itself (hylozoism) or to an intelligent creator external to nature (theism).

15. Philonenko, "L'Antinomie du jugement téléologique," in *Etudes kantiennes,* 21.

16. Philonenko gives an excellent formulation of this in his *Etudes kantiennes,* 21.

17. Ibid.

18. Notably in "Kant und die Ordnungen des Reellen," as well as, more elliptically, in "Kant et la philosophie biologique," *Etudes kantiennes,* 35.

19. Philonenko, "Kant et la philosophie biologique," 118–29.

20. Ibid.

21. Philonenko, "L'antinomie du jugement téléologique," 35.

22. Ibid., 24.

23. I repeat Philonenko's expression who himself uses it in its Fichtean sense. See "L'antinomie téléologique."

24. This is why dogmatism is unable to resolve the problem of the connection between self-consciousness and object-consciousness, as Fichte showed in a persuasive way. See Meiner edition of *SK* 66.

25. See §77 of Kant's *Critique of Judgment.*

26. See the end of Philonenko's "L'antinomie du jugement téléologique," where he suggests that Kant might have yielded to the temptation of "cynical" relativism. I must say that this is the only point where I disagree with Philonenko's interpretation: the viewpoint of reason *cannot not be posited,* which does not mean that it relativizes the viewpoint of reflection.

27. See Schelling, *Ideen zu einer Philosophie der Natur als Einleitung in das Studium dieser Wissenschaft* (Leipzig, 1797), 368–70. Here I am inspired in large part by a commentary of Rivelaygue about this text in a seminar on Schelling held in 1981.

28. Kant, *Critique of Judgment,* §77.

29. See Ferry, "Sublime et système chez Kant."

30. On this distinction, see chapter 3.

31. Which no one has seen better than Fichte, as is shown by his profound criticism of dogmatic realism and idealism. See *SK* 66 (Meiner ed.).

32. On the importance of this theme in Rousseau, Kant, and Fichte, see Philonenko's introduction to *Réflexions sur l'éducation,* his French translation of Kant's *On Education* (Paris: Vrin, 1966).

33. Fichte, "Lectures on the Vocation of the Scholar," *SW* 6:304.

34. Ibid., pp. 115–25; this passage is located in chapter 2 of *SK.*

35. See Philonenko, "Kant und die Ordnungen des Reellen."

36. See the first volume in this series, *Political Philosophy, 1: Rights, The New Quarrel between the Ancients and the Moderns.*

37. See the well-known example of the papercutter in Sartre's "Existentialism Is a Humanism."

38. Quoted and discussed by Philonenko, "Kant et la philosophie biologique," 121.

39. Ibid., 122. See also the analysis of the antinomy of taste in volume 2 of Philonenko's *L'Oeuvre de Kant.*

40. On taste as the mark of absolute individuality, see the third volume of Philonenko's *L'Oeuvre de Kant* (an analysis of the antinomy of esthetic judgment).

41. I understand the term here in the Husserlian sense, as an *immediate* analysis of the meaning of our perceptions, in contrast with what is usually called "intellectualism."

42. See *Kant's Logic,* trans. Robert Hartmann and Wolfgang Schwarz (Indianapolis: Bobbs-Merrill, 1971), 71, and also his *On Education,* the first few pages of which follow Rousseau.

43. Kant, *Education,* 2, 5.

44. See Philonenko, "Kant und die Ordnungen des Reellen," 317.

45. *SW* 3:80ff.: this passage should be compared to Kant's "Conjectural Beginning of the Human Race."

46. I shall come back to this point, essential for the understanding of the controversies about the epistemology of the social sciences, in *Political Philosophy 4: Historicism and the Social Sciences.*

47. See Kant's *Metaphysics of Morals.*

48. See the final page of volume 2 of his *Das Erkenntnisproblem.*

CONCLUSION

1. See in the introduction the discussion of the problems created by the moral view of the world, notably by its essentially naïve character compared to the other philosophies of history.

2. Alain Renaut and I have shown how a *criticist* understanding of the "ontological difference" was possible as a feeling of *wonder* and even *admiration* in the face of the indissolubly *contingent* and *signifying* character of the real. See Ferry and Renaut, "D'un retour à Kant."

3. I have already discussed, though obliquely and without elaboration, these two questions in an article written with Alain Renaut, "Penser les droits de l'homme," *Esprit,* March 1983, as well as in my report presented to the Congress of the AFSP in October 1981 (published as "Stalinisme and historicisme").

INDEX

INDEX

Dogmatic metaphisics, 100–101, 114–15, 132, 156–58, 188n.35, 36
Dogmatism, 95, 100–101, 113–16, 125, 147, 155, 172
Druet, Pierre-Philippe, 126–27

Engels, Friedrich, 22
Ethical view of the world. *See* Moral view of the world
Existence, 12, 26, 49, 52, 55, 58, 62, 64, 75–82, 84–86, 89, 128–30, 132–33, 142–43, 149, 160–64. *See also* Ontology

Fallenness, Heideggerian, 66–67
Fichte, Johann Gottlieb, 1, 13–14, 16–17, 19, 37–44, 46–48, 50–53, 55–60, 62, 66–67, 71–74, 96–97, 99–103, 147–51, 158–61, 163–70, 188n.34; and antinomy of self and not-self, 131–40; criticism of Kant, 105–22; criticism of Rousseau, 122–27; and determinism, 112–122; and French Revolution, 177n.10; and human finitude, 188–89n.38; and idea of future, 140–46; method and the Golden Age, 128–40; and philosophy of history, 27–29, 128–46, 189n.50; and Rousseau's romanticism, 122–27; and state of nature, 191n.73, 191n.77; on war, 189–90n.51
Finality. *See* Purposiveness
Finitude, Human, 17, 21, 39–45, 52–59, 64, 86, 88, 94, 126, 128, 130–36, 140, 142–44, 151, 155, 160–63, 183n.1, 188–89n.38; and Kant, 82–83
Freedom, Human, 13–15, 22, 24, 28–29, 37, 40, 48, 55, 95, 99–107, 108, 110–21, 124, 137, 139, 143–46, 159, 163–71, 187n.24, 189nn.45, 46, 191n.75; and determinism, 147–51; history and, 14
French Revolution: and Copernican revolution, 99–103; and idealism, 24–31
Freud, Sigmund, 20
Future, idea of, 140–46

Galileo, Galilei, 23
Gelassenheit, 21–22, 66

Gentz, Friedrich von, 25
Geraets, Théodore 52–53, 55
God, 11, 13, 44–45, 76–79, 80–89, 92, 155–65
Golden Age, 128–40
Gueroult, Martial, 141

Habermas, Jürgen, 49, 51–52, 54, 172
Häring, Theodor, 35
Haym, Rudolf, 49
Hegel, Georg Wilhelm Friedrich, 1, 4–7, 10–13, 28–30, 40–60, 68, 72–74, 81, 95, 102, 106, 109–12, 124, 130–31, 152, 155, 158, 161; and contingency in history, 35; criticism of, 50–60; and cunning of reason, 37–46; and ethical view of politics, 21–24; on Fichte and Schelling, 177n.10; and freedom, 39–40; and French Revolution, 46–50, 176n.2, 178–79n.25, 179–80n.35; and idealism, 38–39; and Kant, 42; and liberalism, 178–79n.25; and moral view of the world, 177n.11, 180–81n.54; and naturalism, 45–46; philosophical development, 176–77n.2, 178–79n.25; philosophy of history, 14–18; and praxis, 39; and principle of reason, 37; and the real and the rational, 39–40; and Robespierre, 179n.32; and the will, 42
Heidegger, Martin, 2, 5–7, 9–12, 17, 19–21, 23, 30, 33, 76–78, 81, 148; and moral view of the world, 63–67; phenomenology of, 67–74; and reason, 11–12; and humanism, 61–63; and praxis, 61–74
Heine, Heinrich, 1
Heinrich, Friedrich, 25
Herder, Johann Gottfried, 143
Herz, Markus, 131
Historicism, 5, 7, 23, 29, 59, 73, 93, 95, 172
Historicity, 5, 8, 17–18, 29, 48–49, 75–76, 79, 89, 92–94
History: antinomy of historical, 75–95; and human freedom, 14; deconstruction of, 17–18; and Hegel, 37–59; and "revolutionary science," 16–17. *See also* Philosophies of history

198

INDEX

Hobbes, Thomas, 23, 191n.73
Human body and individuality, 159–70
Humanism, 7, 21, 61–63, 66
Husserl, Edmund, 164
Hylozoism, 157

Idealism, German, 1–3, 5, 23, 35, 38, 44, 47, 73, 76, 108, 122, 132–33, 140, 143, 147, 154, 156, 162, 166; and philosphies of history, 24–31; and tasks of philosophy, 8–13
Ideas, Kantian, 88–96
Iliad, 117
Illusion, metaphysical, 85–88
Indeterminacy, 76, 93–95, 170
Individuality and the human body, 159–70
Irrationalism and praxis, 61–74

Jacobi, Friedrich Heinrich, 25–27

Kant, Immanuel, 1, 10–14, 18, 21–24, 33, 35, 40–42, 44, 47–48, 56–57, 100–103, 124, 126, 128–35, 140, 143, 148–50, 152, 154–57, 159–62, 164–66, 167–70; and Fichte's criticism, 105–22; and French Revolution, 179–80n.35, 188n.32; and critique of metaphysics, 75–96; and human finitude, 82–83; on peace, 187n.19, 187–88n.28; philosophy of history, 27–30, 185n.4; on war, 186nn.12, 13, 18
Kaufmann, Walter, 50
Kierkegaard, Søren, 35
Krug, Wilhelm Traugott, 81

Lacan, Jacques, 20
La Harpe, Jean François de, 26
Legality, 5, 110–11, 118–19
Leibniz, Gottfried Wilhelm, 39, 45, 105, 143–44, 165, 174n.29; antecedent and consequent wills, 185n.3

Machiavelli, Niccolò, 23
Mandeville, Bernard, 174n.29
Manent, Pierre, 23
Marx, Karl, 2, 4–5, 17, 35, 40, 93, 173n.9
Materialism, 2, 4, 11, 40, 100
Mechanism, 29–30, 105–8, 148–49, 150, 165, 170–71; and finality, 151–59; limits of, 151–59
Mendelssohn, Moses, 25–26
Merleau-Ponty, Maurice, 5, 164–65
Metaphysics, 5–8, 12, 17, 21–22, 60–73, 115, 118–19, 128, 129–30, 140, 158, 161, 172; critique of illusion, 85–88; Kant's deconstruction of, 75–96
Modernity, 2, 12, 23, 30, 65, 68
Montesquieu, Charles de Secondat, Baron de, 15
Moral view of the world, 7–8, 12, 14–17, 20–25, 28, 30, 38, 42–44, 47, 50, 58–66, 72, 74, 95–96; esthetic interpretation of, 147–70; and Heidegger, 63–67; and history, 99–172; and terror, 8, 15
Morality, 13, 41–42, 105, 107–11, 119–20, 145, 148, 170

Nietzsche, Friedrich, 21, 23, 50, 65
Nonrationality of the real, 82–83
Not-self. *See* Self and not-self
Novelty and reason, 4–5

Ontological Argument, 75–76, 80, 84–85, 128
Ontology, 14–23, 39, 44, 61–62, 65, 68–69, 71, 75–77, 80, 82, 84–86, 89, 94, 128, 151–52, 156, 164, 170–172; definition of, 9–13; deconstruction of, 11–12; and reason, 12
Ontotheology, 11, 151

Pantheism, 25, 26
Parousia, 69–70
Perfectibility, 109, 169
Phenomenology, 20–22, 30–31, 49, 54, 61, 67, 74, 76–78, 151–52, 88, 95, 147, 159, 164–67, 169–70, 172; and history, 1–5; limits of, 5–8
Philonenko, Alexis, 24, 27, 86, 107–8, 112, 125, 130–33, 141–42, 149, 151–152, 155, 165–66
Philosophies of history: and Engels, 193–94n.22; and Fichte, 27–29, 128–46, 189n.50; and French Revolution, 26–27; and German idealism, 24–31;

199